MW01243922

LEARN ESP32

ARDUINO INTERFACING - A STEP BY STEP GUIDE

PROGRAMMING, Internet Of Things Projects, Email Alert Based on
Sensors Reading

By

Janani Sathish

TABLE OF CONTENTS

2

INTRODUCTION

The ESP32 development board, which was released as a successor to the ESP8266 chip, made a huge impact on the IoT industry as it integrated Bluetooth with WiFi and utilized a dual-core processor. ESP32-S3 is the latest addition to Espressif's microcontroller series, specifically designed for AIoT applications. In this video, we will look into the specifications of ESP32-S3 and its applications. Espressif announced the ESP32-S3 microctroller on 1st December 2020. It features a dual-core Xtensa LX7 CPU, while its previous iteration, the ESP32-S2, was based on a single-core Xtensa LX7 CPU. The S2 model was considered a bridge between the ESP8266 and ESP32 microcontrollers regarding performance and cost. For more details on ESP32-S2, check out our previous video in the link provided below. The latest version gets a significant boost in performance and retains the improved hardware-level security of the S2 family. It also includes other features of the ESP32-S2, such as USB On-The-Go support and an improved touchpad sensor implementation. Now, let us have a detailed overview of the features. The ESP32-S3 has 384 KB of RAM and an additional 512 KB of SRAM. The dual-core CPU has a clock speed of up to 240 MHz. It comes built-in with 2.4 GHz, 802.11 b/g/n WiFi, and 40 MHz of bandwidth support. It features Bluetooth Low Energy 5.0 connectivity capable of long-range communication over 1 km through the coded PHY layer. it also supports higher transmission speeds and data throughput with 2 Mbps transfer support. An impressive feature of the ESP32-S3 is that both WiFi and BLE have a superior RF performance even at high temperatures. The ESP32-S3 has a total of 44 programmable GPIO pins, which is ten more than that of the ESP32-S2, and it supports a rich set of peripherals like SPI, I2C, UART, I2S, PWM, RMT, ADC, DAC, SD/MMC host and TWAI. 14 GPIO pins can be configured for HMI or Human Machine Interface applications. Also, the chip comes with an ultra-low-power (ULP) core that supports multiple low-power modes. The ESP32-S3 is made very secure as it supports AES-XTS-based flash encryption, RSA-based secure boot, digital signature, and HMAC. It also has a "world controller" peripheral that implements a trusted-execution environment by providing two fully-isolated execution environments. A major highlight of the ESP32-S3 would be its powerful AI acceleration features and support for AIoT applications. The term AIoT stands for Artificial Intelligence plus the Internet of Things. With the vast amount of data collected from IoT devices, the future of AI based applications looks promising. AI is indeed the key factor in unlocking IoT's full potential. Major AIoT markets include wearables, smart industry, smart home, and smart city sectors. The Xtensa LX7 core has been extended with vector instructions. Vector instructions are essentially a class of instructions that enable parallel processing of AI datasets, thereby improving performance and power efficiency. Such instructions can be leveraged for digital signal processing and neural network computing. Developers at Espressif are currently working on updates for the ESP-WHO library for face detection and the ESP-Skainet library for voice recognition. However, the code for ESP32-S3 SoC is still a work in progress and is not ready for the public yet. Espressif has released a video demonstration of the speech recognition capabilities of ESP32-S3 using Amazon's built-in Alexa Voice Service (AVS) with blind source separation (BSP) and acoustic echo cancellation (AEC) features. The fact that there are no external DSP chips interfaced with ESP32 proves how powerful it is for AIoT applications. Check out the video demo in the link provided below.

Espressif's IoT Development Framework or ESP-IDF also provides support for the ESP32-S3 model. The platform has rigorous testing features for building applications, and it also has a great support policy as it gets frequent updates. Developers can easily migrate their applications to the ESP32-S3 platform and continue working with popular ESP-IDF tools. With support for such libraries in the future, AI applications like object detection and image recognition will be easier to implement with the ESP32-S3.

Will guide you through making your first internet-connected electronics project using a Wi-Fi breakout ball that is available almost everywhere. You will study the complex workflow of hardware and software that makes smart objects successful through basic examples of step-by-step. We will take examples of the most common things you want to wake up, such as sensors or buttons that trigger email or tweet. We will also take examples of circuits that display FITCHETT information online and how to combine sample codes to build your project ideas. So whether you are a software engineer just dipping it at all into hardware or beginners who only have basic knowledge and Arduino, you will explore the Cloud service to quickly and easily link your DIY circuit with other Internet Things devices, social media websites and A more. The Internet of Things is now a trending topic, so I strongly recommend that you join this reason to get the knowledge you need to start as a freelancer IoT or just to start your career on the internet.

HARDWARE AND SOFTWARE REQUIREMENTS

Hardware and software requirements. Now. The first thing you need to have is E.s. P 30 Toolbelt, which is a board that we will use to connect our project or our sensors to the internet. This is a board that deals and looks like an Arduino board but has the ability of Wi-Fi and more features we will discuss. And the use section. You also need other fruit and clothing accounts. And we will explain how to get a free account on these two websites because we will need it for our automation or automation. You will need some basic electronic components, resistors, buttons, whatever you need to start with a new board, you will need Arduino Aldy, which is the original programming environment. Because we will use it for the program or ESPORT, you will need a sensor. If you have a motion detector or other type of sensor, you can use it. And you start with this board and you need a jumper cable to connect different elements to this board. But I can assure you that everything can be done just by using the ball without additional elements. You need a VSP Bold board and an idea programming environment. These are the two most important components of hardware and software.

ESP 32 PINOUT V1 DOIT

ESP32 DEVKIT V1 – DOIT
version with 30 GPIOs

The stimulus on energy will talk about E.s. P 30 to open, which is the output pen input objective, which you must use now? This is how the physical layout of the board ESP and as you can see, it is very similar to Arduino Nano, but has wi-fi built and now they are the first speed to peripherals, including 18 digital converters or ADC channels, where You can receive analogueue signals and these signals can be converted to internally digital. It also has three interfaces S.P.I for communication and three, your art interface for communication and all to see the interface for Seattle communication. So this, say, eight modules or eight pens can be used to allow cell communication with several devices that support the S.P.I eye to see or accuracy of your eyes and art. It also has 16 pwi output channels that help produce analogueue output from the load. It also has two digital channel converter and two eyes to the US interface. It also has 10 capacitive sensings, output special-purpose input. I provide more data and more details about each of these pens in resource lectures, but because we have many of them, we don't want to be trapped in details. Now, all we need to know is the pan itself. As you can see, this is the display of the board. This is a USPI board and you will connect your Glaspie connector here and the other side will be connected to your computer. As you can see, this is a pen, g.p. I mean, the real purpose, output input. Now, there is more than one general-purpose, input-output, as you can see here. And each pen has more than one function. As you can see, usually Bend comes with many names such as PII and ADC and digital converters and general goals and exits so you can use it as an output pen input or to receive analogueue signals or for all to be seen. So the choice is yours now, as you can see, this pen, everything is numbered for easy access so you can easily find out which pen is connected to each. Now, besides, there is a pen with specific features that make it suitable or not for certain projects. The following demonstrations show you some of these pens. And I will talk about each of these pens in detail and if they can be used as input or output. Now, the pen is highlighted green here. I will show the table to summarize this information.

GPIO	Input	Output	Notes
0			outputs PWM signal at boot
1	TX pin		debug output at boot
2	OK	OK	connected to on-board LED
3		RX pin	HIGH at boot
4	OK	OK	
5	OK	OK	outputs PWM signal at boot
6			connected to the integrated SPI flash
7			connected to the integrated SPI flash
8			connected to the integrated SPI flash
9			connected to the integrated SPI flash
10			connected to the integrated SPI flash
11			connected to the integrated SPI flash
12		OK	boot fail if pulled high
13	OK	OK	
14	OK	OK	outputs PWM signal at boot
15	OK	OK	outputs PWM signal at boot
16	OK	OK	

Again, the PIN is highlighted in green ok to use the highlighted with yellow ok to use, but you need to pay attention because they may have unexpected behaviour, especially at both time, while the PIN is highlighted to be used as input or output. Now, that the output PIN of the general goal input is zero, as you can see, ok to use. But you need to get extra attention because it might have unexpected behaviour at both times so that it can be used as an interesting input or as an output. This produces signal output, but nothing can be used as an IT expert for communication or output when debugging output. Number two is ok to be used as input or output and is usually connected to the onboard so you can use it to test the code or to test our basic function because you don't need to connect additional components at all you make and cause. Number three is ok to use it as input, but you cannot use it as an output. This is high output. So it will read one output. Ben, number four and five are ok to be used as input to output and PIN five also the SPW output and signal output pins from six to 11 are connected to the integrated S.P.I flash. So you can't use it as input or output. But No.12 is OK to use, but both will fail if it must be high, so it's okay to use it as input. But you need to get extra attention for this instead. And if you connect it as an output, it's okay. You have no problem. Pins from 13 to 16 are ok to be used as input or output without paying extra.

Now as you can see, the same Fourpence from 17 to 33, while 34, 35, 36 and 39 only enter the input, you cannot use it as output. Now, in our example and our training test, we will use the number two PIN, which has been built and placed on the board, built and led and using it on the board, the built and LED will make it easier for us to test or try different things if We make Auberge with a stick to control it through the internet. Now it's for a pin out. Now I will add additional information, uh, so tell you more information about the place of input-output general purpose. But for me, what I want you to know at this time is that we have a trash can that can be used easily without extra attention as output input, which is released for up to four, five to 16 to thirty-three. And if we want the input only trash, we can use 34, 35, 36 or 39. Now, if we need additional features, if we need BW, UM, ADC or DSE, if we need a capacitor activated bin or BW, and then We can continue and check this scheme. And from this trash can you can see that in our case, Sharp Elbows PIN Thirty-Six can be used as an ADC or Douceur converter. As you can see, and have the only country, you can use this scheme that is printed to refer whenever you need to do something. Same for here. You can see from this picture that PIN 25 can be used as a digital to analogueue converter and PIN 26 can also be used as a Central Converter or Digital Converter. So it depends on what you need or what your final goal is, you will check this scheme and ensure that you choose a PIN that suits your needs. So, if you are going to use a PIN as an output, you can't use PIN 34 because as you can see here, it's just input, just a pin. And if you want to use, say, analogueue to the digital converter, you can't use this number 17 pin because it only supports zero communication and input-output, regular digital input-output or output digital input. So before using any pin, uh, take one or two minutes to make sure it supports what you will do and the sensor or things you will connect, and whether it's analogueue or digital, they input like pushbutton or output like LEDs, You need to connect the element to the right pin before starting coding to avoid problems in the future. After you start testing your code, if you have questions or if you have a project that you don't know which PIN is suitable for the project, I will be more than happy to help answer all your problems.

DOWNLOAD AND INSTALL ARDUINO ESP AND USB DRIVER

Now, let's start with setting software, hanging into your keyboard and mouse. This section may be wavy following carefully because we configure and upload our first day, the Iwai Wi-Fi software is connected. Will install package E.S.P eight six six Balde in our Arduino software. We will also install device drivers for board communication chips and upload the Arduino sketch that connects to your home wireless network. The good news is that once you have finished the steps, you don't need to do it anymore. You use the same computer and the same ball, you don't need to reconfigure and reinstall one of the software that we will install and the software.

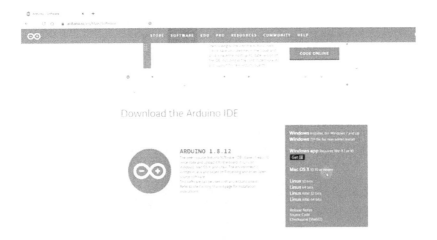

So the first step will install Arduino software. As you know, hardware is available for free on Arduino, the Cissie website. So the first step will go to Arduino, Cissie goes to the software section, click Download. And from here, choose your operating system, in our case, this Windows operating system, we can use the Windows Installer, all windows, and I installed the window. This is it.

```
char serialData;
int pin = 13;

void setup() {
  // put your setup code here, to run once:
  pinMode(pin, OUTPUT);
  Serial.begin(9600);
}

void loop() {
  // put your main code here, to run repeatedly:
  if(Serial.available() > 0)
```

Now, by default, the supporting chip Arduino application uses the official Arduino board, but not the E.S.P. board. This board can be programmed from the box because the Arduino application already knows about each and its properties. One cool thing about Arduino is you can add support for other bolts and all you have to do is tell and we know where to find their priorities. The first step of the process is to provide you with additional board managers. Now. You have to go to Edit, and from there you need to go to the File menu and choose preferences, you will be able to see this window. As you can see here, we have an additional board manager. You are Alts and you must be aspecific based. You are all in the window.

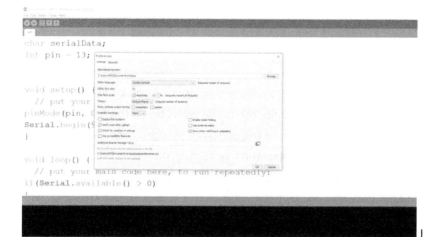

will provide this lecture resource, but here. Let me copy and paste you. This is the original E.s. P, you are all for this package. Now, if the box is not empty where you open the preference window, you might have installed several other boards. If it's the problem, I contact Xbox with the above, we all use commas to separate different Yahels. So you can add this one and add commas and add another. But because we only have it, I will be based here after doing it. Click OK to play to close the preference window. Now the original application we know where to find its info about the sport in general.

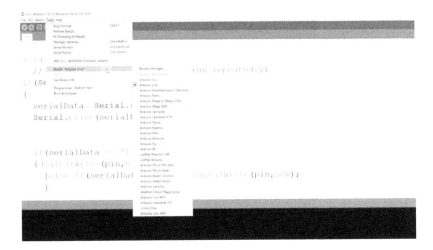

So let's go to the tool. And from there. Go to the board manager. And here and the boss manager, you need to write E.S.P. Now, as you can see here, we have E.S.P.

```
void loop() {
    // put your main code here, to run repeatedly:
    if (Serial.available() >
    {
        serialData= Serial.re
        Serial.print(serialDa

        if (serialData == '1')
        {digitalWrite(pin, HIG
        }else if (serialData
    }
```

Eight two six-six, all you need to do is click Install. It will take time to download around 34 megabits of data to your Arduino library folder, and once finished, it will show you a message that shows that everything is done. Now, after it's finished, as you can see, he said it was installed here, you can click on the lid. And if you want the Board manager, you can see that now we have E.S.P eight two, six, six, and E.S.P eight to eight-five and other E.S.P balls. Most of them are here now, all you need to do is start using it and I have mentioned that we have. At hand is e.s.p fair to eight to six six million now? To ensure that it is recognized when connecting a USB port, you need to install additional drivers from the Sealab website. I will give you a link to this driver too. So, you need to go and check your operating system. And we have Indusind Universal.

So we will use this software, click Download VCP. The download will begin, you just click download, after that you can install. Driver, depending on your operating system, that's all. Now, we have installed the hardware hardware hardware E.S.P for Arduino and USB drive drivers.

WHAT IS ESP32 BOARD

SB Development Board 32. E.s. P 32 is a low-cost system in the chip series made by the system. This is an increase in E.S.P eight to six six six which is widely used in Internet of Things projects. Their Aspy, 32, has the ability of Wi-Fi and Bluetooth, which makes it chip all that is rounded for the development of the internet project and the embedded system engineer. You will learn how to start e.s.p 32 and learn how to use it to scan a Wi-Fi, LED, button, sensor or sensor on our page along with other examples.

Specifications - ESP32 DEVKIT V1 DOIT	
Number of cores	2 (Dual core)
Wi-Fi	2.4 GHz up to 150 Mbit/s
Bluetooth	BLE (Bluetooth Low Energy) and legacy Bluetooth
Architecture	32 bits
Clock frequency	Up to 240 MHz
RAM	512 KB
Pins	30
Peripherals	Capacitive touch, ADCs (analog-to-digital converter), DACs (digital-to-analog converter), I²C (Inter-Integrated Circuit), UART (universal asynchronous receiver/transmitter), CAN 2.0 (Controller Area Network), SPI (Serial Peripheral Interface), I²S (Integrated Inter-IC Sound), RMII (Reduced Media-Independent Interface), PWM (pulse width modulation), and more.

Now, some of the main specifications for E.s. P 32, when it comes to chip specifications, you will find that it has a dual-core, which means that it has two processors. It also has Wi-Fi and Bluetooth built. And you don't need to plug every use of B Dongle to activate Wi-Fi or get a module. It runs a 32-bit program. The clock frequency can rise to 240 megahertz and have 512 kilobytes of this special board have 30 or 36 rounds, 15 in each row. It also has various kinds of peripherals available, such as capacitive touch sensors and digital converters, digital analogueue converter Universelle, asynchronous series communication modules, SPI, ice squirty and more than this board are equipped with effects and saws built and built and built temperature sensors, So this board is everything you need to start in a short time on the internet world. Now, to start programming sports, you need software or programming environments. You simply use the original idea, it's very easy to use software and most people are familiar with him. And if you are even if you are not used, this is the easiest software to use when you want to program. Yes, but there is also an expressive software idea of software. This is an interactive thing, the development framework they provide for their boards. There is also a JavaScript micro python, although it requires some adjustments to install the ESP library, everything will be explained in detail in a separate section where you will learn how to download and install the library needed for different ISP boards and. True steps to do it. Now to prepare your board. For those who are already known, there is an addition to the Arduino idea that allows you to program E.S.P 32 using the platform, the same platform that you can use to program Arduino can also be used to program E. P. P. Using the Arduino programming language, so out of the box and ready for you to use, and then we will explain that it is better to find out how many pins there, how to recognize the PIN and PIN functions which will be used when you want to connect the input-output. PWI signal or sensor.

STEP BY STEP INSTRUCTIONS TO UTILIZE STM32 SHEETS WITH ARDUINO IDE

STM 32 processors are utilized in a lot more industrially accessible item than the ESP 8266 or the ESP 32. This should have an explanation perhaps we creators can benefit on the off chance that we know it. This is the reason this video will cover the accompanying subjects. We will get an outline of the STM 32 chips and an outline of the accessible advancement sheets. We will speed test the ordinary delegates. Here we will see words like Fortran and Vax MIPS. The more established folks among us hear what I'm saying. We will program diverse STM 32 sheets with the Arduino ID. Here we will become familiar for certain stunts. We will perceive that it is so natural to do inline troubleshooting with stage IO. Furthermore, shock us with the board likewise referenced by watchers. We should begin with the outline. st microelectronics is settled in Switzerland, they make a ton of stuff. Today, we are just keen on their 32 bit chip units beginning with a five lectors st m 32. Every one of them are quicker and more proficient than the Arduino Uno

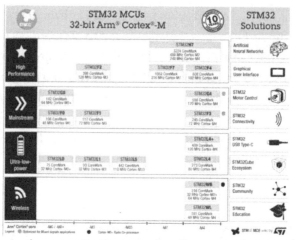

or then again the mega By the way, they fragment their reach in ultra low force standard, superior and remote. Here you as of now see a distinction to espressif. While they just have four MCs st Microsystems has 1090 of all dependent on ARM centers. Also, this may be the principal motivation behind why they are so effective in business applications. We will later check whether this additionally moves to us producers. Since I didn't perceive any sheets with remote chips promptly accessible for producers. With the exception of a Laura module from rack remote, I will focus on the remainder of the contribution. A more intensive glance at the naming shows that all low force chips have a L after the STM 32. Most others have a F It appears to be that the following number has to do with the center. Yet, here you need to focus. In the event that four chips truly utilize m four centers, however f1 chips use em three centers, so check before you choose. a general guideline discloses to us that the higher the center number, the more speed and different capacities. This is acceptable to know for us producers when we need to choose

Figure 9. STM32F103xx performance line UFQFPN48 pi

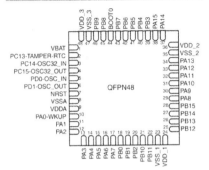

Figure 10. STM32F411xC/xE UFQFPN48 pinout

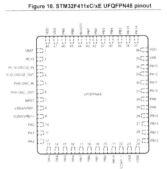

which board to utilize. Another intriguing truth in the event that we for instance, start our improvement with a modest f 103 c 86 chip with 64 kilobyte streak and later find that we need more we can choose the chip with a comparable pinout with more memory or speed. Or on the other hand we start with an incredible MCU for improvement. Furthermore, when completed quest for the least expensive conceivable chip which has sufficient memory for our item. A couple of pennies saved. Is this significant for producers not all that much since we as a rule purchase sheets and not chips and don't have to shave off each penny. A certain something anyway is huge. We can program many of those chips with our Arduino IE,

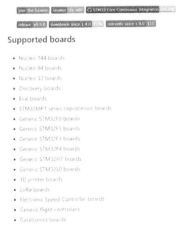

Arduino core support for STM32 based boards

Supported boards

- Nucleo 144 boards
- Nucleo 64 boards
- Nucleo 32 boards
- Discovery boards
- Eval boards
- STM32MP1 series coprocessor boards
- Generic STM32F0 boards
- Generic STM32F1 boards
- Generic STM32F3 boards
- Generic STM32F4 boards
- Generic STM32H7 boards
- Generic STM32L0 boards
- 3D printer boards
- LoRa boards
- Electronic Speed Controller boards
- Generic flight controllers
- Garatronics boards

you find a list on the STM 32 duino project get up and the number grew from release to release.

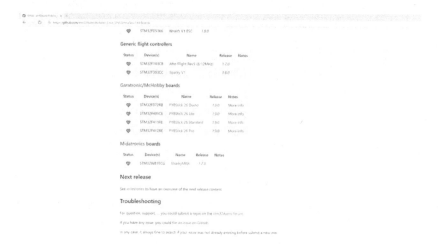

STM itself supports the SDM duino project. The initial project of Roger Clark is no more man The next question for us is, what kind of boards are available on the market? Here we have to distinguish between two very different sources, the Chinese and STM. Let's start with the Chinese.

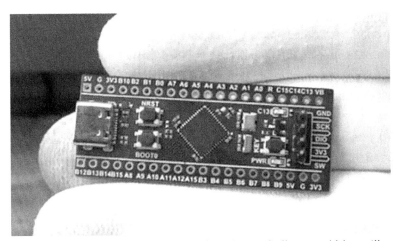

Most of the recent discussions on this channel all around blue pills and black pills, because they are relatively cheap.

If you search for other boards, you also get them but check first if the Arduino ID supports the chip before you order. The blue pills use the f 103 c h d six chip mentioned before they run on 72 megahertz have 64 kilobytes of flash and 20 kilobyte RAM, which is ridiculously small compared with a four megabyte flash of the ESP s. The black pills come in two versions. Both use f four chips and a floating point coprocessor to speed up calculations. The F 401 CCU runs on 84 megahertz has 256 kB flash and 64 kB ram the one with an F 411 CPU chip runs at 100 megahertz has 512 kilobyte flash and 128 kilobyte Ram.

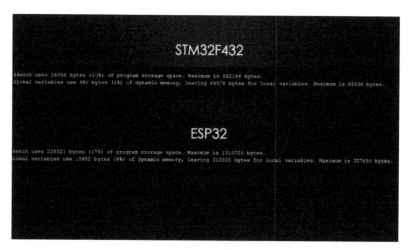

Is this flash sufficient? Here I compiled one of the benchmarks for an STM 32 F 432. It uses 27 kilobyte or 10% flash and 1% of RAM. The ESP 32 needs much more 17% and 4%. Maybe this has to do with the underlying artists and Wi Fi code of the ESP 32. We makers see that the STM 32 memories are smaller, but we also can build big sketches like with the ESP 32. At least with the F four chips. If we compare prices,

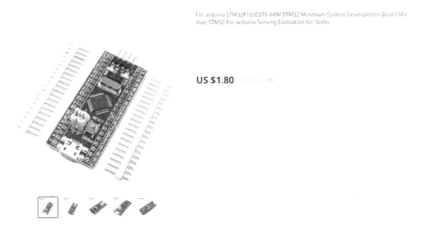

For arduino STM32F103C8T6 ARM STM32 Minimum System Development Board Module STM32 For arduino Sensing Evaluation for Skiller

US $1.80

we see that we get a blue pill for around $3 including shaping in single quantities that black pills are

STM32F401CCU6

STM32F401 STM32F411 Development Board V3.0 STM32F401CCU6 STM32F411CEU6 STM32F4 Learning Board 84Mhz 64KB RAM 256KB ROM
★ ★ ★ ★ ★ 5.0 · 101 Reviews · 303 orders

US $2.46

$3.83 respectively. $4.96. A typical ESP 32 Development Board costs around $5. Similar to the most expensive pill, as I said before st

STM32F401 STM32F411 Development Board V3.0 STM32F401CCU6 STM32F411CE
STM32F4 Learning Board 84Mhz 64KB RAM 256KB ROM

★ ★ ★ ★ ★ 5.0 - 101 Reviews 303 orders

ESP-32S ESP-WROOM-32 ESP32 ESP-32 Bluetooth and WIFI Dual Core CPU with L
Power Consumption MCU ESP-32

★ ★ ★ ★ ★ 4.9 - 2137 Reviews 6456 orders

US $3.39 ~~US $3.99~~ -15%

microelectronics also sales development boards, they are called nucleo and come in three versions with 3264 and 144 pins.

The 32 pin versions are slightly bigger than an Arduino Nano, the 64 pin versions are slightly bigger than the you know, and the 144 pin versions are similar to the maker. Also here you get a lot of different versions pay attention, the Arduino IDE supports not all of them.

Nucleo 144 boards

Status	Device(s)	Name	Release	Notes
♡	STM32F207ZG	Nucleo F207ZG	0.2.0	
♡	STM32F429ZI	Nucleo F429ZI	0.1.0	
♡	STM32F767ZI	Nucleo F767ZI	1.4.0	
♡	STM32F746ZG	Nucleo F746ZG	1.9.0	
♡	STM32F756ZG	Nucleo F756ZG	1.9.0	
♡	STM32L496ZG	Nucleo L496ZG	1.3.0	
♡	STM32L496ZG-P	Nucleo L496ZG-P	1.3.0	
♡	STM32L4R5ZI	Nucleo L4R5ZI	1.4.0	
♡	STM32L4R5ZI-P	Nucleo L4R5ZI-P	1.4.0	
♡	STM32H743ZI	Nucleo H743ZI(2)	1.5.0	Nucleo H743ZI2 since 1.6.0

This f 722 board would have been nice for a test ride, but it is not supported. I ordered an F 746. And my supplier returned the money because it was his fault. He said that the F 746 could not be exported to Switzerland, because it is dual use. This means that it can be used for civil as well as for military applications. I'm sure it would have improved the capabilities of our Swiss Army. Together with its famous Swiss Army knives. It would be unbeatable, I think. Now this board with a big chip weight still it is supported in the future version. Or maybe I will learn how to tweak the board's dot txt file.

25.58
STMicroelectronics STM32
★★★★☆ 2 Bewertungen

●○○
3 Bilder

I

would not mention those sports if they were expensive. They are not sourced in Switzerland. The big ones are below $30 including shaping. The small ones are around

STMicroelectronics STM32
Nucleo-32 Board L031K6 32K Flash
☆ ☆ ☆ ☆ ☆ 0 Bewertungen

●
1 Bild

$20. Maybe prices vary in your country. The main difference between the Chinese and the boards from st microelectronics is this part. All boards come with a built in so called St link. And now we are already in the next topic. How do we program our boards. Here things are straightforward with the Arduinos and DSPs. All are programmed via serial connection. Most boards have a USB to serial adapter on board.

Some of them not. Then you need a USB to serial adapter, sometimes also called ftdi adapter. The STM 30 twos are different. Some of them can be programmed via USB right out of the box. Others need a bootloader which you have to install when you get them on If you break them, if you use an st link adapter, you are offered additional programming possibilities.

The original adapter is not extremely expensive, but we also get cheap clones.

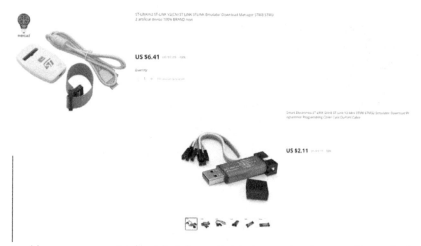

And here comes a trick. st link is available in version two and two dash one. My Arduino ID he did not accept these small st link B two adapters. The bigger ones look very similar to the original, and they can be upgraded to the newest release using this STM 32 pube

programmer, a software which has to be installed before you can use STM 32 chips with the Arduino, you just press this button, then this one And lastly, upgrade. Now it's on the newest version and can be used with the Arduino ID. So I would spend a little more and not buy one of those.

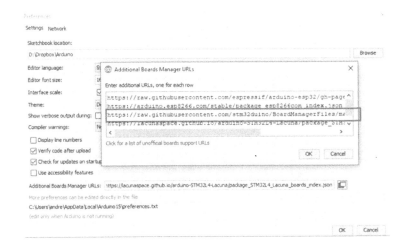

Obviously, we need to introduce the STM 32 programming climate for the Arduino ID. I leave a connection in the portrayal on the most proficient method to do it. It is like the ESP 32. The primary method of programming offered by these connectors is SW D sequential wire investigate. Its connector just has four pins, and all pills offered this association. SW D consistently works regardless of whether you break your chip some way or another, and it tends to be utilized for inline investigating. The following method of writing computer programs is the H ID bootloader. This is the path for blue pills impact. martic made a video on the most proficient method to streak the bootloader and how to transfer your sketch, you discover the connection in the portrayal. The H ID bootloader is just required for the blue pills. In any case, I didn't care for this cycle, I just would program them inside st interface. This boot loader thing was not truly stable for my situation and focus for the test. I additionally purchased clones with ck s 103 chips rather than STM 30 twos, I had the option to program them with s WD. However, my PC never perceived USB. You can maintain a strategic distance from this problem by not accepting blue pills. Perhaps you have an alternate involvement in them. Kindly remark. Next we go to the dark pills.

They already have a bootloader on the chip and I did not hear of clones with different shapes. Very good. You get two versions according to your needs. Both behave the same. First you block the board into USB and select these parameters according to the chip on board.

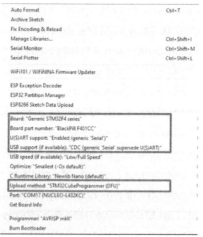

Now you have to do a similar procedures as on some ESP boards. Brace the boot zero and n rst buttons together. Wait for the USB disconnected tone. Let the reset button go and wait for the USB connected tone.

> 🖶 Print queues
> 🖶 Printers
> 🖥 Processors
> 🛡 Security devices
> 📲 Software components
> 📱 Software devices
> 🎙 Sound, video and game controllers
> 🖴 Storage controllers
> 🖥 System devices
> 🖦 Universal Serial Bus controllers
∨ 🖦 Universal Serial Bus devices
    🖦 STM32 BOOTLOADER
> 🖶 WSD Print Provider

Now you should see STM bootloader in the device manager and can hit upload. After uploading you should see the virtual comport your black pill created. This is the Chinese way to program the boards. Now we go to this waste way. As I said all nucleo boards have an st link on board as before you connect the board via USB and select the parameters like that. Currently, I use a small nucleo 32 f 432.

⬤ Mass Storage

STM32CubeProgrammer (SWD)

STM32CubeProgrammer (Serial)

STM32CubeProgrammer (DFU)

For the upload you can choose whatever method you want. Even the mass storage works because the Japes create a disk drive on your PC. Hit upload and make sure you connect to the right comport if you want to use serial. By the way, if you do not choose these two parameters, serial will not work. simple and efficient. No button pricing, no bootloader flashing, but I should not show off with these switch features. Why? After a few days of perfect working all my boards refused to show anything on cereal anymore. I tried nearly everything. I even installed the environment on a different computer. Maybe you have an idea of how to correct this flaw. Anyway, I found out that the serial two pins internally are connected to the SD link. When I use serial two, I got serial output via USB.

By the way, the serial two pins are also connected to the pins labeled our x t x on the Arduino connector of the nucleo 64 boards. The serial one pins are on D six and D eight. Another trick if you use serial on pins, not via USB, you have to use different parameters in the board menu. Now I was able to go on with my speed tests. In my last video, these tests also gave cause for complaint.

Arduino > Stm32 Examples

Name	Date modified	Type
e-tinkers_Test	16.09.2020 21:06	File folder
Communication	23.07.2020 10:10	File folder
NonReg	23.07.2020 10:10	File folder
Benchmarking	23.07.2020 10:10	File folder
Boards	23.07.2020 10:10	File folder
Peripherals	23.07.2020 10:10	File folder

So this time I use the official STM benchmark. It consists of three parts, a dry stone and two whetstone sketches, one with single and the other with double precision. The dry stone is an integer benchmark, and the whetstone uses floating point numbers.

Dhrystone

From Wikipedia, the free encyclopedia

Dhrystone is a synthetic computing benchmark program developed in 1984 by Reinhold P. Weicker intended to be representative of system (integer) programming. The Dhrystone grew to become representative of general processor (CPU) performance. The name "Dhrystone" is a pun on a different benchmark algorithm called Whetstone.[1]

Whetstone (benchmark)

From Wikipedia, the free encyclopedia

The **Whetstone benchmark** is a synthetic benchmark for evaluating the performance of computers.[1] It was first written in Algol 60 in 1972 at TSU (The Technical Support Unit of the Department of Trade and Industry - later part of the Central Computer and Telecommunications Agency or CCTA in the United Kingdom). It was derived from statistics on program behaviour gathered on the KDF9 computer at NPL National Physical Laboratory in the United Kingdom, using a modified version of its Whetstone ALGOL 60 compiler. The workload on the machine was represented as a set of frequencies of execution of the 124 instructions of the Whetstone Code. The Whetstone Compiler was built at the Atomic Power Division of the English Electric Company in Whetstone, Leicestershire, England.[2] hence its name. Dr. B.A. Wichman at NPL produced a set of 42 simple ALGOL 60 statements, which in a suitable combination matched the execution statistics.

Looking at the sketches you see Copyright 19 188, more than 30 years old. Then a little further down, you find the word Fortran.

Fortran was the accepted norm for logical counts during the 60s and 70s. What's more, was likewise utilized subsequently for that reason. It was the main programming language I learned in the 1900 and 70s. At the point when we were permitted to utilize the incredibly costly IBM 360 centralized computer of our administration. During the daytime, it determined assessments, yet it was normal in those days to turn the PCs off when individuals returned home. Our Professor knew the opportune individuals, and got the way in to the PC room like that we had a PC only for us. The evenings were short, however we had loads of fun, and we caught on quickly. The other fascinating thing here is the yield Vax MIPS. What's the significance here? Vax was the best departmental PC in the 1900 and 80s. Worked by Digital Equipment Corporation, can likewise was something like Elon Musk today. In those days he beat the unbelievably huge and incredible IBM from various perspectives, and was named America's best enterpreneur by Fortune Magazine, and I was one of his pleased workers. In any case, I digress the Vax 11 780 was the main model have a long column, it was a major machine cost 1,000,000 dollars rapidly and created correctly one Vax MIPS. Furthermore, presently we are in the presentation test. I utilized these games for STM 32 f four sheets with three unique cycles. Two distinctive STM 32 f1 sheets with various processors, and one STM 32 low force port. Obviously, I contrast them and the ESP 8266 and the ESP 32. I likewise attempted to contrast it and an

Arduino Uno. Sadly, this sketch was too huge. So we don't get an Arduino MIPS For correlation, the twofold exactness whetstone didn't run on my L zero 31 board. In the event that we analyze the number exhibition,

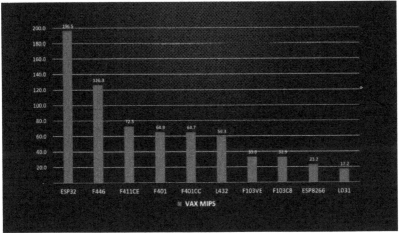

we see that even the low power chip for a few dollars beats the Vax of 1978 by a factor of 17. But the top of the row still is the ESP 32. With nearly 200 bucks MIPS. The three of the four f four chips are very similar, the F 446 is much faster. This proves that the Chinese pills have comparable performance as the nucleo boards with similar processors. astonishingly, the low power f4 is also quite fast. The ESP 8266 is slower than the F 103 chips and compatible with a low power l zero 31. But how do they compare if they can use their co processors to crunch floating point numbers?

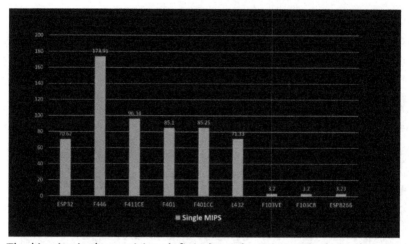

The king in single precision definitely as the F 446. It is more than two times faster than the ESP 32. Again, the other f4 chips are similar in performance. And the F 103. And the ESP 8266 are much much slower because they have no coprocessor.

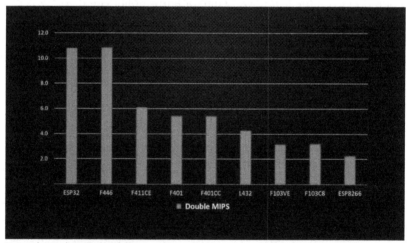

But what about double precision? Here, the ESP 32 has a similar performance as the F 446. The low power I 432. loses a little. But interestingly, the slow f 103 chips are not slow in this benchmark. But if we have a closer look,

Board	VAX MIPS	Double MIPS	Single MIPS
ESP32	196.5	10.8	70.62
F446	126.3	10.8	173.91
F411CE	72.5	6.1	96.34
F401	64.9	5.4	85.1
F401CC (Blackpill)	64.7	5.4	85.25
L432	59.3	4.3	71.33
F103VE	33.0	3.2	3.2
F103C8 (Bluepill)	32.9	3.2	3.2
ESP8266	23.2	2.2	3.23
L031	17.2		1.55

we see that the single and the double precision MIPS are the same for these two processors. Also for the ESP 8266. The difference between the two benchmarks is tiny. Maybe the compiler cheats and uses the same precision for both benchmarks. Please comment if you know more.

The last point I needed to show you is cool in the event that you use stage IO all things being equal. The Arduino ID, you can investigate all STM 32 sheets, as demonstrated in video number 274. You can do that with ESP 32. In any case, the Arduinos and the ESP 8266 don't have this component, or if nothing else not in a usable design. Here, we just interface the st connection to the SW D port and add these lines in stage IO speck ini. Since the nucleo sheets as of now have the st interface inherent, we just need to plug them into a USB port, convenient. Furthermore, incidentally, here, the little and modest st connect v2 connectors work abnormal. I need to say I like inline troubleshooting with breakpoints and variable assessment a great deal. It improves on my work and I'm exceptionally profitable. summed up. The STM 32 family is tremendous and has around 1000 individuals. Contrasted and this decision. The expressive family with four individuals is little, however the expressive chips have a great deal of highlights, particularly Wi Fi. This is the reason we love them. The STM 32 chips are accessible with a few ARM centers with totally different properties and paces. The chip numbering is some way or another instinctive. By and large, greater numbers are all the more remarkable chips. Sadly not generally. They additionally have a low electrical cable, which is adequately intriguing to take a gander at later on. We can either purchase Chinese or nucleo sheets from st microelectronics, the most acclaimed Chinese STM 32 sheets are the blue and the dark pill. I don't prescribe to purchase blue pills, they have no local bootloader their clones don't work accurately, and they are difficult to deal with. The dark pills are the better decision they have a worked in bootloader are a lot quicker have more memory, and the F 401 isn't considerably more costly than the blue pill. The nucleo sheets, particularly the greater ones are not pricey and a decent decision essentially in light of the worked in st interface, which likewise works with just a USB link. The Arduino ID works almost perfectly with upheld sheets. Nonetheless, focus that you don't accepting unsupported sheets. The boundaries in the sheets menu must be changed. Particularly in the event that you need to utilize sequential print you need to utilize the correct mix. Something else, zero print won't work in my current circumstance zero cerebrum abruptly quit working. So far I didn't discover an answer bad by the privilege st connect. Else, you won't program the Chinese game with the Arduino ID nor with the STM 32 center developer. Coincidentally, the speed correlation uncovers that my watchers were correct. The f4 tapes are a lot quicker than the F 103 shapes utilized in video number 345. The quickest f 446 utilized in my correlation is pretty much as quick as an ESP 32. Be that as it may, remember the ESP 32 has a subsequent center if necessary. All STM 32 chips can be repaired utilizing stage IO and a SD interface. Something final a few watchers may have missed the small 4.1 board introduced in my last mailbag. It is small expense around $30 and has a M seven center its clock speed of 600 megahertz guarantees very some force. I would not like to remember it for the examination, since it has no STM 32 center and it is very quick.

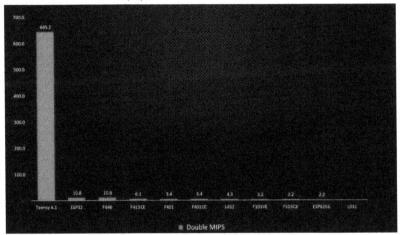

The curves would have been useless to compare the rest of the chips, but we can assume that the fastest STM 32 chips are comparable in speed. For integers.

Board	VAX MIPS	Single MIPS	Double MIPS
Teensy 4.1	1'751	548.8	645.2
ESP32	196	70.62	10.8
F446	126	173.91	10.8
F411CE	73	96.34	6.1
F401	65	85.1	5.4
F401CC (Blackpill)	65	85.25	5.4
L432	59	71.33	4.3
F103VE	33	3.2	3.2
F103C8 (Bluepill)	33	3.2	3.2
ESP8266	23	3.23	2.2
L031	17	1.55	

It has nearly 10 times more Vax MIPS than the fastest f 446. And for double precision, it is unbelievable 60 times faster than the F 446 or the ESP 32 What a surprise, I can also would be pleased to see such a small burger if he would still be alive. And now you probably understand why I do not want to sell hardware anymore.

DOWNLOAD AND INSTALL ARDUINO ESP32 V1 DEVELOPMENT ENVIRONMENT

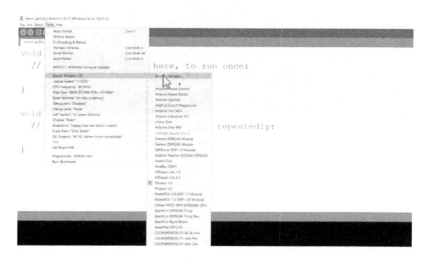

Know if you have a board like we have, which is the version of E.S.P 32, you have to go to the tool and from the tool menu, you just go to the board, select the manager section and from E.S.P. Thirty-two now. If you don't get any results, you need to do one thing before continuing, you need to add that SB 32 Package Digest on the file link to the preference window. So let's click the file.

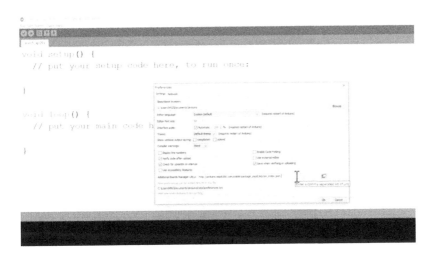

Preferences and here are coma, then the second length. I will give all this link in a resource lecture again, go to the Board Sports Manager tool and here.

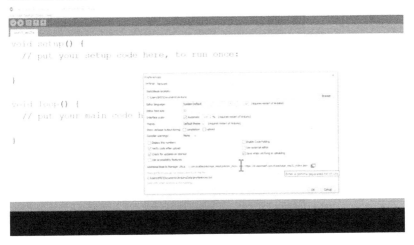

Cut e.s.p. 32. And this is it, you just click installed to install this, Paul. It will take time. Now, after you are done, you will see here, click Close and go to the tool menu.

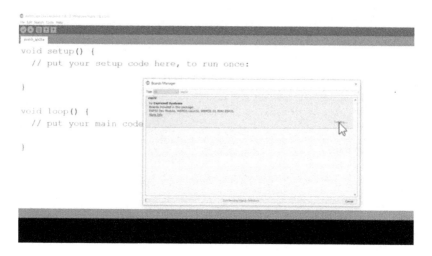

```
void setup() {
    // put your setup code here, to run once:

}

void loop() {
    // put your main code
}
```

From there, you can check the board you want to connect and you can see what we have. List of balls here, you need to choose that match your configuration in our case. OK sorry. In our case, it will be it. E.S.P and we need to choose SB 32, so let's scroll up.

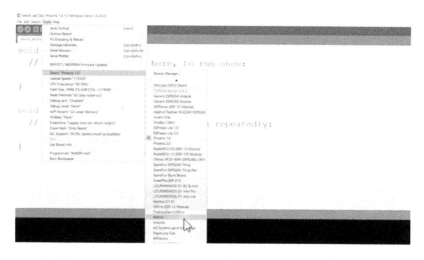

OK, here we have E.S.P,32 people get ready for this module and we have other E.S.P 32 modules, as you can see here. We need word E.S.P to get version one, which is the one we have here and our lab. And we recommend this to everyone who just started on the Internet of Things.

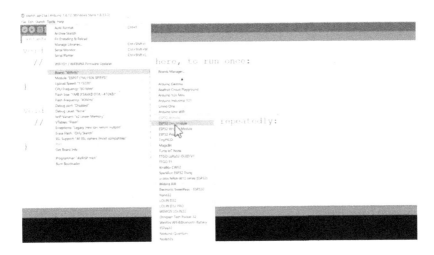

So choose, then go if you do not see your ball. I have it on my OSPI board, I have connected the ball, but I do not see the board here in that regard.

You need to download and install this and your USB to your art bridge driver now, not what matches your operating system. Be sure to write this name when you look for it if your board is E.S.P 32, depending on your board. There are other drivers. So click, download. Again. Click Download here won't take time, double-click.

LOAD YOUR FIRST CODE TO ESP32 BOARD

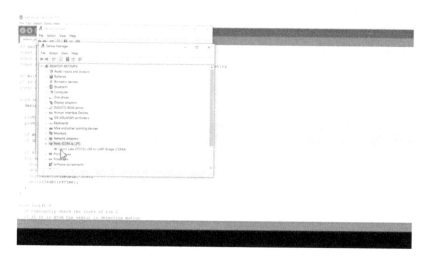

Now, if you have everything connected correctly and if you go to the device manager, I do connect my board so that you will see your board and compare on the name of the sea or silicon labs, which we just installed and before.

Now we know that our bodies are connected to come to return to our software, make sure that you choose the right board. Perform E.S.P 32 a difficult version and come back again to select the board.

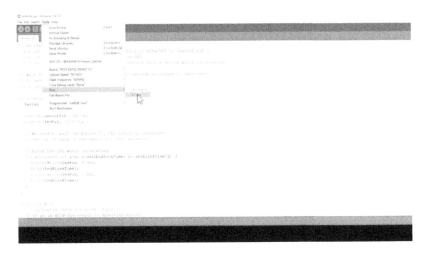

Select Confort. Now, you can go to the example and check out some examples of wi-fi. As you can see here, we have more than one, you can check examples of wi-fi scanning.

Now, this is our new sketch, as you can see, it uses a Wi-Fi library. You don't need to know. All previous experiences, to use this example, all you need to do now is upload.

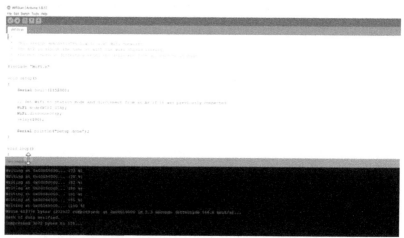

Now combining sketches and uploading the SB 30 sketch style to bald. Usually, takes time because of how you know, isn't the original coding application for ESPN? As you can see, it connects, using Confort. To write e.s.p. The current code attracts a code of four per cent, 100 per cent.

Now it's hard to sit VSP boards, as you can see from this menu, show all the details. Again, the writing process takes time. Now, as you can see, upload. So continue, open the cereal monitor.

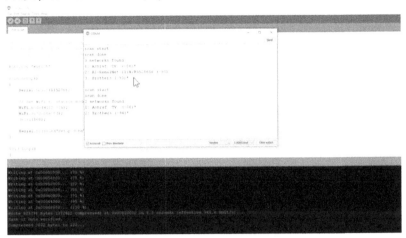

Make sure you have selected a tripod, right, as you can see, you know it, yes, people start scanning wildfire and after completion, it will show you the network available in your area. I have these three networks, as you can see, one of which has a very weak signal. That's why it comes and goes.

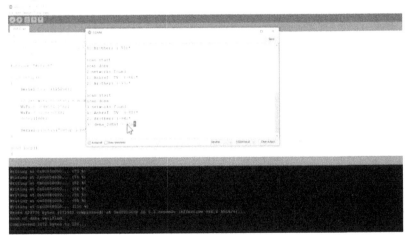

So this is my network and this is a network of someone. Now we have three networks. So. As you can see, we just uploaded our first call to the E.S.p to 32 board, and this is a quote, an example of the Wi-Fi scan process. Next, we will dig deeper and start talking about how to test the lead on the board and how to control different elements using the port. Then we will turn to Auberge.

WIFI ACCESS POINT

```
#include <WiFi.h>
#include <WiFiClient.h>
#include <WiFiAP.h>

#define LED_BUILTIN 2   // Set the GPIO pin where you connected your test
LED or comment this line out if your dev board has a built-in LED

// Set these to your desired credentials.
const char *ssid = "yourAP";
const char *password = "yourPassword";

WiFiServer server(80);


void setup() {
  pinMode(LED_BUILTIN, OUTPUT);

  Serial.begin(115200);
  Serial.println();
  Serial.println("Configuring access point...");

  // You can remove the password parameter if you want the AP to be open.
  WiFi.softAP(ssid, password);
  IPAddress myIP = WiFi.softAPIP();
  Serial.print("AP IP address: ");
  Serial.println(myIP);
  server.begin();

  Serial.println("Server started");
}

void loop() {
  WiFiClient client = server.available();   // listen for incoming clients
```

```
if (client) {                    // if you get a client,
  Serial.println("New Client.");   // print a message out the serial port
  String currentLine = "";         // make a String to hold incoming data
from the client
  while (client.connected()) {     // loop while the client's connected
    if (client.available()) {      // if there's bytes to read from the client,
      char c = client.read();      // read a byte, then
      Serial.write(c);             // print it out the serial monitor
      if (c == '\n') {             // if the byte is a newline character

        // if the current line is blank, you got two newline characters in a row.
        // that's the end of the client HTTP request, so send a response:
        if (currentLine.length() == 0) {
          // HTTP headers always start with a response code (e.g. HTTP/1.1 200
OK)
          // and a content-type so the client knows what's coming, then a blank
line:
          client.println("HTTP/1.1 200 OK");
          client.println("Content-type:text/html");
          client.println();

          // the content of the HTTP response follows the header:
          client.print("Click <a href=\"/H\">here</a> to turn ON the
LED.<br>");
          client.print("Click <a href=\"/L\">here</a> to turn OFF the
LED.<br>");

          // The HTTP response ends with another blank line:
          client.println();
          // break out of the while loop:
          break;
        } else {    // if you got a newline, then clear currentLine:
          currentLine = "";
        }
      } else if (c != '\r') {  // if you got anything else but a carriage return
character,
        currentLine += c;      // add it to the end of the currentLine
      }

      // Check to see if the client request was "GET /H" or "GET /L":
      if (currentLine.endsWith("GET /H")) {
        digitalWrite(LED_BUILTIN, HIGH);           // GET /H turns the LED
on
      }
      if (currentLine.endsWith("GET /L")) {
```

```
        digitalWrite(LED_BUILTIN, LOW);            // GET /L turns the LED
off
      }
     }
    }
    // close the connection:
    client.stop();
    Serial.println("Client Disconnected.");
   }
 }
```

WHAT AMOUNT IS OPEN SOURCE FEATURING THE NEW ESP32-C3

when I got these new RISC five ESP 32 boards in my mail, I asked myself, is this new technology really revolutionary as written everywhere? What are the advantages for a typical maker, time for a closer look, but pay attention, it will be a rough ride and not for the faint hearted because we will talk about stacks, IP ecosystems, and a lot about standardization.

RISC-V (pronounced "risk-five"[1][1]) is an open standard instruction set architecture (ISA) based on established reduced instruction set computer (RISC) principles. Unlike most other ISA designs, the RISC-V ISA is provided under open source licenses that do not require fees to use. A number of companies are offering or have announced RISC-V hardware, open source operating systems with RISC-V support are available and the instruction set is supported in several popular software toolchains.

According to Wikipedia, risk five is an open standard instruction set architecture based on established risk principles. Unlike most other iaasa designs, the RISC five is a is provided under open source licenses that do not require fees to use. Sounds cool, open source and no fees, who does not love these words? So it's worthwhile to start digging into the topic. Let's start the digging with the word RISC, reduced instruction set computers, its rivals or Sisk. Complex instruction set computers simply say it Sisk chips have very powerful

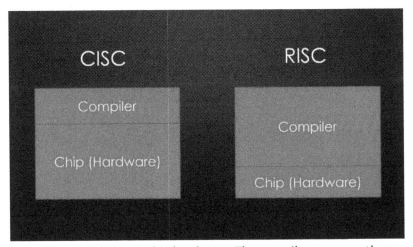

instructions implemented in hardware. The compilers can use these instructions and so half less work. The earlier computers like the Intel x86 were Sisk. Then came RISC, which implemented only basic instructions in hardware, the compilers had to take over a lot of work to assemble the complex comments using hardware basic instructions. Obviously, the code became longer. Back then memory was already cheaper. And because RISC was much faster than Sisk. The technology gained acceptance, the simple RISC chips had much higher clock speeds, and the compiler sat optimization possibilities to increase speed even further. In the 1990s. All workstations and high end computers used risk. But the Sisk processors survived because they borrowed some concepts from risk and risk processors became more complex.

A

typical example for risk is the arm instruction set, where each generation added more instructions. We will cover arm later. It's crucial for RISC five. Today, the most important Sisk processors still are based on Intel's x86 architecture, and are produced by Intel and AMD. They are pretty fast too. And now we have to go back to the last century. Back then, risk was an excellent way to attack Microsoft and Intel's dominance using risk and Unix, IBM,

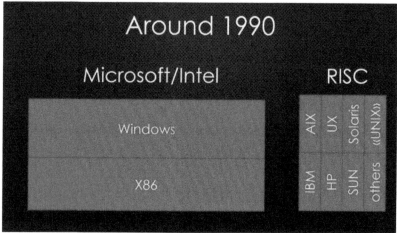

HP son and others tried to create their chips. They could not break the monopoly of the x86 architecture because they hated each other too much and were not able to cooperate. Also Linux as a more unified Unix operating system was not invented or adopted yet. Chips are not

everything. As we saw, we need operating systems to run applications,

```
Application

Operating system, Compiler

Chip Architecture

Silicon
```

which at last will be utilized by the clients on cell phones or PCs, and the processor structures are executed on silicon chips. The outcome is a few layers of various innovations. Each level relies upon The level underneath and interfaces To associate with levels, I consider this drawing that innovation stack, we will lay to put organizations on this stack. We should begin with the UI. Since the client and the application designers are not the equivalent, a UI should be characterized. Today, a couple of UIs endure, which has a great deal of benefits for us clients. The following level is the working frameworks like Android, Windows, Linux, and iOS. I incorporate the compilers or device chains. Likewise here. The applications run on these working frameworks. Once more, we need an interface definition to ensure that applications immaculately run on all PCs utilizing a specific working framework. This interface utilizes application programming interfaces, or API's. Here, Windows was the principal working framework that had the ability to compel numerous application designers to revamp their applications on the off chance that they needed to endure. This made it conceivable that today, everyone can utilize PCs. Why? Prior to windows, each equipment provider had its own stack. Also, in light of the fact that no standard API interface existed, application, engineers needed to choose which stack they needed to help with their applications. Due to this fracture, their business sectors were restricted. The quantity of uses sold little, and the costs in this way high.

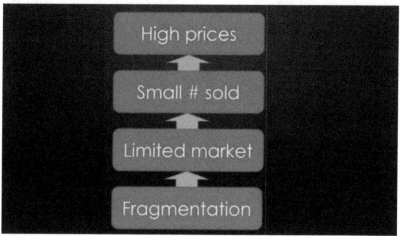

The users had a lot of incompatible applications in their lab or factory. Young people cannot imagine how miserable life was back then. Did I say standard? Yes, I said it. But who wants to be standardized and follow strict rules. Only one smartphone to choose? No Macs, only PCs. Everybody has to wear the same trousers. No, not jeans, we do this voluntarily. Standards are the contrary of flexibility and restrict our freedom. Right. Right on our level. If we open our point of view, and include the level below us things change. Standardization on the lower level becomes the basis for flexibility on the higher level. using Linux, for example, we get the flexibility to choose whatever application we want to use.

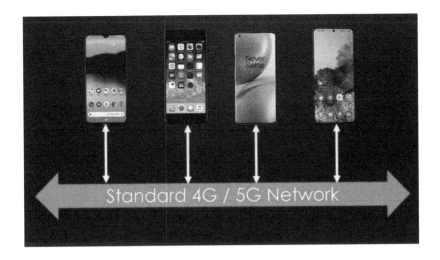

Another model, normalized network interfaces empower our cell phones to work wherever on the planet. The older folks actually recall when us telephones didn't work in the remainder of the world, and the other way around. Due to various organization principles. You can stretch out these guides to shape holders or traffic. What might occur if everyone demanded the adaptability to utilize the roadside they like most, or if half of the vehicles had the speed increase and the brake pedals exchanged. Like this Bentley from 1928. Brian Johnson, the front man of ACDC actually drives one, I expect he changed the setup to the current norm. Else, he presumably would be dead at this point. Simply because the UI of vehicles is pretty much normalized, we get the adaptability to lease a vehicle wherever on the planet, we Swiss simply need to pay somewhat more consideration. In the event that we go to the UK or Ireland and a couple of different nations. Since we drive on the correct side, they should drive on some unacceptable roadside. As we saw with a Bentley, it's frequently undeniably less basic, which standard is picked. More significant is that a standard is characterized. Except if you're an architect, we are acclaimed for beginning almost strict conflicts about such things. The learning is on the off chance that we need adaptability on one level, we need to normalize the level underneath. On the off chance that you keep a certain something, this is it, and you can stop on the off chance that you would prefer not to understand what this inside has to do with hazard five, or did you as of now discover obviously,

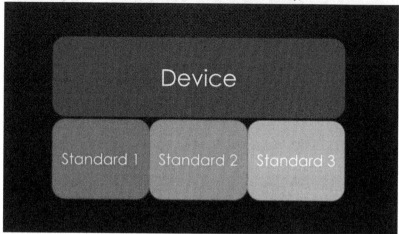

the upper level could be built to support different standards on a lower level. Unfortunately, this creates a lot of complexity and costs. As an example, all companies have to offer an app for Android and iOS. Let's continue with our stack.

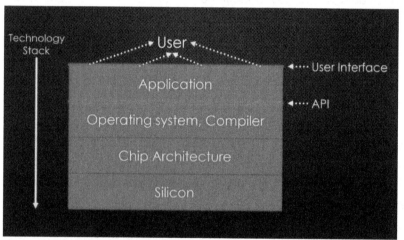

The next level is vital for RISC five. It is the level of chip architectures. On this level, we find all risk is as like power PC or MIPS. And we find the arm and Intel is as Did you ever ask yourself why windows only run

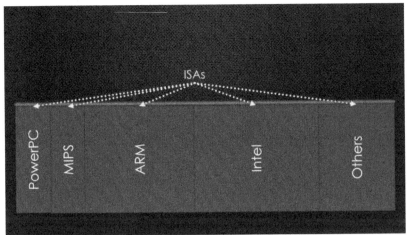

on Intel compatible chips because it uses the standard it As a published by Intel and AMD, all other chips have other ISS and Microsoft until recently only supported Intel's ISC.

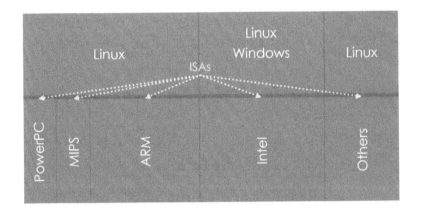

Linux on the other hand, runs on several ISS. So they solve the problem and of course are much better than Windows right? A little bit. You still have to compile your operating system and all your applications for the is a of choice. They are not compatible Percy.

If we search for Debian on Docker Hub, we find a different version for each is a by the way, arm needs two different versions. Unfortunately, again, we must make a detour to understand why arm is so successful. This time into strategies of companies. Each company buys stuff from suppliers adds some value, sometimes partners with other companies and sell their products to their customers. Competitors try to do the same,

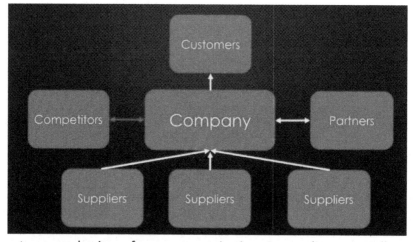

yet, remove business from our organization. Accomplices generally are on a comparable level. They either work with similar clients or purchase a similar innovation. Frequently, organizations are made by more modest organizations to rival a lot bigger contender.

Organizations like to purchase a normalized item. Why? buy items as a rule are one level underneath. Also, normalized items frequently are called wares, since they are compatible. Utilizing products has a great deal of benefits for organizations. The first is that they can get lower costs since they have providers all sell practically identical items and need to contend on cost. What's more, they don't rely upon one provider alone, which builds adaptability. organizations don't care for restraining infrastructure providers by any stretch of the imagination. How about we apply this reality to our chip designs. IBM, HP and different constructing agents needed to buy chips. You can envision how much their buys loved Intel and AMD with an extensive piece of the overall industry in the PC and the worker business they directed the guidelines. Hence, the two organizations attempted to do a regressive reconciliation and began to deliver their own chips to turn out to be less subject to Intel. Since both were wild contenders and privately owned businesses, they couldn't accomplice. They additionally didn't discover numerous clients since all more modest organizations on a similar level dreaded them and rather purchased from Intel or AMD. These two organizations were providers and not contenders for them. In mid 1990. A little UK organization called arm teamed up with Apple and made a danger is a remembering licensed innovation or IP for how to execute the semiconductors on silicon arm never have fabricated chips and offered its IP to little organizations that couldn't go through the cash to construct their own ISP. As of not long ago, we had Intel and AMD for PC chips, IBM, HP and some all were their own ISS and a couple of little players that dependent on their chips on ARM design. Furthermore, we had a couple of free organizations like pic or atmail, which delivered little chips for particular applications.

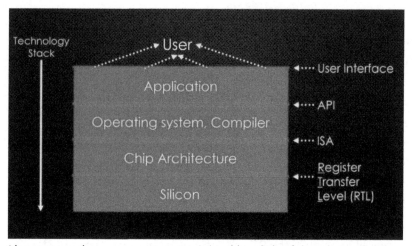

Also, presently we are on most minimal level the fabs who make the chips as indicated by the client's outlines. Worldwide foundries or tsmc are instances of organizations zeroed in on this level. Since arm didn't sell chips, they were viewed as accomplices to the chip merchants. Furthermore, on the grounds that all had Intel and AMD as shared adversary arm was fruitful, and today has a 80% piece of the overall industry in the IoT territory. Obviously, it helped that Intel zeroed in on the more productive PC and worker business. The market of little chips in those days was not fascinating for the huge folks. The interface to the silicon level is called RTL or register move level data and depicts how to construct the chip in silicon. here by the manner in which you discover Verilog and VHDL dialects, which are likewise used to program FPGAs. For little arrangement, we can utilize FPGAs rather than plain silicon. This reality regularly is utilized to test new plans before a ton of cash is given to the fabs in conjunctions with RISC five. This reality is interesting for us. Another piece of the IP is the way to do confirmation. This is the undertaking to confirm that the recently constructed silicon chip consents to the characterized is a detail.

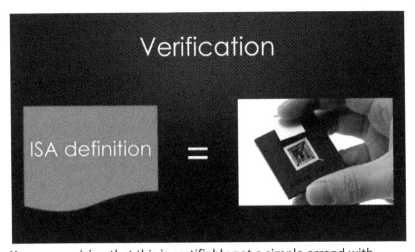

You can envision that this is certifiably not a simple errand with complex processors. ghost and emergency come into memory where mistakes were found on the silicon level after huge number of chips were sold. Along with numerous different apparatuses like compilers, these check suites are known as the environment of n is a you even could tally all the prepared plan specialists and fanboys of a specific is an in as indicated by least fatty, Torvalds, the designer of Linux, the biological system is the most basic segment of an ISP. Yet, where fits hazard five. On this site, we have Intel and AMD. Also, here we have arm both with a high piece of the overall industry in their individual business sectors. They need an extra contender like an opening in their mind. Furthermore, as we saw previously, they have positively no requirement for open source. They need to ensure their restraining infrastructures to the extent that this would be possible. So who is keen on hazard five, if not, the folks with the most expertise the following degree of organizations, as we saw previously, is a lot of intrigued that a normalized is an arises on the grounds that it would normalize the level beneath them and increment their adaptability. It will likewise give them haggling force and cost decrease. The equivalent applies to Linux, where huge organizations like SAP put a great deal of cash into Linux. They were situated on the application layer and needed an item working framework since it made their lives simpler and their pockets Fuller. They even made the greater part of the Linux augmentations they created open source like that Linux turned into a dependable working framework rapidly. Additionally for business applications. We previously saw some open is as in the mid 2000s, which were not fruitful. My hypothesis is that race fives timing is wonderful in light of the fact that every one of the allies have a shared adversary, arm like arm during the 1990s against Intel and AMD RISC five is presently the development against arm. This is the reason I figure it will be effective. One organization anyway is missing. In the event that you Google STM and RISC five, you discover no hits.

Why RISC-V for Falcon Next

RISC-V is the only architecture that meets all our criteria
https://riscv.org/wp-content/uploads/2016/07/Tue1100_Nvidia_RISCV_Story_V2.pdf

Item	Requirement	ARM A53	ARM A9	ARM R5	RISC-V Rocket	NV RISC-V
Core perf	>2x riscv	Yes	Yes	Yes	Yes	Yes
Area (16ff)	<0.1mm^2	No	No	Yes	Yes	Yes
Security	Yes	T2	T2	No	Yes	Yes
TCM	Yes	Yes	No	Yes	No	Yes
L1/D$	Yes	Yes	Yes	Yes	Yes	Yes
Addressing	64bit	Yes	No	No	Yes	Yes
Extensible ISA	Yes	No	No	No	No	Yes
Safety (ECC/Parity)	Yes	Yes	Yes	Yes	Yes	Yes
Functional (Emulation mode)	Yes	Yes	No	No	No	Yes

STM is one of the more critical arm clients and perhaps they rest similar profound and comfortable rest as Intel during the 1900s and 90s, where they made a huge load of cash and under appraised arm as the newcomer. This is my view on the set of experiences and the current circumstance. However, is this bologna? Or then again does it contain a trace of legitimacy? We should check and take a gander at the rundown of allies of the last danger five occasion normally following the progression of cash assists with comprehension. On this slide, we see Calista redmont, the CEO of the danger five Foundation. The establishment as of late moved to Switzerland, incidentally. Also, here is the rundown of the supporters of the occasion. The most intriguing is the flake-out and Vidya one of the establishing individuals and the large enthusiast of hazard five as we see on this slide from 2017. Meanwhile, they bought arm and appear to be not any more an excess of keen on supporting RISC five. The acquisition of arm by the way is a traditional in reverse incorporation where an organization purchases its essential provider which in some cases bases its accomplice off. We will perceive how Intel and friends will respond to this buy. Unmistakable allies of the occasion Western Digital Seagate who have an and micro processor the Arduino chips producer, these organizations share practically speaking that they are for the most part clients have arm and they don't care for their imposing business model. At that point we see psi five and andis both sell IP around hazard five. Indeed, they sell something which clearly isn't open source lightpath and different organizations sell instruments into the RISC five market. Indeed, they sell it and it's not open source. So what is genuinely open source around hazard five. For the occasion,

ISA base and extensions (20191213)

Name	Description	Version	Status[n]
	Base		
RVWMO	Weak Memory Ordering	2.0	Ratified
RV32I	Base Integer Instruction Set, 32-bit	2.1	Ratified
RV32E	Base Integer Instruction Set (embedded); 32-bit, 16 registers	1.9	Open
RV64I	Base Integer Instruction Set, 64-bit	2.1	Ratified
RV128I	Base Integer Instruction Set, 128-bit	1.7	Open
	Extension		
M	Standard Extension for Integer Multiplication and Division	2.0	Ratified
A	Standard Extension for Atomic Instructions	2.1	Ratified
F	Standard Extension for Single-Precision Floating-Point	2.2	Ratified
D	Standard Extension for Double-Precision Floating-Point	2.2	Ratified
Zicsr	Control and Status Register (CSR)	2.0	Ratified
Zifencei	Instruction-Fetch Fence	2.0	Ratified
G	Shorthand for the IMAFDZicsr Zifencei base and extensions, intended to represent a standard general-purpose ISA	N/A	N/A
Q	Standard Extension for Quad-Precision Floating Point	2.2	Ratified
L	Standard Extension for Decimal Floating-Point	0.0	Open
C	Standard Extension for Compressed Instructions	2.0	Ratified
B	Standard Extension for Bit Manipulation	0.92	Open
J	Standard Extension for Dynamically Translated Languages	0.0	Open
T	Standard Extension for Transactional Memory	0.0	Open
P	Standard Extension for Packed-SIMD Instructions	0.2	Open
V	Standard Extension for Vector Operations	0.9	Open
N	Standard Extension for User-Level Interrupts	1.1	Open
H	Standard Extension for Hypervisor	0.4	Open
Zam	Misaligned Atomics	0.1	Open

only the is a definition for these four cores and some extensions for different purposes like F and D, which provide floating point operations. The scores and extensions enable companies to build custom made microprocessors. They even are allowed to extend these instructions with their own ones. Extension G, by the way, is a general purpose iaasa and include these extensions. We also find the rest of open source course as we will lay to see how can we order our custom made RISC five chip, just go to the sci fi homepage and start to design your own desire chip, hit Enter, and you will get the specification for

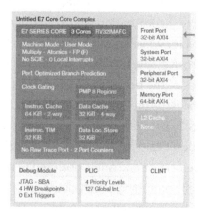

your chip and a big invoice, then you can contact the fab and order the chips, they will tell you that the minimum order size is a few 1000 chips, and their offer is even more expensive. Millions of dollars seem to be the dimensions these companies calculate. So probably not for the average maker. So let's stick with the ESP 32 c three, a less expensive possibility to play with RISC five its core complies with our v 32 i m c.

3.1.1 CPU

ESP32-C3 family has a low-power 32-bit RISC-V single-c

- four-stage pipeline that supports a clock frequency

  `RV32IMC ISA`

- 32-bit multiplier and 32-bit divider
- up to 32 vectored interrupts at seven priority levels
- up to 8 hardware breakpoints/watchpoints
- up to 16 PMP regions
- JTAG for debugging

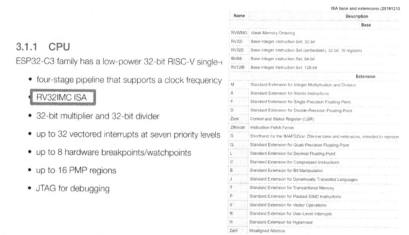

ISA base and extensions (20191213)

Name	Description
	Base
RVWMO	Weak Memory Ordering
RV32I	Base Integer Instruction Set, 32-bit
RV32E	Base Integer Instruction Set (embedded), 32-bit, 16 registers
RV64I	Base Integer Instruction Set, 64-bit
RV128I	Base Integer Instruction Set, 128-bit
	Extension
M	Standard Extension for Integer Multiplication and Division
A	Standard Extension for Atomic Instructions
F	Standard Extension for Single-Precision Floating-Point
D	Standard Extension for Double-Precision Floating-Point
Zicsr	Control and Status Register (CSR)
Zifencei	Instruction-Fetch Fence
G	Shorthand for the IMAFDZicsr Zifencei base and extensions, intended to represent
Q	Standard Extension for Quad-Precision Floating-Point
L	Standard Extension for Decimal Floating-Point
C	Standard Extension for Compressed Instructions
B	Standard Extension for Bit Manipulation
J	Standard Extension for Dynamically Translated Languages
T	Standard Extension for Transactional Memory
P	Standard Extension for Packed-SIMD Instructions
V	Standard Extension for Vector Operations
N	Standard Extension for User-Level Interrupts
H	Standard Extension for Hypervisor
Zam	Misaligned Atomics

Now we know what it means. It is a 32 bit processor with extensions for integer multiplication and divisions and the extension for compressed instructions, which increases execution speed. It has no floating point operations on silicon. The chip contains lots of peripherals like Wi Fi and Bluetooth in addition to the RISC five core and a big part is cryptographic hardware acceleration.

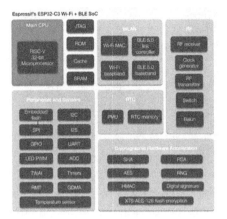

The chips target market is a secure Wi Fi or Bluetooth connection for IoT devices, the same purpose as the ESP 8266 heart when it came to market.

ESP32-C3 family is an ultra-low-power and highly-integrated MCU-based SoC solution that supports 2.4 GHz Wi-Fi and Bluetooth® Low Energy (Bluetooth LE). It has:

- A complete Wi-Fi subsystem that complies with IEEE 802.11b/g/n protocol and supports Station mode, SoftAP mode, SoftAP + Station mode, and promiscuous mode
- A Bluetooth LE subsystem that supports features of Bluetooth 5 and Bluetooth mesh
- State-of-the-art power and RF performance
- 32-bit RISC-V single-core processor with a four-stage pipeline that operates at up to 160 MHz
- 400 KB of SRAM (16 KB for cache) and 384 KB of ROM on the chip, and SPI, Dual SPI, Quad SPI, and QPI interfaces that allow connection to external flash
- Reliable security features ensured by
  - Cryptographic hardware accelerators that support AES-128/256, Hash, RSA, HMAC, digital signature and secure boot
  - Random number generator
  - Permission control on accessing internal memory, external memory, and peripherals
  - External memory encryption and decryption
- Rich set of peripheral interfaces and GPIOs, ideal for various scenarios and complex applications

So it is the replacement of the ESP 8266 not of the ESP 32. With this drawing, we can assess the current risk five and amount of open source.

The danger five establishment characterizes just the iaasa of this center, the IP on the best way to fabricate the center isn't open source, and likely must be bought by expressive and all peripherals are shut source to and their IP either has a place with expressive or another particular organization.

Likewise, every one of the instruments must be bought by expressive. So the open source a piece of the C three is small, frustrating for me, I had expected more since all the promotion around the RISC five, I anticipated a lot greater impression of open source. Yet, there is trust. Jaron Elias sprite tm made the group for the keep going hackaday occasion dependent on an open source center. Furthermore, he added some open source peripherals and consumed them into a FPGA. So his chip was totally open source. very cool. Possibly you watch his superconference discourse, in the event that you leave a couple of moments with him, you will find that he is likewise an interesting moderator, we will see a Western Digital or Seagate or others will give part of their work to the establishment. In the same way as other organizations remained with Linux, at that point clusters weep for its quick addition foothold. Yet, are the RISC five chips in any event quicker? No. They utilize similar assembling innovation as ARM processors and are not quicker or better. The lone distinction is normalization where the benefits was talked about before. The possibility we producers will see anything of that is little, in any event for the following years. Possibly genuinely open source RISC five will assume a part for us in FPGAs on the off chance that they become less expensive, and perhaps we will make such a venture once on this channel. What do you think? The evidence of what I just said can be found in the presence of the Raspberry Pi Pico. It contains standard ARM centers and no danger five. Furthermore, what might be said about the ESP 32 c three. On the off chance that it gets firmware that makes it simple for us to associate with Wi Fi or Bluetooth securely. I'm certain I will utilize such a module along with another chip, possibly a PI Pico or a STM 32.

Arduino Announces Raspberry Pi RP2040 Core Port, Arduino Nano RP2040 Connect Board

Arduino for example, at a standard ESP 32 to their board with a PI Pico chip. Maybe it will be replaced by a C three module in the future if it's less expensive conclusiones. Creating a standard is a library risk five is a good idea. not new, but the timing might be right this time because the play is called everybody against arm. Risk five is mainly a topic for chip manufacturers and large chip users. It has not a lot of implications on the end user, at least not for the next years. Only a minimal part of RISC five chips is open source. Most of the design and the tools used to build it are IP of companies and have to be purchased.

7 SENSORS TRIED MEASURING CURRENT WITH MICROCONTROLLERS

we will look at the different methods to measure current, its advantages and disadvantages. We will see where we have to pay attention, we will look at some of the most popular boards. We will build an example with each board to see how they can be used. And in the end, you should know which module is best for your project and how to use it. I said before measuring current as simple, not as simple as voltage or resistance, because we have to think about changing one cable to a different connector. And then usually we have the choice like here milli ampere, micro ampair or 10 ampere.

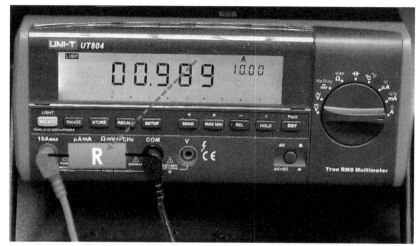

The main inquiry is, the reason do we need to change the connector? What's more, the subsequent inquiry, for what reason do we require two distinct connectors? The principal answer is these multimeters can not actually measure current, they just measure voltage. This is the reason they use ohms law for the current estimations. These meters have a resistor between the left and the correct connector. Furthermore, they measure the voltage across this resistor use ohms law and show you the current straightforward yet for what reason do we need two connectors. It is a result of the weight voltage. In the event that you need to know more, you can watch the video which is presently showing up in the upper right corner. It manages estimating negligible flows like the profound rest flows. More or less, in the event that we draw the full graph of our present meter, including a force source like a battery, and a heap like an ESP 8266, which burns-through around 100 milliamp pair, we can do a few computations.

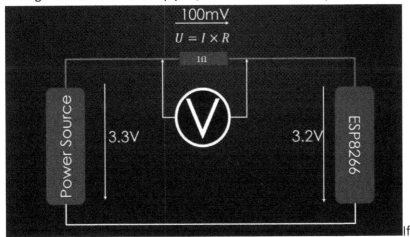

If we need to simplify it for our meter, we utilize a one ohm resistor 100 milliamp pair prompts a voltage of 100 milli volts, which effectively can be estimated by the underlying meter. Tragically, this 100 milli volt is lost in this resistor. In the event that the resistor would be greater, the ESP would no more get sufficient voltage and crash. This is the justification the subsequent connector. Here a lot more modest resistor is between the connectors which prompts a lower trouble voltage. We additionally need to remember the force scattering. On the off chance that we utilize a 0.1 ohm resistor for the 10 ampere range, it would disseminate 10 watts, it would require a significant stout resistor. Here I have an alternate multimeter without these extra connectors for current estimation. Yet, with this cinch, this meter utilizes purported opening sensors to quantify the attractive fields. It estimates the current contactless and without the weight voltage. It is fundamental that you just feed one wire through the clip. On the off chance that you feed both a picked zero on the grounds that the forward and the opposite current are something similar and counterbalance each. How can it function? Current makes an attractive fields around the link and this cinch gets it and in the event that I wind the link multiple times through the brace the current pairs. Yet in addition in the event that I place a magnet close to the clasp, it shows current from nothing. So focus with magnets. The current reach is high up to 600 ampere. It can quantify current both way and furthermore AC yet the exactness is low as we see here. We presently saw two different ways of estimating current with multimeters. What's more, here we make them relate sensors for our MCU project. In the first place, we can quantify flows on the low or on the high side. Presently, you could contend, for what reason do we need an extra sensor, we can embed a resistor and measure the voltage across it with one of our simple information sources. We should give it a shot the low side. In the first place, we embed the resistor. Furthermore, truly, we can gauge a voltage.

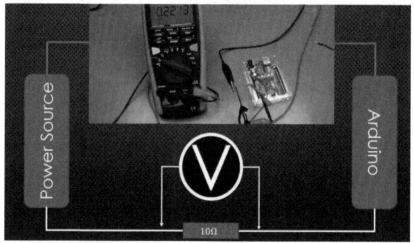

Presently we could associate the simple contribution of the Arduino to the resistor. The principal question is, on which side, the simple contribution of the MCU estimates the voltage corresponding to the ground. On the off chance that we associate the contribution to this side, without a doubt, we get zero volts constantly. So we need to pick the opposite side. In the event that I check with my multimeter, we see that this voltage is negative contrasted with the ground. What's more, shockingly, simple sources of info are obliterated. On the off chance that they get a lot of negative voltage, great I checked before with my multimeter. Presently you can say add an upsetting operation amp and you get a positive voltage. This is valid for course. Yet, just if the operation amp has an or more and less five volts supply, we will require an extra negative voltage not exceptionally advantageous. So I would say we desert this site and attempt the high side. This should work better. I embed a similar resistor on the high side and measure correctly a similar voltage. A similar inquiry here where to interface the info, we recall the simple information estimates voltages according to the ground. So here it generally gauges Vcc of the MCU. Furthermore, here the voltage is higher than Vcc, which again can't be estimated by the simple information. You can say simple at a voltage divider. Indeed, I can add one and it works. I can add a simple contribution to the voltage divider and deduct the two qualities without a middle triumph. We supplanted a current sensor with two modest resistors. Tragically, there is a disadvantage. The voltage across the resistor is the weight voltage. Also, as we saw previously, it must be little. How about we expect a 0.1 ohm resistor 100 milliamp power utilization and five volts, the simple information will gauge 5.01 isolated by two equivalents 2.5 or five volts. In light of the voltage divider, this outcomes in 512 or 513 in the Arduino, due to the 10 cycle ADC, the other will gauge the greatest worth since it estimates BCC 1023 we duplicate the primary occasions two and take away the subsequent worth.

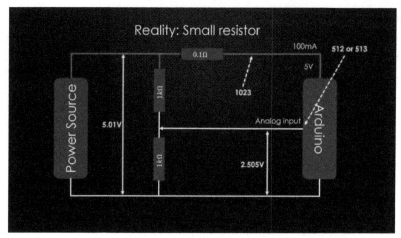

The difference is one. If we were to increase the load to 200 milliampere, we would measure 2.51 volts, which would result in 513 or 514. The difference are two digits for a doubling of the current. very insensitive. Again, you can say at an op amp. Yes, here You're right. But let's look at the selection of the sensors I have here and see how they deal with those problems. The first category, the ones with the resistors are Max 4080 and i n a 169 and i n a to 19 and and i n a 3321. The second category, the ones with hold sensors are the ACS 712, the ACS 758 and the W cs 1800. And a last one, which somehow fits in between

LTC4150
Coulomb Counter/
Battery Gas Gauge

FEATURES

- Indicates Charge Quantity and Polarity
- ±50mV Sense Voltage Range
- Precision Timer Capacitor or Crystal Not Required
- 2.7V to 8.5V Operation
- High Side Sense
- 32.55Hz/V Charge Count Frequency
- 1.5µA Shutdown Current
- 10-Pin MSOP Package

APPLICATIONS

- Battery Chargers
- Palmtop Computers and PDAs
- Cellular Telephones and Wireless Modems

DESCRIPTION

The LTC®4150 measures battery depletion and charging in handheld PC and portable product applications. The device monitors current through an external sense resistor between the battery's positive terminal and the battery's load or charger. A voltage-to-frequency converter transforms the current sense voltage into a series of output pulses at the interrupt pin. These pulses correspond to a fixed quantity of charge flowing into or out of the battery. The part also indicates charge polarity as the battery is depleted or charged.

The LTC4150 is intended for 1-cell or 2-cell Li-Ion and 3-cell to 6-cell NiCd or NiMH applications.

LT, LT, LTC, LTM, Linear Technology, the Linear logo, Burst Mode are registered trademarks and ThinSOT and PowerPath are trademarks of Linear Technology Corporation. All other trademarks are the property of their respective owners.

the LTC 4150 Kulon counter. Most of the sensors of both categories have an analog output and you need an analog input for measurement. The usual MCs have built in analog inputs, and you can use one of those if you are okay with the resolution. If not, you have to add an external ADC. If you create an analog circuit, you are fine without an ADC Of course, to have the sensors come with a built in ADC and an i square C interface. This is quite handy for MCU project. Let's look at the sensors of the first category.

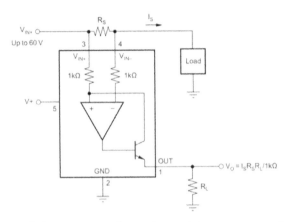

The analog part of the sensors where the resistors are very similar They insert a Small shunt resistor into the top site and contain more or less an op amp. It is not a standard Op Amp though, let's look at the diagram of the ima 169. It can handle voltages up to 60 volts. And because it only measures the voltage difference across the smaller resistor, its common mode rejection and its offset voltage errors have to be very small.

PARAMETER	TEST CONDITIONS	MIN	TYP	MAX	UNIT
INPUT					
Full-scale sense voltage	$V_{SENSE} = V_{RS+} - V_{RS-}$		100	500	mV
Common-mode input range	INA139	2.7		40	V
	INA169	2.7		60	V
Common-mode rejection	INA139: $V_{RS+} = 2.7$ V to 40 V, $V_{SENSE} = 50$ mV	90	115		dB
	INA169: $V_{RS+} = 2.7$ V to 60 V, $V_{SENSE} = 50$ mV	100	120		dB
Offset voltage [1] RTI	INA139		±0.2	±1.5	mV
	INA169		±0.2	±1	mV
vs. temperature	T_{MIN} to T_{MAX}				µV/°C
vs power supply (V+)	INA139: V+ = 2.7 V to 40 V, $V_{SENSE} = 50$ mV		0.5	10	µV/V
	INA169: V+ = 2.7 V to 60 V, $V_{SENSE} = 50$ mV		0.1	10	µV/V
Input bias current			10		µA
OUTPUT					
Transconductance vs temperature	$V_{SENSE} = 10$ mV – 150 mV	980	1000	1010	µA/V
	$V_{SENSE} = 10$ mV		10		nA/°C
Nonlinearity error	$V_{SENSE} = 10$ mV to 150 mV — INA139		±0.01%	±0.12%	
	— INA169		±0.01%	±0.1%	
Total output error	$V_{SENSE} = 100$ mV		±0.5%	±2%	
Output impedance			1 ‖ 5		GΩ ‖ pF
Voltage output	Swing to power supply, V+		(V+) – 0.9	(V+) – 1.2	V
	Swing to common-mode, V_{CM}		V_{CM} – 0.6	V_{CM} – 1	
FREQUENCY RESPONSE					
Bandwidth	$R_{OUT} = 10$ kΩ		440		kHz
	$R_{OUT} = 20$ kΩ		220		kHz
Settling time (0.1%)	5-V step, $R_{OUT} = 10$ kΩ		2.5		µs
	5-V step, $R_{OUT} = 20$ kΩ		5		µs
NOISE					
Output-current noise density			20		pA/√Hz
Total output-current noise	BW = 100 kHz		7		nA RMS
POWER SUPPLY					
Operating range, V+	INA139	2.7		40	V
	INA169	2.7		60	V
Quiescent current	$V_{SENSE} = 0, I_O = 0$		60	125	µA
TEMPERATURE RANGE					

For the ima 169 we can change to a resistor values our S and R I both influence the sensitivity of the chip.

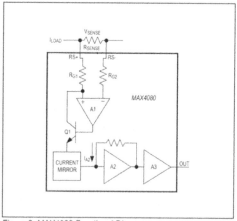

Figure 2. MAX4080 Functional Diagram

The board I have here has rs 0.1 ohms and our I 10k. Which prompts an affectability of one volt for each ampere. We should look at it. I associated with my rs 606 force supply to make some current the heap is in it at 512 A we get exceptionally near one volt for one ampere at four amp pair we just get 3.6 volts. So this design is reasonable for up to around three ampair. A certain something anyway is imperative, you need to interface the ground of the heap to the ground of your sensor and your MCU else, you don't get right qualities. Also, in the event that you are stuck between a rock and a hard place, you obliterate your sensor. On the off chance that we increment the voltage, it doesn't make any difference. The perusing stays something very similar. This operation amp is actually very exact. The base voltage relies upon the current estimated, it goes down to around three volts on the off chance that you stay under one ampere, so it very well may be utilized for a solitary cell ly Eon MCU arrangement. How about we attempt the Max 4080 you just have one resistor to play with our sense. Rather than changing our I you get various renditions of the chip.

- Three Gain Versions Available
  - 5V/V (MAX4080F/MAX4081F)
  - 20V/V (MAX4080T/MAX4081T)
  - 60V/V (MAX4080S/MAX4081S)

I

have here the T adaptation, which has an affectability of 20 volt for each volt. I didn't discover a breakout port for this chip. This is the reason I have it on a breadboard. I utilize two one ohm resistors in equal as our sts which brings about 0.5 ohms. one ampere ought to make 0.5 volts duplicated with the affectability of 28 is 10 volts. You see this is an extremely touchy chip, and in this arrangement, I just can compare around 400 milli ampere. With a 0.1 ohm resistor I could quantify around two ampere. The two chips are subsequently appropriate for little sun based tasks, for instance, else, I have no inclination. How about we view the I n a 219. It has a supposed programmable addition enhancer, which is tantamount with our operation amps from previously. There are two contrasts, as the name says its benefit can be changed. Furthermore, as we can see here, its info likewise can be exchanged. Notwithstanding the previous two chips,

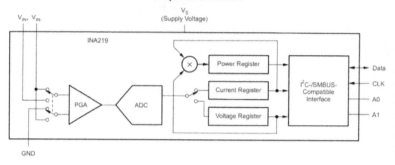

Simplified Schematic

it has a built in analog to digital converter, and then I square C interface. This seems to be a neat chip. Let's look at how we can connect it to our project.

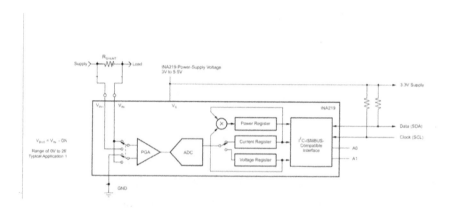

As before we add a resistor into the hot side here called our shunt and connect V in plus and v n minus two this resistor all as before. Fortunately,

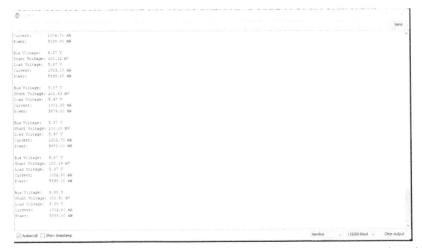

we get a ready made library for the chip and we can start it up. It not only shows the current it also shows a voltage. This is because of this switch.

If switched, the ADC measures the voltage of V n minus two grand cool with these values, we can also calculate power. Just to rant a little. This sketch makes us the bus voltage add the load voltage, the load voltage obviously have to be lower than the bus voltage. The breakout board also has a 0.1 ohm resistor,

```
// Initialize the INA219.
// By default the initialization will use the largest range (32V, 2A). However
// you can call a setCalibration function to change this range (see comments).
ina219.begin();
// To use a slightly lower 32V, 1A range (higher precision on amps):
//ina219.setCalibration_32V_1A();
// Or to use a lower 16V, 400mA range (higher precision on volts and amps):
//ina219.setCalibration_16V_400mA();

Serial.println("Measuring voltage and current with INA219 ...");
```

- 32V, 2A (default)
- 32V, 1A
- 16V,400mA

and the Adafruit sketch offers these three ranges.

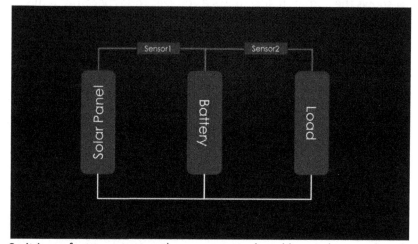

So it is perfect to measure the current produced by a solar panel or the current used from a battery, or both using two iron a 219. I also like the I squared c interface, because we can put the sensitive analog stuff close to the action and use longer digital wires to our MCs if needed. This leads us to the ima 3221 board. This chip has three sensors like the ima 219 on one chip, which in principle would be perfect for a solid project where as we saw before need to iron a 219. Unfortunately, the designer of the board had a different scenario in mind and connected all vn plus paints together like that we only can use it in such a configuration,

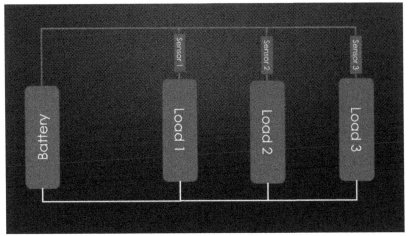

one battery with three loads, not very intelligent. This one here seems to be better designed, but I do not have it right now,

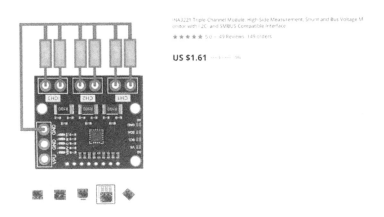

INA3221 Triple Channel Module, High-Side Measurement, Shunt and Bus Voltage Monitor with I2C and SMBUS Compatible Interface

★ ★ ★ ★ ★ 5.0 · 49 Reviews · 149 orders

US $1.61

before you order look at the difference here. The bed one has two ground pins and the other one three different pins.

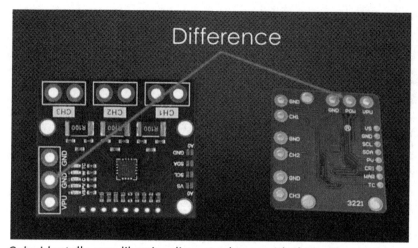

Coincidentally, you likewise discover sheets with the eye and a two to six, which is very much like the I n a to 19 it has a somewhat higher greatest voltage and an extra alarm pin for overcurrent security. Each of the five sensors can't gauge invert flows. Presently we go to the sensors which use opening components. As we saw previously, they have three critical benefits. The estimating circuit is electrically not associated with your stock link. So they work on the low side just as on the high side they ought not make a weight voltage since they simply utilize the attractive fields. However, two of the three sensors in the test actually must be embedded in line. So apparently they additionally make a little weight voltage. They typically measure in the two ways and hence, now and then they additionally can be utilized to gauge AC. In the event that we take a gander at their specs, we see that they are intended for high flows, which likewise implies that they are not exact for little flows and they can be affected by magnets as I appeared with my brace meter. How about we start with the littlest chip the ACS 712 it comes in three variants 520 and 30 ampere, it is just a small chip and 30 amps is by all accounts a considerable amount for this gadget.

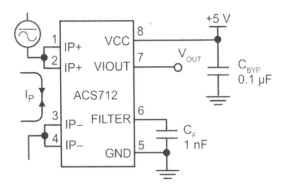

Even if it uses two pines each for the connection to the load on the battery, I probably would stick to the five ampere version also because of the sensitivity of the stronger ones is smaller.

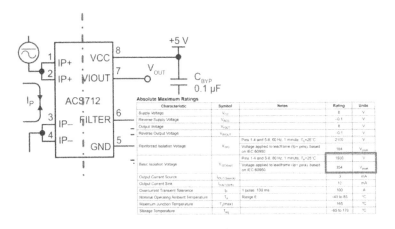

Theoretically, you can connect it to mains because the pins involved in the measuring are isolated from the pins connected to our MCU however, I would not trust such a small chip and small distances. Anyway, I do not like too much working with means let's hook it up. The first thing we see is that we get 2.5 volts out at zero amperes which is half of the five volt input voltage. If we increase the current eight adds around 0.18 millivolts per ampere and ends at 3.4 volts, the full swing is about 0.9 volts. If I reverse the direction, the voltage goes down and ends at around 1.6 volts. Also a point nine volt difference. So it seems to work the same company produces a bigger brother or is it a bigger sister,

Selection Guide

Part Number [1]	Package		Primary Sampled Current, Iₚ (A)	Sensitivity Sens (Typ.) (mV/A)	Current Directionality	T_OP (°C)	Packing [2]
	Terminals	Signal Pins					
ACS758LCB-050B-PFF-T	Formed	Formed	±50	40	Bidirectional		
ACS758LCB-050U-PFF-T	Formed	Formed	50	60	Unidirectional		
ACS758LCB-100B-PFF-T	Formed	Formed	±100	20	Bidirectional	−40 to 150	
ACS758LCB-100B-PSF-T	Straight	Formed	±100	20	Bidirectional		
ACS758LCB-100U-PFF-T	Formed	Formed	100	40	Unidirectional		
ACS758KCB-150B-PFF-T	Formed	Formed	±150	13.3	Bidirectional		
ACS758KCB-150U-PSF-T	Straight	Formed	150	26.7	Unidirectional	−40 to 125	34 pieces per tube
ACS758KCB-150B-PSS-T	Straight	Straight	±150	13.3	Bidirectional		
ACS758KCB-150U-PFF-T	Formed	Formed	150	26.7	Unidirectional		
ACS758ECB-200B-PFF-T	Formed	Formed	±200	10	Bidirectional		
ACS758ECB-200B-PSF-T	Straight	Formed	±200	10	Bidirectional		
ACS758ECB-200U-PSF-T	Straight	Formed	200	20	Unidirectional	−40 to 85	
ACS758ECB-200B-PSS-T	Straight	Straight	±200	10	Bidirectional		
ACS758ECB-200U-PFF-T	Formed	Formed	200	20	Unidirectional		

the ACS 758 you get them for significantly higher flows up to 200 amperes I have the in addition to short 50 ampere type it ought to make 40 million sets for every ampere how about we check truly 2.5 volts with zero ampere and 2.7 volts at five ampere I truly need a more strong force supply to test this monster. While I proceed to take for a more grounded power supply you can hit the approval fasten or buy in if not done at this point. What's more, truly I discovered one which is useful for 20 ampere. So we can proceed with the outcome is true to form around 3.3 volts at 20 ampere so the sensor appears to work and the distances are likewise a lot greater. So in the event that you need something for mains, this is likely the better decision. The last one the WCS 1800 looks similar to my brace meter. It tends to be sleeved into a mains link without cutting it. Its reach is 35 ampere. On the off chance that we connect it to the 20 amp pair he picked 2.4 or five volts at zero amp air and 3.7 volts at 20 ampere so the affectability is around 60 millivolt for each ampere. For a primary situation I would utilize this one likewise in light of the fact that I don't have to cut a wire which is lawfully not permitted all over. The last game is somewhat uncommon. They call the LTC 4150 a kulambu counter. It is a basic gadget. Which is appended to a battery.

LTC4150
Coulomb Counter/
Battery Gas Gauge

FEATURES

- Indicates Charge Quantity and Polarity
- ±50mV Sense Voltage Range
- Precision Timer Capacitor or Crystal Not Required
- 2.7V to 8.5V Operation
- High Side Sense
- 32.55Hz/V Charge Count Frequency
- 1.5µA Shutdown Current
- 10-Pin MSOP Package

APPLICATIONS

- Battery Chargers
- Palmtop Computers and PDAs
- Cellular Telephones and Wireless Modems

DESCRIPTION

The LTC®4150 measures battery depletion and charging
in handheld PC and portable product applications. The
device monitors current through an external sense resistor
between the battery's positive terminal and the battery's
load or charger. A voltage-to-frequency converter transforms the current sense voltage into a series of output
pulses at the interrupt pin. These pulses correspond to a

Coulomb

From Wikipedia, the free encyclopedia

For other uses, see Coulomb (disambiguation).

The **coulomb** (symbol: **C**) is the International System of Units (SI) unit of electric charge.

$$1\ C = 1\ A \times 1\ s$$

The chip counts the charges which go into and come out of the battery. It can be used to calculate the charging status of a cell in percentage. The chip simply generates a interrupt signal for each charge. According to another pin, the MCU gets the direction of the charge. If the battery is charged, it adds

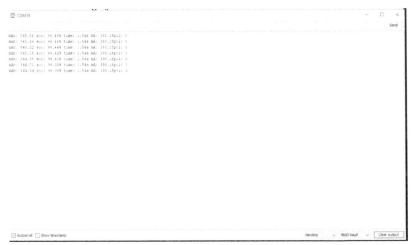

furthermore, if the battery is released is deducted from the real rate. So it is a mix of two current sensors and one voltage sensor. summed up today we tried two kinds of flow sensors, the shunt type, which estimates a voltage across a little resistor, and opening sensors which are electrically separated from the force link. The shunt types just work on the high side and make a weight voltage. They are electrically

85

associated with the force source and don't work for mains. They likewise just can gauge current one way. Their reach is movable, yet generally simply up to a couple of amperes. On account of this more modest reach, their exactness is higher. You additionally get them with an inherent ADC and an I squared c interface. An ideal blend for low force microcontroller projects like sun oriented force, these chips can likewise gauge the voltage, you even get the I n a three to one with three inherent channels. Awesome in the event that you need to gauge more than one current focus on which form you request. The opening sensors are made for higher flows and in this way less touchy and less exact. You get them for exceptionally high ampere goes up to 200 ampere. They can be utilized on the high just as on the low side. What's more, they likewise can gauge flows in the two ways. The vast majority of them actually must be electrically circled into the electrical cable. I would not confide in the more modest ones for mains applications. The WCS 1800 worked with a totally separated opening sensor. What are my top choices, certainly the I n a 219. Or on the other hand on the off chance that I need more than one of them, the ima 3221. For simple undertakings, I would likely utilize either the iron a 169 or the Max 4080 for the ACS seven twelves and the ACS 758. I don't see a ton of necessities. Since I have no task with enormous engines.

CODING LED BLINK

As usual, the first thing we did when we started exploring new hardware was to lead empty or to write programming sentences, which are Hello, the worst case for our hardware, namely SB 32, for example, it will be led flashing. So let's go to the example menu and an idea of Arduino and open the sketch example or sample class now.

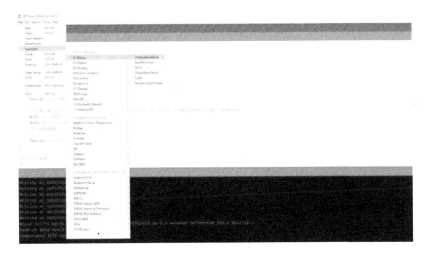

As you can see, we have many examples here, you can go to the base and click Blink. Now, let's close this window. Let's open this one now.

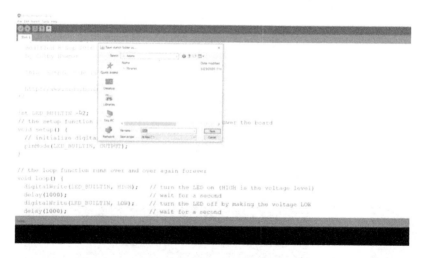

As you can see in this code, let me zoom in. We have a lid set to default, which is led number 13 in Arduino, so we need to change this number. As you know, SB 32 has a default lid connected to the Gilberto input-output. Number two, it is important to check whether LYD pollution is automatically recognized by IDC. If not, you have to add to call a line like this. Good. And. And the right letter is properly copied and inserted here and now you have to write to make sure the code

will be saved for PIN two, which is an internal lid pin in sports. Now let's save our code. Let's leave the name empty. And let's roll this. Now, as you can see, it is the same court that we use and you have two methods,

Sound regulation method and sound method. The sound method is basically where you set things to like here we have a number two-pin, which is a variable, and we can replace it with number two here. But because we use variables, we can apply the variable name here and here. We can assign it as input or output because we deal with it as output. So we write output and we use the Benmore function to ensure that we set number two as output in the loop setup. Now the loop function of the name is, it will continue to repeat. The loop function runs repeatedly forever. After you stop the program or stop turning off the power, it will stop running. Now the digital right will write digital value. Height means one logic or turns on to the round, which has become number two that has internal. And then the delay sentence will wait for a second and we will write the same sentence. We will write additional values, which are low or zero or off, and we will wait second. So we will turn it on. Wait a minute. Turn off and wait second again now. Plant this court, we need to go and make sure that we have it that does the SB 32 version, one selected, and we need to make sure we have the right combat. After that, we just click upload. It will take time.

```
int LED_BUILTIN = 2;
// the setup function runs once when you press reset or power the board
void setup() {
  // initialize digital pin LED_BUILTIN as an output.
  pinMode(LED_BUILTIN, OUTPUT);
}

// the loop function runs over and over again forever
void loop() {
  digitalWrite(LED_BUILTIN, HIGH);   // turn the LED on (HIGH is the voltage level)
  delay(1000);                       // wait for a second
  digitalWrite(LED_BUILTIN, LOW);    // turn the LED off by making the voltage LOW
  delay(1000);                       // wait for a second
}
```

OK, as you can see, you now have an error because this is a system variable, we cannot change it with another name led.

```
int LED2 = 2;
// the setup function runs once when you press reset or power the board
void setup() {
  // initialize digital pin LED_BUILTIN as an output.
  pinMode(LED2, OUTPUT);
}

// the loop function runs over and over again forever
void loop() {
  digitalWrite(LED2, HIGH);   // turn the LED on (HIGH is the voltage level)
  delay(1000);                // wait for a second
  digitalWrite(LED2, LOW);    // turn the LED off by making the voltage LOW
  delay(1000);                // wait for a second
}
```

Let's try again. As you can see now, it wrote the code, finished uploading it. Now, if you have a board, you can see that there is a blue light that blinks and dies. There he is. This is how simple to turn on or turn off Alland you can use another PIN or connect an external lid if you have it. But that is for this.

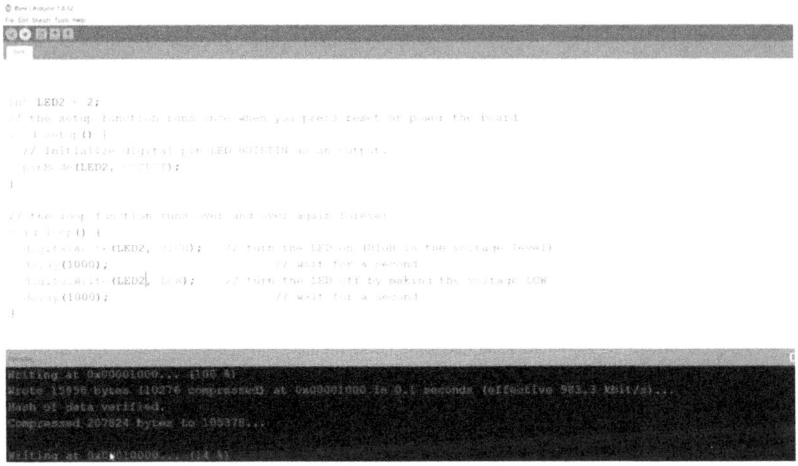

As you can see, it is the same code that we use and Arduino. So it's very simple. It's easy to start with this board. You don't have a lot of knowledge, only coding basic knowledge and Arduino. And if you don't have basic knowledge, I've explained every line of code in this sketch. If you have questions about anything.

LED SOFTWARE FADE

```
int brightness = 0;    // how bright the LED is
int fadeAmount = 5;    // how many points to fade the LED by

// Arduino like analogueWrite
// value has to be between 0 and valueMax
void ledcAnalogueWrite(uint8_t channel, uint32_t value, uint32_t valueMax = 255) {
  // calculate duty, 8191 from 2 ^ 13 - 1
  uint32_t duty = (8191 / valueMax) * min(value, valueMax);

  // write duty to LEDC
  ledcWrite(channel, duty);
}

void setup() {
```

```
// Setup timer and attach timer to a led pin
ledcSetup(LEDC_CHANNEL_0, LEDC_BASE_FREQ,
LEDC_TIMER_13_BIT);
ledcAttachPin(LED_PIN, LEDC_CHANNEL_0);
}

void loop() {
// set the brightness on LEDC channel 0
ledcAnalogueWrite(LEDC_CHANNEL_0, brightness);

// change the brightness for next time through the loop:
brightness = brightness + fadeAmount;

// reverse the direction of the fading at the ends of the fade:
if (brightness <= 0 || brightness >= 255) {
fadeAmount = -fadeAmount;
}
// wait for 30 milliseconds to see the dimming effect
delay(30);
}
```

DEALING WITH ANALOGUE SIGNALS

ESP32 DEVKIT V1 – DOIT
version with 30 GPIOs

The stimulus on energy will explain how to deal with analogueue and both VSP 30 Toolbelt now to test the analogueue input value signal. There are around 18 12 with an ADC input channel. You can easily recognize them from the wiring diagram, which we have mentioned, all the pain out there we explained before, and there was only one thin bit and a digital converter on MCU. Now, depending on the ball you use, this pen can be in a different location. Let me show your pin now, as you can see in this picture. You can see the ADC. Pins, so all of this is a pen capable of our digital converter and there are other pens too. Again, this is AC1 and Aissatou, a very different channel and you can recognize it, with the general-purpose input-output PIN starting from the pin. As you can see here, PIN has an ADC pin for pin 15 pin one does not have an ADC. So it's something from zero then you can continue. Who has been to 12, 13, 14, 15 and so on? We only need one pin for this Lassonde. So to read it and what you will use the same as Arduino boards, we will use our analogueue and coding function.

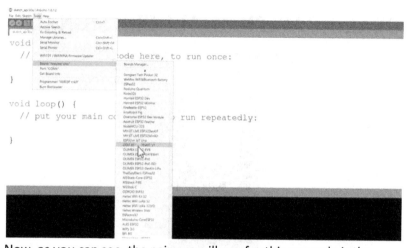

Now, as you can see, the pain we will use for this example is the
output of the general-purpose input 36. It has eight six six zeros or zero
channels now to release value. We need to use an analogueue read
function and we see analogueue values on variables. It is very
important to note that speed analyst 32 is the converter has 12-bit
resolution versus 10 bits on E.S.P eight two, six, six and Arduino. So the
total line of reading analogueue conversions to digital can go to 4000
zero nine or 095 five instead of 1,000 zero twenty-seven on Arduino
and SB eight two six-six when a maximum of three-point three volts
are applied to the input. So, you can expect more values that can rise
to 4000. Now for input, let's use it, I think, you are on a potential
meter or any analogueue sensor we have and we can connect it from
three-point three volts and ground. Now let's use the output of its
variables to be input from the band E.s. P 32 ADC to start. Let's open
our software. Go Arduino IVI. Now, after opening Padrino Idee. OK, let
me open another software. OK, this is him. Hardware and software.
Now, the first step we will do is create a new sketch, let's make sure
that our board is connected and recognized, as you can see, at
convenience, and let's make sure that we have the right port selected.
Our case, SPF 30 too. As you can see, do it when we set it to the gate
and we have another library that can cover this. Now, this is our board.
Let's start coding, the first thing we need to do is go to Void Setup and
initialize the serial serial serial and we can choose whatever moderate.

Let's choose eleven thousand five hundred and five thousand two hundred. Um, now let's add a delay to this supply. CIA communication with your prints, a sentence that shows that we use E.S.P. 32 Analogue Flowers Now here, let's initialize variables, save data, become analogueues. Equal to zero, then in the void loop, right, and the same value as and agreed upon, just like Arduino. And from here, we need to choose a pin.

```
int analogValue = 0;
void setup() {
  // put your setup code here, to run once:
  Serial.begin(115200);
  delay(1000);
  Serial.println("ESP32 Analog Pin Test");
}

void loop() {
  // put your main code here, to run repeatedly:
  analogValue = analogRead(36);
```

In Our case, it's a general-purpose. And what output? PIN 36. After that, let's print the read analogueue value, so the cereal is printed. Now, it's based on the creed, which has done value and it's sturdy. Five hundred milliseconds.

```
  // put your setup code here, to run once:
  Serial.begin(115200);
  delay(1000);
  Serial.println("ESP32 Analog Pin Test");
}

void loop() {
  // put your main code here, to run repeatedly:
  analogValue = analogRead(36);
  Serial.println(analogValue);
  delay(500);
}
```

Ok, let's verify. Let's save the code, just call it ... it takes time to compile the sketch. Now, let's upload sketches to our E.S.P board, make sure your board is connected.

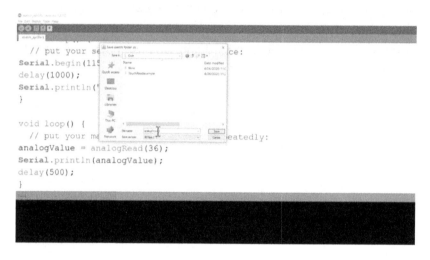

And you have selected the right board and the right comport.

```
    // put your setup code here, to run once:
Serial.begin(115200);
delay(1000);
Serial.println("ESP32 Analog Pin Test");
}

void loop() {
    // put your main code here, to run repeatedly:
analogValue = analogRead(36);
Serial.println(analogValue);
delay(500);|
}
```

Global variables use 15388 bytes (4%) of dynamic memory, leaving 312292 byte
esptool by v2.6
Serial port COM4
Connecting........

OK, as you can see, it's uploading. OK, writing, OK, done uploading now if we went and open up here, Serializer. OK, we have this science chance, the moderate to.

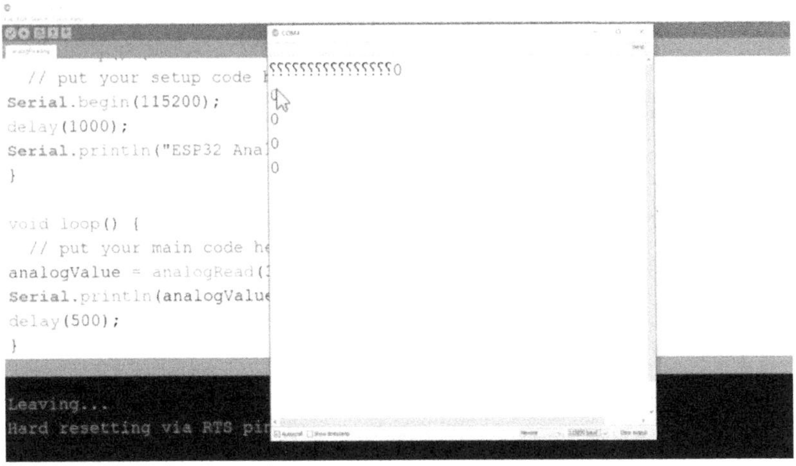

```
// put your setup code
Serial.begin(115200);
delay(1000);
Serial.println("ESP32 Ana
}

void loop() {
// put your main code h
analogValue = analogRead(
Serial.println(analogValu
delay(500);
}

Leaving...
Hard resetting via RTS pi
```

One hundred and fifteen thousand two hundred, as you can see here, we have zero value now, if you play with analogue potential meters, you will get a value of up to 4000 and that's it. This is how easy it is to use an analogue pin on the USB port, the same Arduino coding, the same structure. And I will have every line.

TOUCH SENSOR

```
int LED2 = 2;
// the setup function runs once when you press reset or power the board
void setup() {
    // initialize digital pin LED_BUILTIN as an output.
    pinMode(LED2, OUTPUT);
}

// the loop function runs over and over again forever
void loop() {
    digitalWrite(LED2, HIGH);    // turn the LED on (HIGH is the voltage level)
    delay(1000);                 // wait for a second
    digitalWrite(LED2, LOW);     // turn the LED off by making the voltage LOW
    delay(1000);                 // wait for a second
}
```

```
Wrote 3072 bytes (128 compressed) at 0x00008000 in 0.0 seconds (effective 2457.6 kbit/s)...
Hash of data verified.

Leaving...
Hard resetting via RTS pin...
```

Now we are finished with a slightly flashing example, let's move on to the touch sensor, for example. This is a new cool feature available on E.S.P 32 bawls, VSP 32 has an internal alten, internal capacitive touch sensor. We have explained or shows that round. We have shown. Well, plans come out depending on the speaker wiring layout to listen, but let's talk about them again now. This East Eastern Antenna capacitive touch sensor can be used as a button. And what are the numbers from general goals and output? Number four zero to 12, 13, 14, 15 at 23 or 32, 33 and 27. This is a pen. I will show you the bend number in a minute, okay? OK, this is him.

```
T0: GPIO 4
T1: GPIO 0
T2: GPIO 2
T3: GPIO 15
T4: GPIO 13
T5: GPIO 12
T6: GPIO 14
T7: GPIO 27
T8: GPIO 33
T9: GPIO 32

void setup() {
    // put your setup code here, to run once:

}

void loop() {
    // put your main code here, to run repeatedly:

}
```

And you can refer to the layout of the cable or PIN diagram where you can see this PIN. These are 10 internal capacitive touch sensors that you can use easily to read this PIN. All you need to do is use the touch function. Good. And this function will only take one variable, which is basically a function and usually takes one variable, which is the PIN, serial number four, number five and so on. So. To use this function first, we need to set a variable. Now we can write an int value. And the right touch of Reed in the vehicle, like any number, we can use the output of the objective input which is the first touch because Sorte zero. And now let's make a code where we read this touch sensor state and send it on the Syrian monitor to do this. First, you need to. Initialize communication in the settings method, as you can see, between these two curly brackets. The right dot series starts and is used and what rates can we use a hundred and fifteen thousand two hundred. And let's add a delay to help stabilize. One second now. Let's try this nonsense, let's try serial, not print. Yes, be fair. This touch now we have to regulate the atmosphere for the US as an output, we want to use the lid as an indicator for the Dutch or Dutch country since all countries. So we have number two, who have the lid, and we need it as output. We also need to write value and make sure it is zero. We want to make sure that the lid is dead. To do it. We need to write a PIN and write law. Use this line.

We ensure that when the E.S.p board starts, it will ensure that it dies. This will only be a loan if there is a touch or if the sensor touch is active. OK, now what we need to do next is to read the value, touch, read using touch, read and see in the value. Now we want to ask questions. If the value is above or below a certain value, we can turn it on or off. But before we do that, we just print the judge, read all the values we get from the touch screen sensor, which is a capacitive touch sensor on the Syrian monitor. So let's do this serial dot online and in it. We need to do the value. After that, we can add delays in the second delay.

```
© sketch_apr26b | Arduino 1.8.12
File Edit Sketch Tools Help

T7: GPIO 27
T8: GPIO 33
T9: GPIO 32

void setup() {
  // put your setup code here, to run once:
  Serial.begin(115200);
  delay(1000);
  Serial.println("ESP32 Touch Sensor Test");
  pinMode(2, OUTPUT);
  digitalWrite(2, LOW);
}

void loop() {
  // put your main code here, to run repeatedly:
  int value = touchRead(4);
  Serial.println(value);
  delay(1000);|
}
```

Now, let's try combining our code. Let's store it inside. Our coding folder, it's called Touch Screen Example. OK, let's remove this. Now, let's come back again.

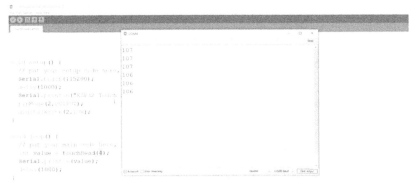

```
T0:  GPIO 4
T1:  GPIO 0
T2:  GPIO 2
T3:  GPIO 15
T4:  GPIO 13
T5:  GPIO 12
T6:  GPIO 14
T7:  GPIO 27
T8:  GPIO 33
T9:  GPIO 32


void setup() {
  // put your setup code here, to run once:
  Serial.begin(115200);
  delay(1000);
  Serial.println("ESP32 Touch Sensor Test");
  pinMode(2, OUTPUT);
  digitalWrite(2, LOW);
}
```

```
exit status 1
'T0' does not name a type
```

OK, done compiling now let's upload the code to our E.S.P board. By the way, you can use number four, which is the PIN, or you can use to zero to one, three to up to T10,

```
107
107
107
106
106
106
```

```
Leaving...
Hard resetting via RTS pin...
```

Because we have mentioned that we have, uh, ten touch sensors. Now, let's open the serial monitor. OK, as you can see, as much as that value here is 100. And seven, and if we touch it, it will change. Let me do that. OK, now, as you can see, we have 74, 37, 71, 70. Now let me touch it, Ben. As you can see, once I touch the value below. And when I left it. Go again, up to seventy-seven to two, so I think we have a constant value here. If the value is below 50, that means that I touch the pen. If above 50 means I don't touch the pen, we can adjust our code accordingly. Now, let's do it. Now, let's go here and add to the current statement and the statement, we will ask questions, value, at all, equal to 50. And this is more than this. So the current policy, in that case, we need to activate red. And Odelay. Ms If the value is. Under 50, we need to turn off the lid. OK, now let's verify our quotation.

```
Serial.println("ESP32 Touch Sensor Test");
pinMode(2,OUTPUT);
digitalWrite(2,LOW);
}

void loop() {
  // put your main code here, to run repeatedly:
  int value = touchRead(4);
  Serial.println(value);
  if(value >= 50)
  {
    digitalWrite(2,HIGH);
    Serial.println("LED ON");
    delay(1000);
  }else if(value < 50)
  {
    digitalWrite(2,LOW);
    Serial.println("LED OFF");
    delay(1000);
  }
```

Sketch uses 214005 bytes (16%) of program storage space. Maximum is 1310720 bytes.
Global variables use 15428 bytes (4%) of dynamic memory, leaving 312252 bytes for local variables. Maximum is

Oh, and let's print the sentence in 12 this statement using serial print. So here we will lead. And here we will present a lot, let's slander the call again. OK, now let's upload the code to the ISP circuit board again, the process takes time. Now connect to the board. Now writing code. Ok, it's finished uploading now if we open a serial monitor, as you can see, the lights are on and if you see your board, you can see that the lid is active.

Now, let me touch the touch pen, as you can see, the value is under 50 and the lid is dead. There he is. This is how easy you can use and adjust the touch sensor in the E.S. P 32 ball. It's built so you don't need to connect any additional components. This is how amazing and how easy it is dealing with this ball. If you have questions about this pin. I am here to help you.

HELLO WORLD – BLINK FOR ESP32

```
int ledPin = 2;

void setup()
{
   // Set LED as output
   pinMode(ledPin, OUTPUT);

   // Serial monitor setup
   Serial.begin(115200);
}

void loop()
{
   Serial.print("Hello");
   digitalWrite(ledPin, HIGH);

   delay(500);

   Serial.println(" world!");
   digitalWrite(ledPin, LOW);

   delay(500);
}
```

ESP32 PINS ARE PROTECTED TO UTILIZE

we will get an overview of all panes of the ESP 30 to learn which panes have particular purposes, and therefore have to be treated with care. Learn the real universally usable Prince create a strategy on how to use the many pins for our project and do some programming examples. The most important source of wisdom for parts always is the datasheet. If we consult

the ESP 32 data sheet, it looks like the chip has 40 GPIO pins numbered from GPIO zero to GPIO 39 GPIO, by the way, means general purpose input output pins. I copied this overview sheet into Excel like that we can filter and sorted as we wish. Of course you find a link to it in the description.

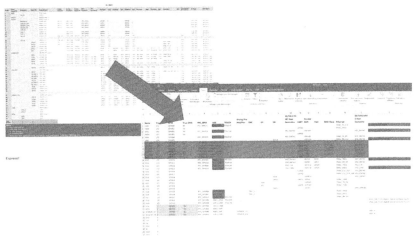

If we have a close look, we see that only 32 pins are labeled GPIO GPIO 2024 28 through 3137 and 38 do not exist.

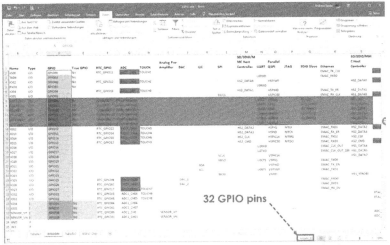

32 GPIO pins

Please don't ask me why. But still 32 is a lot compared with the ESP 8266 Or the Arduino Uno. The next surprise, not all those panes are general purpose as the name implies GPIO 34 through 39 should be called GPIO pins, they cannot be used as output pins, mostly 34 and 35 are dangerous, if you do not pay attention and try to use them for output, no warning will pop up and after hours, you think you are stupid GPIO 36 and 39 usually are labeled as sensor VP and sensor v n. We will later see that they have a special function. So there are 28 through GPIO pins left ESP 32 modules like the V room or the V rover use an external flash memory chip to store data. So GPIO six to 11 are connected to this flash chip and are forbidden for us. Unless you exactly know what you do. Still 22 potentially through GPIO pins are left.

Table 3: Strapping Pins

		Voltage of Internal LDO (VDD_SDIO)			
Pin	Default	3.3 V		1.8 V	
MTDI	Pull-down	0		1	
		Booting Mode			
Pin	Default	SPI Boot		Download Boot	
GPIO0	Pull-up	1		0	
GPIO2	Pull-down	Don't-care		0	
		Enabling/Disabling Debugging Log Print over U0TXD During Booting			
Pin	Default	U0TXD Active		U0TXD Silent	
MTDO	Pull-up	1		0	
		Timing of SDIO Slave			
Pin	Default	FE Sampling FE Output	FE Sampling RE Output	RE Sampling FE Output	RE Sampling RE Output
MTDO	Pull-up	0	0	1	1
GPIO5	Pull-up	0	1	0	1

Next are the so called strapping pins, they have a function during boot up and if wrongly connected, prevent your ESP 32 from booting GPIO zero is well known to us. Sometimes we have to press a boot button which tells the chip that we want to flash a new firmware definitely not a general purpose pin. We should not use it unless we absolutely need it. And then make sure it is always high during boot GPIO two also has a hidden function.

GPIO15 low

If you pull it hide during boot, you are not able to flash new content also here you will search for the error for a long time GPIO five also seems to have a function but I did not see a disadvantage by pulling it low or high other than the MT d o or GPIO 15. If you pull this pin low, the ESP 32 does not show the lock anymore at boot up. If you do not know it you probably will search for a problem which in reality is non GPIO zero and GPIO two should not be used for projects without need 20 pins or left. Most development boards use our x dx for flashing and debugging. These are GPIO one and three, we should not touch them to 18 pins left. Often we need an i squared c interface. The ESP 32 has two such interfaces.

- 34 × programmable GPIOs
- 12-bit SAR ADC up to 18 channels
- 2 × 8-bit DAC
- 10 × touch sensors
- 4 × SPI
- 2 × I²S
- 2 × I²C
- 3 × UART
- 1 host (SD/eMMC/SDIO)
- 1 slave (SDIO/SPI)
- Ethernet MAC interface with dedicated DMA and IEEE 1588 suppor
- CAN 2.0
- IR (TX/RX)
- Motor PWM
- LED PWM up to 16 channels
- Hall sensor

Because we can attach up to 112 sensors to one connection. We usually only need to one.

Extension of the I2C Specifications

Standard mode of I2C bus uses transfer rates up to 100 kbit/s and 7-bit addressing. Such I2C interface is used by many hundred I2C-compatible devices from many manufacturers since its introduction in the 80s. However, with the advance of the technology, needs for higher transfer rates and larger address space emerged. There are cases where large amount of data needs to be transferred. Many complex embedded boards contain a large number of different I2C devices. In some cases it is very hard to avoid address collisions since 7 bits for I2C addresses allow only 127 different addresses where only 112 can actually be used. Some I2C devices on the board, despite address pins, have the same address. This resulted in few upgrades to the standard-mode I2C specifications:

The standard pins are GPIO 2122 and can be changed with this command to most other GPIO pins. For displays. For example,

108

SPI Bus

SPI	MOSI	MISO	CLK	CS
VSPI	GPIO 23	GPIO 19	GPIO 18	GPIO 5
HSPI	GPIO 13	GPIO 12	GPIO 14	GPIO 15

the fast SPI interface is the right choice. The ESP 32 has two usable SPI interfaces that use the following pins. The third SPI bus is used for the flash memory chip by the way. Standard libraries use the V SPI pins as shown in the SPI examples catch. Because many sensors offer an i squared c interface. I usually do not use these two pins for other purposes. 16 pins left. If you plan to debug your sketch using the inline debugger of platform IO, you have to spare GPIO 12 to 15 out for your project 12 pins left. This is my priority one pins list.

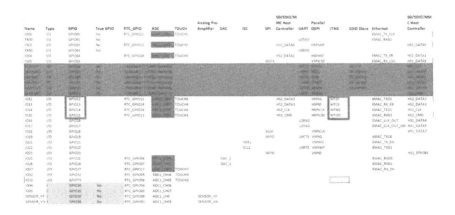

I always start to use these pins. Only on PCB layouts, it might be handy to use other pins, or if you really need a lot of pins.

Priority One Pins

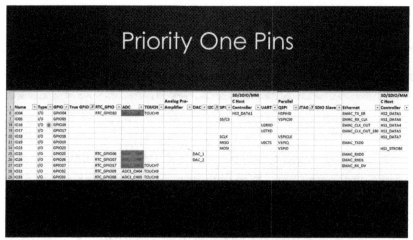

Then you can use the flexibility of the ESP 32 to change pins for functions like i square C, serial or SPI. Next we have a look at the secondary function of pins. For example,

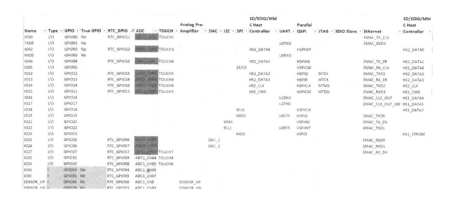

the datasheet shows us many ADC pins. Unfortunately, all pains starting with ADC two cannot be used if we use Wi Fi and who is not using Wi Fi with the ESP 32. A good thing GPIO 34 through 39 can be used as ADC input pins. My preferred solution to relief my priority one pin list. Just keep in mind the ESP 32 ADC results are not excellent as shown in video number 340. But good enough to measure battery voltage for example,

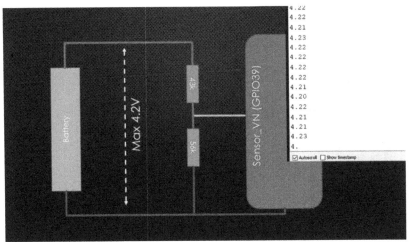

you can easily add two resistors and monitor a 4.2 volts lie on battery. The ESP 32 also has two Eight HD AC outputs on GPIO, 25 and 26. They are very simple to program just use this command and the results are okay as we see here.

```
void setup() {
  Serial.begin(115200);
  // initialize digital pin LED_BUILTIN as an output.
  pinMode(LED_BUILTIN, OUTPUT);
  Serial.println("Start");
}

// the loop function runs over and over again forever
void loop() {
  digitalWrite(LED_BUILTIN, HIGH);
  digitalWrite(LED_BUILTIN, LOW);
  for (int i = 0; i < 256; i++) {
    dacWrite(26, i);
    delay(10);
  }
  delay(100);
}
```

We can also create sine waves for example, with this function. Next comes p w m. In this mode pins generate a square wave signal with a variable on off ratio.

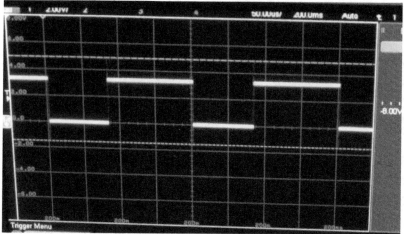

Such signals are used to control servos, for example, or the LVDS. Fortunately, we can use all GPIO O's for p w m, just a curiosity, the ESP 32 never got the same implementation as the Arduino where analog right is used. Also not the best choice if you ask me.

Reference > Language > Functions > Analog io > Analogwrite

analogWrite()

[Analog I/O]

Description

Writes an analog value (PWM wave) to a pin. Can be used to light a LED at varying brightnesses or drive a motor at various speeds. After a call to analogWrite(), the pin will generate a steady rectangular wave of the specified duty cycle until the next call to analogWrite() (or a call to digitalRead() or digitalWrite()) on the same pin.

BOARD	PWM PINS	PWM FREQUENCY
Uno, Nano, Mini	3, 5, 6, 9, 10, 11	490 Hz (pins 5 and 6: 980 Hz)
Mega	2 - 13, 44 - 46	490 Hz (pins 4 and 13: 980 Hz)
Leonardo, Micro, Yún	3, 5, 6, 9, 10, 11, 13	490 Hz (pins 3 and 11: 980 Hz)
Uno WiFi Rev2, Nano Every	3, 5, 6, 9, 10	976 Hz
MKR boards *	0 - 8, 10, A3, A4	732 Hz
MKR1000 WiFi *	0 - 8, 10, 11, A3, A4	732 Hz
Zero *	3 - 13, A0, A1	732 Hz
Nano 33 IoT *	2, 3, 5, 6, 9 - 12, A2, A3, A5	732 Hz
Nano 33 BLE/BLE Sense	1 - 13, A0 - A7	500 Hz
Due **	2-13	1000 Hz
101	3, 5, 6, 9	pins 3 and 9: 490 Hz, pins 5 and 6: 980 Hz

But the ESP 32 implementation is even more adventurous. It seems that somebody wrote a function to them elegies, and then it stayed like that. First we have to define the frequency and the resolution of a channel. Then we have to attach this channel to a pin. After that, we can start to write to this channel. As we see here, the ESP 32 can create relatively high frequencies, which might be interesting for some projects. Anyway, these were the typical usages of GPIO pins in

112

projects with one exception. interrupts. interrupts are a great functionality of most MC use, we can interrupt any running sketch with an external signal,

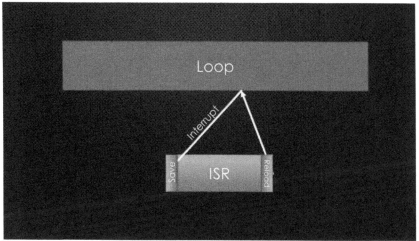

which can drastically simplify some sketches. As we saw in video number 328. The ESP 32 is not very fast in this discipline. But we can use all panes for that purpose very flexible. If you never used it, I strongly suggest trying interrupts at least once.

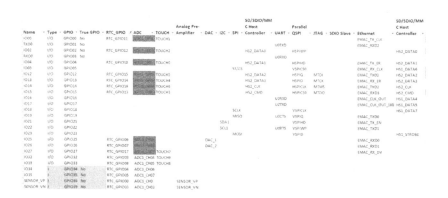

If we want to use an interrupt pain to wake the ESP 32 from deep sleep, we have to use so called RTC GPIO pins. Here we see like with the ADCs that we can use GPIO 34 through 39 to save our priority one pins. Now we definitely come to the exotic usages of pins. The first being touch sensors, 10 pins can be used for that purpose. If we exclude the special pins, we still get eight pins. So far, I had no projects with them, I only played around. Maybe you now have cool projects using these pins. And the last even more exotic function is a whole sensor. Here I have no idea why it is built in. Definitely a solution on the search for a problem, because even strong magnets do not influence the whole sensor over distance. So I prefer to use such a small hole sensor chip that can be mounted where the action is and keep the ESP 32 away in a safe case, just in case you want to use this whole sensory. It is connected to GPIO, 36 and 39. You must leave these pins open if you want to use the sensor.

30.4.3 Functional Description

The Hall sensor converts the magnetic field into voltage, feeds it into an amplifier, and then outp SENSOR_VP and pin SENSOR_VN. ESP32's built-in ADC converts the voltage into a digital valu by the CPU in the digital domain.

The inner structure of a Hall sensor is shown in Figure 147.

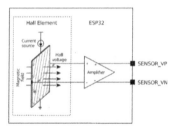

That's it. The last remaining question is how do I choose the pins. I start with my priority one list. If I expect that they will not be sufficient. I use the GPIO pins for analog input or wake up. I try to stick with a standard i square C or SPI pins, as some libraries do not allow to change pins, especially libraries coming from the Arduino. Only use wire begin which use standard pins. Only in rare cases, I switch standard pins. For example, if I need three serial connections, standard serial one pins are mapped to pins used by the flash chips. If I design PCBs, I sometimes use the flexibility of changing pins to ease the design.

PWM SIGNALS

In this case, we will take a PWI campaign from the E.S.P board, all 36 of the output of the general-purpose input E.S.P 32, Penns has the ability. This is a very good thing. But we must use a more complex code to achieve the same results in other pens. So let's program one of the general goals and output with the output signal. Now, if you want this schematic, all these pots come out for various people, you can see that all these pins can be used to produce PWI and signals. The first thing you need to think about when signal programming is the frequency. You need to generate that signal at certain or specific frequencies. We will use a 5000-hertz value that works well with our literature. We also have to determine the PWI channel and task cycle resolution. I want. Explain that, because you must have basic knowledge of BWL signals, but what is needed is only a resolution, channel, and frequency. So after determining the task cycle, using the resolution and frequency and channel, we can start programming, we can choose the channel from zero to 15 and the resolution between one and sixteen bits. We will use zero channels and eight-bit resolutions. So let's start. That is good. According to a new sketch. And this is a new sketch. Let's specify multiple variables. First, we need to define frequency and frequency and let's make 5000. Then we need a little channel. Let's make zero. And we need that resolution. And let's make eight. Now let's use the general goal, the input-output will number two, where we have advantages or connect or attached externally. It also has an innate lid that can be used. So this parameter must be defined in the settings function. So let's go. And why is this code? Now, what we will do in the setting function will not be something we usually do. We will see the Pin Toph and Lizzi set. Now pinch Lizzi pin and let's use it. There is a function for arm configuration. They are very similar to the right analogue function on Arduino. So now they are aspy. Do not support the underground function, but it supports a much better, which is the one you have mentioned. Let's see that time. Come see. Functions like very similar to analogue, true. It also requires two parameters and channels that we want to write the value. And it's a BWL value. We want to write to selected channels. Now, let's finish the settings function, now let's look at the settings function. We will take three parameters, the first will be the main channel. The second will be the frequency. The third will be a resolution, which we have found there. Next, we will set a link to the channel. So let's look at the Penn hat now the Penn that we have chosen is to and we want to attach it to the channel we have chosen. This is it. This is how you have finished setting up that BW, UM, frequency resolution and channel and how you can attach it to any output pin. Now to turn on the lid, which is connected to PIN two, using a red channel out of BW um, signal, we need to adjust certain brightness now to turn on or turn off the lights.

```
int freq = 5000;
int ledCh = 0;
int resolution = 8;    // 0 - 255
int dutyCycle = 0;

void setup() {
    // put your setup code here, to run once:
ledcSetup(ledCh, freq, resolution);
ledcAttachPin(2, ledCh);
}

void loop() {
```

We must define the task cycle, for example, the closing round that each cycle must be zero and close the function of seeing the rights we have mentioned can be used indoors to adjust the brightness to zero. Now. We can use that function now. That's right, let's see. Good. This is exactly like analogue, right? And two parameters are needed. The first is the main channel, which is this variable, and the second is the task cycle. Now, you can add a task cycle here. And zero, this will die valid because we have since zero. To the main channel, which has become number two, and it will set a protest to zero now different values of the news cycle. We will turn on the lead with a different priority now, this variable can be from zero to 255 after the resolution used is eight bits. If we use a 10-bit resolution, it can switch from zero to 1024 or 1023 and so on. We have already mentioned that you can choose a resolution between one and until 16. So that choice is yours. But you need to make sure that you choose a cycle that matches your resolution. So in a better solution, the cycle will be between zero and 225 255. OK, now we are finished with this, we can use that potential. We connected to analogue pins from before to control the brightness of the advantage. Or we can simply send the present value to test this. Let's complete the code. Let our first menu and settings. Add serial dow biggin and select a moderate one hundred and fifteen hundred two hundred, then add Odelay delays as usual for one second after delay. Let's write a sentence to make sure everything works correctly.

```
int freq = 5000;
int ledCh = 0;
int resolution = 8;    // 0 - 255
int dutyCycle = 0;

void setup() {
  // put your setup code here, to run once:
  Serial.begin(115200);
  delay(1000);
  Serial.println("Testing PWM");
ledcSetup(ledCh,freq,resolution);
ledcAttachPin(2,ledCh);
```

The trend line and let's limit this to be read ok. Now we have a valid setting and Penh top pen and we can use it. Let's look here. And the first value to be written is zero so it will die now in a void loop. We can send other values that we can send. Cycle. Let's define this cycle here plus. The same plus one and let's add Odelay. Let's make 15 milliseconds. OK, now let's move this line here, it will start with zero, then it will be added one or let's make it blasting and it will continue to move until it reaches 255.

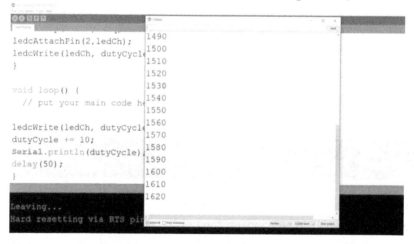

```
ledcSetup(ledCh, freq, resolution);
ledcAttachPin(2, ledCh);
ledcWrite(ledCh, dutyCycle);
}

void loop() {
    // put your main code here, to run repeatedly:

ledcWrite(ledCh, dutyCycle);
dutyCycle += 10;
Serial.println("Testing PWM");
delay(50);
```

We can add and if the Bartletts statement calls. First of all, let's upload the code or verification to make sure it doesn't have an error. Let's save it. BW about this. OK, Duncan, compare now let's upload the code. So we have to underline to ensure that we will prevent the cycle. We want to combine cold, but for now. Let's put it so we can get the cycle here now. Let's recompile the code for the fight. Now, let's.

```
ledcAttachPin(2, ledCh);          1490
ledcWrite(ledCh, dutyCycl         1500
}                                 1510
                                  1520
void loop() {                     1530
    // put your main code h        1540
                                  1550
ledcWrite(ledCh, dutyCycl         1560
dutyCycle += 10;                  1570
Serial.println(dutyCycle)         1580
delay(50);                        1590
}                                 1600
                                  1610
                                  1620
Leaving...
Hard resetting via RTS pi
```

Okay, now. As you can see, it goes beyond 155 very quickly, so we need to control this. After the cycle reaches, the cycle is more than the same as 125. We need to reset to zero. Now, let's call it again. Now, let's upload. Okay, don't, now, as you can see, after reaching 255, it resets to zero, and from your ball E.S.P,

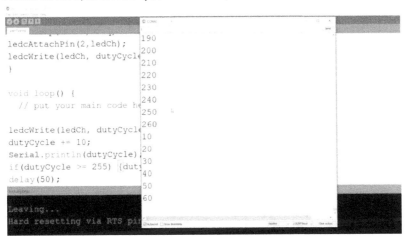

You can see that reproach and let all speed up that your connection fades in and out using this very simple code now. Now, let's concise what we do. This. We have set a 5000 frequency. We have chosen the channel to zero and we have chosen the resolution to eight, which means that we must have a cycle between zero and 255. We start with zero cycles and ultimately zero communication here. We use new functions. Let's use setting to set B. frequency channel and resolution. And top of this Lizzi has attached that function to us and a particular PIN, which has become number two here. And the LCD is basically like analogue. Good. Channels are needed and that you are cycling and its value for that channel. Now, in this fight, Lou, we have used a tin channel, which has been installed here to number two, and it will rotate and we continue to improve the cycle with 10. And printed on Tehran monitor. Now, once the music reaches 255, which is the limit here, we say that the cycle is zero to repeat the process. And that's the way you can adjust and use the PWI signal. You can apply this to another. You can choose a better resolution. In this case, if you select 10 better resolutions, you will get a value between zero and one thousand twenty-three.

```
int freq = 5000;
int ledCh = 0;
int resolution = 8;    // 0 - 255 >> 10 0 - 1023
int dutyCycle = 0;

void setup() {
  // put your setup code here, to run once:
  Serial.begin(115200);
  delay(1000);
  Serial.println("Testing PWM");

  ledcSetup(ledCh, freq, resolution);
```

```
Leaving...
Hard resetting via RTS pin...
```

So in this case, this statement will be a thousand twenty-three instead of set 255. That said, I know that this is a long class, but I want to explain. I use an example. I hope everything is now described well to you. If you have questions about whatever you can ask. This is Ashraf. So you are next, learn happily. This is an educational engineering team.

SERVO MOTOR CONTROL USING PWM SIGNAL IN ESP32

Now, let's control yourself, water, use the ability of our E.S.P 30 to the code basically will be the same as that used to control the brightness. First, it is important to remember that the frequency to work with a micro servo motor is 15 Hertz. So we have to edit the first value, which is a frequency, and we must change it to 15 or 50 instead of five thousand. We also have to determine that the channel and PWI job cycle resolution. We will set or reuse the zero channel and eight resolution. Come on, use this code and create a new sketch. Let's base it and save it. Same location. Come on, call it, the PWI is responsible. Now, let's close this. And let's open this one. GOOD.

```
int freq = 5000;
int ledCh = 0;
int resolution = 8;    // 0 - 255 >> 10 0 - 1023
int dutyCycle = 0;

void setup() {
    // put your setup code here, to run once:
    Serial.begin(115200);
    delay(1000);
    Serial.println("Testing PWM");

ledcSetup(ledCh, freq, resolution);
```

Now, here's our quote, We need to change this to 50 and the same. Charles Watson fled, let's call it Servoz. Now, we have used Channel Zero, Resolution eight news cycle zero, and let's connect our greatest things here, disconnect our service to PIN five.

```
Serial.println("Testing Servo");

ledcSetup(ledCh, freq, resolution);
ledcAttachPin(5, ServoCh);
ledcWrite(ledCh, dutyCycle);
}

void loop() {
  // put your main code here, to run repeatedly:

ledcWrite(ServoCh, dutyCycle);
dutyCycle += 10;
```

So we need to edit us, see the pinch pin to the server, which is the number five-pin, and change the channel with the server channel. Now we have everything ready, we have used the same parameters for the channel frequency resolution and number five PIN, which we use to connect our servers and server channels, which we have mentioned here, zero channels for signals. Same here, serve the channel and you will spin now.

```
  // put your setup code here, to run once:
  Serial.begin(115200);
  delay(1000);
  Serial.println("Testing Servo");

ledcSetup(ServoCh, freq, resolution);
ledcAttachPin(5, ServoCh);
ledcWrite(ServoCh, dutyCycle);
}

void loop() {
  // put your main code here, to run repeatedly:
```

To position serve at a certain angle, we must define the task cycle. For example, the position we have is around 90 degrees that each cycle must be around 21. And Lizzi's function. Good. It must be used to send that value through the PWI channel so we can say twenty-one here and will be sent using this lid.

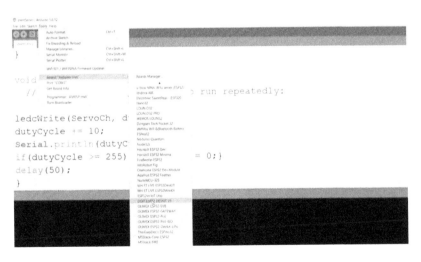

```
int freq = 50;
int ServoCh = 0;
int resolution = 8;   // 0 - 255 >> 10 0 - 1023
int dutyCycle = 21;   // 10

void setup() {
  // put your setup code here, to run once:
  Serial.begin(115200);
  delay(1000);
  Serial.println("Testing Servo");

  ledcSetup(ServoCh, freq, resolution);
```

Right. So it will be at 90 degrees. Now, different values of the cycle well-positioned to serve all different angles, this variable, each cycle should vary from 10 to 30. And this range was gotten manually, so it will be between 10. I wanted to. Now to simply out this code after.

```
void
//                                         run repeatedly:

  ledcWrite(ServoCh, d
  dutyCycle += 10;
  Serial.println(dutyC                    = 0;}
  if(dutyCycle >= 255)
  delay(50);
}
```

Writing it, you need to go to the tools, check the port and choose the compost where you yes, people disconnected and from this menu choose that the whiteboard that we are using, do it E.S.P 30 to defecate where one or any other word that you are using and then upload your code to that board. It will take some time to compile the code and then upload it to the ISP board.

```
void loop() {
    // put your main code here, to run repeatedly:

    ledcWrite(ServoCh, dutyCycle);
    dutyCycle += 10;
    Serial.println(dutyCycle);
    if(dutyCycle >= 255) {dutyCycle = 0;}
    delay(50);
}
```

Global variables use 15396 bytes (4%) of dynamic memory, leaving 31228
esptool.py v2.6
Serial port COM3
Connecting........

Now connecting. OK, now done uploading and we open up the serial monitor. Change the board rate.

Now you can see that the surface water is rotating and receding, now you can increase the delay, you can make it 100 to slow down the rotation. But as you can see, this is how easily you can control a cell phone water using an ISP ball. Now, if you have any question regarding anything, I'm here to help you.

SIMPLE WIFI SERVER

```
#include <WiFi.h>

const char* ssid     = "yourssid";
const char* password = "yourpasswd";

WiFiServer server(80);

void setup()
{
    Serial.begin(115200);
    pinMode(2, OUTPUT);      // set the LED pin mode

    delay(10);

    // We start by connecting to a WiFi network

    Serial.println();
    Serial.println();
    Serial.print("Connecting to ");
    Serial.println(ssid);

    WiFi.begin(ssid, password);

    while (WiFi.status() != WL_CONNECTED) {
        delay(500);
        Serial.print(".");
    }

    Serial.println("");
    Serial.println("WiFi connected.");
    Serial.println("IP address: ");
    Serial.println(WiFi.localIP());

    server.begin();

}

int value = 0;
```

```
void loop(){
WiFiClient client = server.available();   // listen for incoming clients

  if (client) {                    // if you get a client,
    Serial.println("New Client.");        // print a message out the serial port
    String currentLine = "";              // make a String to hold incoming data
from the client
      while (client.connected()) {         // loop while the client's connected
       if (client.available()) {          // if there's bytes to read from the client,
         char c = client.read();          // read a byte, then
         Serial.write(c);               // print it out the serial monitor
         if (c == '\n') {             // if the byte is a newline character

    // if the current line is blank, you got two newline characters in a row.
    // that's the end of the client HTTP request, so send a response:
    if (currentLine.length() == 0) {
      // HTTP headers always start with a response code (e.g. HTTP/1.1 200
OK)
      // and a content-type so the client knows what's coming, then a blank
line:
      client.println("HTTP/1.1 200 OK");
      client.println("Content-type:text/html");
      client.println();

      // the content of the HTTP response follows the header:
      client.print("Click <a href=\"/H\">here</a> to turn the LED on pin 2
on.<br>");
      client.print("Click <a href=\"/L\">here</a> to turn the LED on pin 2
off.<br>");

      // The HTTP response ends with another blank line:
      client.println();
      // break out of the while loop:
      break;
      } else {    // if you got a newline, then clear currentLine:
      currentLine = "";
      }
    } else if (c != '\r') {  // if you got anything else but a carriage return
character,
      currentLine += c;      // add it to the end of the currentLine
      }

    // Check to see if the client request was "GET /H" or "GET /L":
    if (currentLine.endsWith("GET /H")) {
      digitalWrite(2, HIGH);          // GET /H turns the LED on
      }
```

126

```
  if (currentLine.endsWith("GET /L")) {
    digitalWrite(2, LOW);          // GET /L turns the LED off
  }
 }
}
// close the connection:
client.stop();
Serial.println("Client Disconnected.");
 }
}
```

HARDWARE AND SOFTWARE REQUIREMENTS

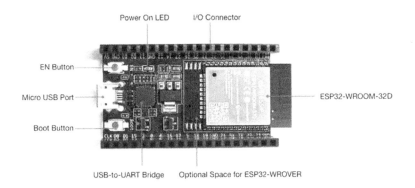

Hardware and software requirements, now we need an ISP 32 ball and we also need Arduino boards. This is a hardware requirement and we will connect it. Yes, people with Arduino. But we also need it, uh, say, level shifta, because e.s.p deal with three-point three volts while Arduino deals with five times. And because we need to be connected, there are these two balls, Cyrille, we need a converter and we will explain it in the circuit design section. Now, you also need a cable. You can connect your Arduino ball to your computer. And I know that you speak can connect your USB port, your computer, and we will need an amputated brokerage account. I will explain how you can do that. How you can create an account and what is the amputation protocol and why we need it. We will also need the Arduino Arcudi development environment, and I will explain how you can install it and how you can add a library. We need to apply for this project now. Again, there are five to three-volt level-level converter points to convert. The signal level is very important in this project. If not, you can damage your board and. These are the things you need to have before moving forward if you just want to get knowledge, but if you want to do this practically, you need to have these two boards and converters too.

REPEAT TIMER

```
hw_timer_t * timer = NULL;
volatile SemaphoreHandle_t timerSemaphore;
portMUX_TYPE timerMux = portMUX_INITIALIZER_UNLOCKED;

volatile uint32_t isrCounter = 0;
volatile uint32_t lastIsrAt = 0;

void IRAM_ATTR onTimer(){
  // Increment the counter and set the time of ISR
  portENTER_CRITICAL_ISR(&timerMux);
  isrCounter++;
  lastIsrAt = millis();
  portEXIT_CRITICAL_ISR(&timerMux);
  // Give a semaphore that we can check in the loop
  xSemaphoreGiveFromISR(timerSemaphore, NULL);
  // It is safe to use digitalRead/Write here if you want to toggle an output
}

void setup() {
  Serial.begin(115200);

  // Set BTN_STOP_ALARM to input mode
  pinMode(BTN_STOP_ALARM, INPUT);

  // Create semaphore to inform us when the timer has fired
```

```
timerSemaphore = xSemaphoreCreateBinary();

// Use 1st timer of 4 (counted from zero).
// Set 80 divider for prescaler (see ESP32 Technical Reference Manual for
more
// info).
timer = timerBegin(0, 80, true);

// Attach onTimer function to our timer.
timerAttachInterrupt(timer, &onTimer, true);

// Set alarm to call onTimer function every second (value in microseconds).
// Repeat the alarm (third parameter)
timerAlarmWrite(timer, 1000000, true);

// Start an alarm
timerAlarmEnable(timer);
}

void loop() {
  // If Timer has fired
  if (xSemaphoreTake(timerSemaphore, 0) == pdTRUE){
    uint32_t isrCount = 0, isrTime = 0;
    // Read the interrupt count and time
    portENTER_CRITICAL(&timerMux);
    isrCount = isrCounter;
    isrTime = lastIsrAt;
    portEXIT_CRITICAL(&timerMux);
    // Print it
    Serial.print("onTimer no. ");
    Serial.print(isrCount);
    Serial.print(" at ");
    Serial.print(isrTime);
    Serial.println(" ms");
  }
  // If button is pressed
  if (digitalRead(BTN_STOP_ALARM) == LOW) {
    // If timer is still running
    if (timer) {
      // Stop and free timer
      timerEnd(timer);
      timer = NULL;
    }
  }
}
```

WHAT IS MQTT AND WHY WE NEED IT

In this case, we will introduce the Cutesie protocol and why we need it. The rise protocol stands for messages that enter basic transportation. Now, this is a lightweight messaging protocol for small sensors and optimized cellular devices for high latency or unreliable networks, allowing smarter projects and devices. And purity is a symbol messaging protocol, it is designed for obstacle devices with low bandwidth, so this is the perfect solution for the Internet of Things. Applications and security allow you to send commands to control output, read and data from science or not, and more. Therefore, it makes it very easy to build communication between several devices. If you like home automation and you want to build a complete home automation system, you can easily do it using Cutesie now. To use Kutty, you need to know Man's command. And this is a common message, topic and broadcast. Now let's start with the main concept of the public. The first concept is the publisher system and subscription and I publish and subscribe to system suggestions can publish messages on topics or can subscribe to certain topics to receive messages so that they can send the value of the temperature sensor online. While the message, which is the second concept, is the information you want to exchange between your device, whether it's a command or it. The third concept here is that OPEX is another important concept. Topics are the way you register interest in ordering or how you determine where you want to publish the message. Topics are served with strings separated by a front tilty. Each forward slash shows the topic level. And you can easily assume this as an example if we add. MCU. And forward Slash, that means that we have this topic, if we add E.S.P after that means that we determine other topics in this one. So this is the main topic and this is one. And we can continue like that. Now, the fourth concept here is brokes. You also need to realize that Broca is mainly responsible for receiving all messages, filter messages, decide who is interested in them, and then publishes messages to all subscribed clients. So this is a very important concept when it comes to multi-level and multi-device systems, but especially we will use publishing. Concept and we will publish data into it and online servers from the ISP and ESB Board will receive data from our ongoing report that says, this is the main concept. This is what I Kutty. Why is it important for you that you can replace it with other APIs like Google Firebase or other APIs? I can work, but you need an encoding experience to adjust the code. Thank you for sharing this. So this is Ashraf from the educational engineering team.

SERIAL TO SERIAL BT

```
#include "BluetoothSerial.h"

#if !defined(CONFIG_BT_ENABLED) ||
!defined(CONFIG_BLUEDROID_ENABLED)
#error Bluetooth is not enabled! Please run `make menuconfig` to and enable it
#endif

BluetoothSerial SerialBT;

void setup() {
  Serial.begin(115200);
  SerialBT.begin("ESP32test"); //Bluetooth device name
  Serial.println("The device started, now you can pair it with bluetooth!");
}

void loop() {
  if (Serial.available()) {
    SerialBT.write(Serial.read());
  }
  if (SerialBT.available()) {
    Serial.write(SerialBT.read());
  }
  delay(20);
}
```

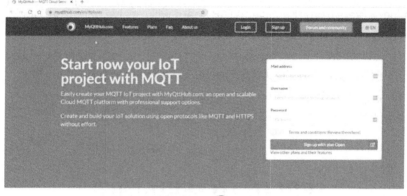

Some features of MyQttHub.com

Now after you already know everything about Cecute, we can use any website provider that activates it and we have this one, for example, my beauty hub starts now. Your internet project with Cutesie, you want to do is write your email address, the username you want and write a password, accept their terms and conditions and register with the option or plan Joplin.

	Open	Micro	Starter	Basic	Standard	Profesional	Premium
Users	100	200	500	1.000	2.000	4.000	6.000
Max connections	50	100	250	500	1.000	2.000	3.000
Storage	10MB	100MB	200MB	500MB	1GB	2GB	2.5GB
Max subscriptions per conn	50	100	100	100	100	100	100
Max subscriptions	250	500	1.250	2.500	5.000	10.000	15.000
Max message size	4KB	32KB	32KB	32KB	64KB	64KB	128KB
Msg measurer size	0.5KB	4KB	4KB	4KB	4KB	4KB	4KB
Messages/minute	300	600	1.000	2.000	3.000	6.000	9.000
Messages/hour	800	2.000	4.000	8.000	12.000	24.000	36.000
Messages/day	10.000	24.000	48.000	96.000	144.000	286.000	432.000
Messages/month	210.000	720.000	1.440.000	2.680.000	4.320.000	8.640.000	13.120.000
MQTT TLS protection	✓	✓	✓	✓	✓	✓	✓
REST HTTPS API	✓	✓	✓	✓	✓	✓	✓

And as you can see here, open the plan. You can make 100 users, maximum conditional, 50 and you have ten megabytes of storage space and free. So, it's a good thing to start, and this is their website, put my hub, that I will add resources from this lecture, click list with the printer package. OK, so the name is not defined. Again, register now. The list only accepts confirmation so click accept. Now you have to go to your email address. Let me open my email to show your confirmation message. Usually have links that you have to click so you can use their services. This is it. This is an email. You just click here. Wait, I can't appreciate success, please, wait until we review your Celtel so that it is activated now, it takes time for them to activate our account after reviewing our details. And they will usually send us another email address, as you can see. Now we can enter. Use the details we provide. For again, OK, from let me check. Okay, now,

After you write your username and password, you will see this dashboard and as you can see, this is the client ID and the admin domain. This is our username and is active. And this is a top priority for our uncute hub. Now, you just add the device by clicking here. You can add client IDs, just call E.S.P 32 click Add device. And as you can see, you can add up to 10 devices.

CREATE MQTT SERVER ACCOUNT CLOUD MQTT

Now let's create a new account, add the Cloud Uncute dot COM website. As you can see, they have many plans that you can choose from depending on your project.

But let's enter using our Gmail account. Without creating a new account, this will give us steps and choose one of my accounts, my email account, to enter this website. Now click Create a new instance, the green button on the right side of the screen.

Now, give your example name and select your package and give a tag. They used to have a free plan, but now they have, uh, five dollars per month the plan you can, uh, try. They have a trial period. And you can contact their support to get it in a certain regime after making this,

You can choose a closer data centre or the closest to you, depending on your location. I will hand it over to default, then click Review.

At this point, you only need to click, create an instance and you will have a stand-alone and ready. This is it. This is called the Ashura test. Now, if you click this instant. You can see the properties click once.

As you can see here, you have the server and the port, and that is this old port. Now go to users and ACL, select a name for your user.

And UNAM. Password for users, I will choose the same thing, Arduino E. P.P. Then clicks, add, now you have a user connected to your instance. Now we need to set our ACLC. You can choose. ACL with topics or patterns? Now, the topic is applied to the user given, and we already have the user you want to apply. ACLC to. So just click the topic, choose your user and make sure that they read and write selected. Oh, we forgot to add a name.

OK, so those are again, add the pattern name. Make sure that they read and write, are selected, then click, add. Now we have the user connected. And has read and write privileges over our insistence.

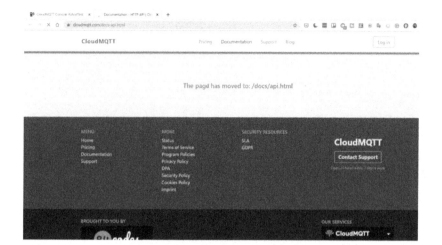

Now you can see their API for further information on this,

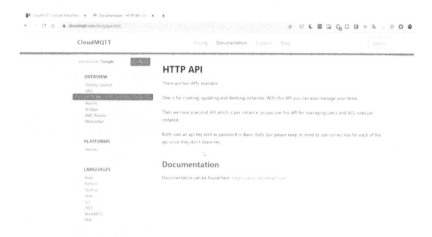

but that's it, this is how to create an instance you.

ARDUINO CODING

Now let's go to our Arduino that can be owned so that it can send data through the series Communication Protocol to our E.s. P board, no one can be found on our Alvino side. We will take samples from analogue digital converters and send them through soft cereal. To do this, first, open Arduino. Now basically will take a reading disc and we will send it through a soft serial communication protocol. Let's make a new code. Not. The first thing we need to do is include a soft serial communication protocol, so it can include it. Soft where the Totex series. Now, Syrian software. Will be done using two pens and let's select a pen, number two and three as an example for the recipient. And Transmission is Russell. So there is ex Ante X will be number two and three pins, number two and three.

```
#include <SoftwareSerial.h>

SoftwareSerial sw(2,3);    // Rx and Tx
void setup() {
    // put your setup code here, to run once:

}
```

Also, here we are not utilizing the equipment sequential. You need to ensure that you comprehend the contrast between programming, sequential and equipment sequential now inside the vocal arrangement. What we need to do is introduce the sequential correspondences that start at a particular moderate.

```
void setup() {
  // put your setup code here, to run once:
Serial.begin(115200);
Serial.println("Project for Interfacing Arduino with
Sw.begin(115200);
}
```

Board at COM8 is not available

At that point, we need to design something to ensure that it's working, so pristine line. What's more, how about we right venture. Or on the other hand interfacing Arduino with E.S.P 32. Presently, whenever you are done, you should begin the product sequential utilizing the item that we are characterized here as W. So as W spot start and we need to allot a board rate, we will utilize a similar board rate. Presently, this sequential is the one that you see when you click the chronic screen and this is the product. So this is the equipment sequential and this is the product arrangement. Presently we should go inside the void circle. We began the equipment and programming sequential. Presently inside the void circle. We need to design something. So we should attempt Serial, the pristine line. Actuated uproars and.

Information to.

```
void loop() {
    // put your main code here, to run repeatedly:
    Serial.println("Send Data to ESP32 Board");
    int adcValue = analogRead(A0);
    Serial.print("");      // {}
}
```

Board at COM8 is not available

PSP 32 purchased. From that point forward, we need to peruse the edit and how about we interface it to a zero or analogous zero. So ADC. The worth will rise to simple 3D. Also, inside it, we can fly zero or a zero now after this, we need to send that to the sequential. So sequential. The Trent. Also, inside it, we should enter information in a particular configuration, so the arrangement will generally be this way, we need to compose OK, similar to this, we need to add Tukur brackets and add slice here. Furthermore, between these two brackets, we need to introduce the sensor information and sensor ID. So to say that we have more than one sensor here, we can characterize an as of now so and sensor as of now rises to, suppose 50. What's more, this likewise one. This is the main sensor that we are adding here. This will be more sensible. Alright, presently inside here, you have attempted that at a particular configuration so E.S.P can get it and send it to the web. Presently. You need to, right precisely like me. We should begin by adding that wavy brackets after adding a slice, at that point add to. 26TH imprints inside them, correct? The name of the variable, which is the thought from that point onward, a slice then between these two checks and twofold focuses, that is it. This is the main line. Presently, the subsequent line will send the. Since we're all worth, so we should pay this variable since Friday thought, this was portrayed

```
}


void loop() {
  // put your main code here, to run repeatedly:
  Serial.println("Send Data to ESP32 Board");
  int adcValue = analogRead(A0);
  Serial.print("{\"sensorid\":");      // {\ sensor data
```

Board at COM8 is not available

in the text on the Syria monitor and this will send its value. After that, we must add a comma. Then we cannot see a real good Trent. After the coma, we need to send the ADC value that we just received, so at last splashier than after this at ADC. Value. OK, Liz. Again, serial. So here you need to add the slash and here you need to add ADC.

```
Serial.println("Send Data to ESP32 Board");
int adcValue = analogRead(A0);
Serial.print("{\"sensorid\":");      // {\ sensor data
Serial.print(sensorid);
Serial.print(",");
Serial.print("\"adcValue\":");
Serial.print();
```

Board at COM8 is not available

Worth and cut, at that point between these two, you need to add twofold focuses, at that point you need to print the worth. So sequential the print. Here will plant this variable, which is the estimation of our sensor, and we need to end this, so we need to compose sequential print. Also, Saadet, we need to add that Carol enclosures, as should be obvious, we began with the brackets and we finished with that end tag for the this currently to end this year, essentially new line, which implies that you have all of you done and the information should be sent. So toward the end, that is it, this is the person that we will ship off the chronic or the equipment vendor Moto. Presently we need to send the very information to the product sequence that we just made. Also, to do that, we simply need to duplicate the same code so we can duplicate the entirety of this and put together it concerning we can compose it once more, however, save time. I will simply duplicate. Friction and to tears. Presently you need to change Syria with S.W. It takes or uses the same innovation. So we will send the same qualities and toward the end, we need to one or the other postponement, we should make it 3000 milliseconds or 4000 milliseconds. Presently we should save our code. We should name it arguido. Paula. Code click saves now what you need to do is essentially transfer this code you are doing on the web. So let me connect my Arduino Ono. Since we have the balls associated, go to the gadget chief. What's more, from here, you can see the part on it, so go to the apparatuses, ensure that order is picked and are doing all, at that point confirm the code to ensure that doesn't have any mistakes.

```
© Arduino/NGCode . Arduino 1.8.12
File Edit Sketch Tools Help

#include <SoftwareSerial.h>
int sensorid = 1;
SoftwareSerial sw(2,3);   // Rx and Tx

void setup() {
    // put your setup code here, to run once:
    Serial.begin(115200);

Sketch uses 4020 bytes (12%) of program storage space
Global variables use 401 bytes (19%) of dynamic memor
```

Presently transfer the code. Presently, all partners hailed. You can work a cereal screen. Also, see with your own eyes the sort of information that is being sent as you can, the obligation to GDP 32 and now since it is one they see esteem is 300 nineteen. Furthermore, that is evolving. Presently, this information will be shipped off the IRS individuals through the chronic or the product convention. Also, we will cover the ESB 32 coding. Presently we are finished with Arduino coding. Presently you can send some other worth relying upon your venture, yet this is it. On the off chance that your distant is showing this, it implies that the cell correspondences are working accurately and you are sending information in the right arrangement, right brackets and opening and shutting the sensor thought between two twofold citations,

```
Project for Interfacing Arduino with "ac
Send Data to ESP32 Board
{"sensorid":1,"adcValue":309}
Project for Interfacing Arduino with ESI
Send Data to ESP32 Board
{"sensorid":1,"adcValue":354}
Send Data to ESP32 Board
{"sensorid":1,"adcValue":319}
Send Data to ESP32 Board
{"sensorid":1,"adcValue":334}
Send Data to ESP32 Board
{"sensorid":1,"adcValue":297}
```

the ADC esteem between two twofold citations, and we have the sensor of significant worth and a similar kind of significant worth and we have a comma here between them. So if you need to send different qualities, you need to add a comma and add information and the same arrangement this and two twofold

focuses then the worth so we can send 100 worth from ALGUIEN to E.S.P. Everything you can even sentence Ansel's perusing relying upon the feeling of ID and the ADC an incentive for every sensor. Yet, here we are just sending two qualities since the thought and the feeling of significant worth, and this is the configuration that you need to send the information. That is it for this.

ESP CODING PART1 DEFINE VARIABLES

the boost cash will court or fare now, the principal thing that we need to do is open up Arduino programming, the product that you will use to program Arduino or E.S.P. Telstra too. Presently, what we need to do this court is first we need to associate with Wi-Fi organization or passage, at that point we need to interface with the, um, QCT broadcast. Furthermore, we additionally need to send each new line got on the Syria line to the MQ DETI. So Alduin all send information to the Syria line and ISP will get this information and it will send it to the amputee dealer or our FBI. Anything you desire, it's up to you. Catch this reason we are utilizing Amcu Deti presently makes another sketch. The principal thing that we need to do is incorporate a few libraries. So we need to incorporate the wi fi library. What's more, we likewise need to incorporate a public subclans library, which is fundamentally a customer library for the SB 32 that offers help for Amcu. Presently attempt to incorporate. Hashtag incorporate them inside it. Right, Bob, some arranged assaults. Presently we need to introduce a few factors before moving onto the setup and circle capacities. Furthermore, we will begin with consistent character.

```
#include <WiFi.h>
#include <PubSubClient.h>

const char* ssid = "SSID";
const char* password = "password";
const char* mqtt_server = "mqtt.eclipse.org";
```

For this current, it's now for our Wi-Fi organization and inside here, you should give it a shot Wi-Fi network name, and we need another consistent character for the secret phrase and we need to compose our secret phrase here, the Wi-Fi secret key. From that point onward, we need the uncute worker interface. So we need to instate Christan character for NQ Treaty Server. Furthermore, inside here, you got a worker name. We can change that later. Presently we need to characterize a few factors, so characterize amputee port for sweetie, Sir Robert. What's more, we need to characterize a username so uncute. Client. Also, here we are, correct, you Kutty ouseley from that point onward, we need to characterize the secret phrase, so I'm certain Deti. Secret key.

```
const char* ssid = "SSID";
const char* password = "password";
const char* mqtt_server = "mqtt.eclipse.org";
#define mqtt_port 1883
#define MQTT_USER "mqtt username"
#define MQTT_PASSWORD "MQTT PASSWORD"
#define MQTT_SERIAL_PUBLISH_CH "/ic/esp32/serialdata
```

Then we need that serial published channel, so we've come to that I define I'm Kutty Serial publish. Challenge. And here we can define it depending on what we have. We can change this later. Serial data and all. OK, now we are done with defining and creating variables and including the libraries, we can move on to. The.

```
#include <PubSubClient.h>

const char* ssid = "SSID";
const char* password = "password";
const char* mqtt_server = "mqtt.eclipse.org";
#define mqtt_port 1883
#define MQTT_USER "mqtt username"
```

```
exit status 1
PubSubClient.h: No such file or directory
```

Set up wi-fi function. But first, let's see if this work. Now, if you did verify your code. You see, there is an error of this library is not defined, no such file or directory. So you need to go to Tool's managed libraries. And here you need to pub. Public subclans have been hit enter and it will.

147

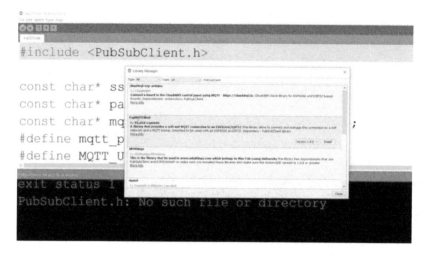

```
#include <PubSubClient.h>

const char* ss
const char* pa
const char* mq
#define mqtt_p
#define MQTT_U

exit status 1
PubSubClient.h: No such file or directory
```

Search for the library, as you can see, this is at E.S.P, I'm Kutty client. Click, install. And click install all. Now, let's verify that point again. As you can see now, it's recognizable. Done combining and we don't have any errors, so that's it, this is the first step. Now let's move on. We need to create a new Wi-Fi client object and we need to create a public sub-client object as well.

```
#include <WiFi.h>
#include <PubSubClient.h>

const char* ssid = "SSID";
const char* password = "password";
const char* mqtt_server = "mqtt.eclipse.org";
#define mqtt port 1883

Sketch uses 1848 bytes (5%) of program storage space
Global variables use 232 bytes (11%) of dynamic memo
```

So wi-fi. It will take a while for my client to choose this one as input and its name will be the client. Now we can verify the quote again. Then combining without it, that's it, this is the first step in calling our E.S.P ball next, we are going to explain how you can create a Wi-Fi connection using various people. Then we will start coding that Sirah communication module. Thanks for sharing this. If you have any questions.

SIMPLE TIME

```
1  #include <WiFi.h>
2  #include "time.h"
3
4  const char* ssid      = "YOUR_SSID";
5  const char* password  = "YOUR_PASS";
6
7  const char* ntpServer = "pool.ntp.org";
8  const long  gmtOffset_sec = 3600;
9  const int   daylightOffset_sec = 3600;
10
11 void printLocalTime()
12 {
13   struct tm timeinfo;
14   if(!getLocalTime(&timeinfo)){
15     Serial.println("Failed to obtain time");
16     return;
17   }
18   Serial.println(&timeinfo, "%A, %B %d %Y %H:%M:%S");
19 }
20
21 void setup()
22 {
23   Serial.begin(115200);
24
25   //connect to WiFi
26   Serial.printf("Connecting to %s ", ssid);
27   WiFi.begin(ssid, password);
28   while (WiFi.status() != WL_CONNECTED) {
29     delay(500);
30     Serial.print(".");
31   }
32   Serial.println(" CONNECTED");
33
34   //init and get the time
35   configTime(gmtOffset_sec, daylightOffset_sec, ntpServer);
36   printLocalTime();
```

```
37
38  //disconnect WiFi as it's no longer needed
39  WiFi.disconnect(true);
40  WiFi.mode(WIFI_OFF);
41 }
42
43  void loop()
44 {
45   delay(1000);
46   printLocalTime();
47 }
```

ESP CODING PART2 WIFI AND MQTT

Since we are finished with the initial segment of our code, we should proceed onward and make a technique so we can interface with Wi-Fi networks effectively tuning in and void who set up wi-fi. Presently, inside this technique to add a postponement of twenty milliseconds and sequential, the brief new line. We should carry something to advise you, however, that we are interfacing with Wi-Fi from the leftovers of. Alright, presently. Truth be told.

```
void setup_wifi()
{
    delay(20);
    Serial.println();
    Serial.print("We are connecting to WiFi Network");
    Serial.println(ssid);
    WiFi.|
```

```
Sketch uses 6494 bytes (20%) of program storage space
Global variables use 375 bytes (18%) of dynamic memor
```

The name of the wi fi. Right is a side after that wi fi spot start to begin interfacing with this wi fi, is this I.D. also, secret word. So it will take the Wi-Fi as ID and secret word and will attempt to interface. Presently, we can't in any case articulation if Wi-Fi the status. It's not associated then we need it to postpone and attempt once more.

```
Serial.print("We are connecting to WiFi Network");
Serial.println(ssid);
WiFi.begin(ssid,password);
while(WiFi.status() != WL_CONNECTED)
{
  delay(600);
  Serial.print();
```

```
Sketch uses 6494 bytes (20%) of program storage space
Global variables use 375 bytes (18%) of dynamic memor
```

And keeping in mind that it's attempting to interface, we need to bring Dot K at this point. After this, after the divider, that divider continues attempting, we'll continue to attempt. Associating with the Wi-Fi network we need to add. Whenever it's associated, it will continue to move this until it's associated. Presently, whenever it's associated, we need to compose a sequential impression. New line now Wi-Fi is associated. Furthermore, we can even print the IP address. What's more, to print it, we need to call a capacity called wi fi speck, neighborhood IP.

```
Serial.print(".");
}
Serial.println("WiFi is Connected");
Serial.println("IP Address: ");
Serial.println(WiFi.localIP());


}
```

```
Sketch uses 6494 bytes (20%) of program storage space
Global variables use 375 bytes (18%) of dynamic memor
```

Furthermore, this will advise the IP address to which our ISP 32 sheets associated and will print it out on the chronic screen. Presently how about we confirm the code to ensure that everything is turned out great. Alright. That is it. Presently, this is the primary capacity. Presently the subsequent capacity is to reconnect now by void, reconnect. Presently we will circle until we are reconnected. So we will add our oil explanation. Also, this is essentially a capacity to ensure that we are associated with the uncute worker. So one player that associated isn't accurate. We need to attempt. To reconnect. So we should attempt to Brent.

```
void reconnect()
{
    while(!client.connected())
    {
        Serial.print("Attempting to reconnect MQ");
    }
```

```
Sketch uses 6494 bytes (20%) of program storage space
Global variables use 375 bytes (18%) of dynamic memor
```

Endeavoring to reconnect and you take an extra. Alright, presently the following line will be on. The distribute inside, it will work out point about how to were. Presently, we should make an irregular customer I.D., solid customer I.D.. How about we call it E.S.P 30 to climb, and you can add anything after that. We can't add customer as of now. In addition, equivalent strength. Thus the strength we can add around work. 06 and for us now, we can ensure that Hicks has the opportunity and this will ensure that each side will have another customer ID,

```
{
    Serial.print("Attempting to reconnect MQTT Conr
    client.publish("outTopic","Hello World");
    String clientID = "ESP32Client-";
    ClientID += String(random(0xffff),HEX);
    }
}
```

```
Sketch uses 6494 bytes (20%) of program storage space
Global variables use 375 bytes (18%) of dynamic memor
```

that is one of a kind since we are getting the worth. What's more, we are adding it to that past esteem so we can move this number and each time it will be in all actuality, it will be this. Besides, the strength that comes out from this line now. How about we endeavor to associate, right on the off chance that proclamation, else. How about we start with that assertion now, inside that proclamation, we need to inquire as to whether a customer that can't work, which normally takes their customer thought to this one, does. Presently we will utilize a capacity called C String, which essentially changes over the substance of a string as a CEO, which is the one that we need for this F articulation. Furthermore, to utilize it, we simply need to compose C, underscore ETR, at that point we can add INF settlement, utilize what is fundamentally the client name for the worker and NQ G.T. secret phrase. Alright, final word now, as should be obvious, uh, it takes the interface work, takes three things the customer ID, the client and the secret phrase after that. In the event that that assertion is valid, we can print the word associated and Barceloneta. So print newline. Alright, presently, when associated, we can distribute a declaration by composing customer, not distribute inside it, we can compose. I see. Rhizomes. What's more, E.S.P, first to. Presently, the declaration will be hi worth. Presently, something else, if this condition didn't hit, we need to go to the EL explanation and inside it we need to Roitfeld.

What's more, we can likewise add a different line that says our see equivalent and leave us space and we will print out the customer state. So sequential, the pattern customer, not state.

```
      }
  else{
      Serial.print("Failed, rc= " );
      Serial.print(client.state());
      Serial.print("Try Again in few seconds");
      de|
      }
```

```
Sketch uses 6494 bytes (20%) of program storage space
Global variables use 375 bytes (18%) of dynamic memor
```

Now. Let's make sure that we have everything correct, that client. The state function. OK, now try again, five seconds. And we can add a delay of five or six seconds to give it time to try again. OK.

```
      Serial.print("Attempting to reconnect MQTT Conr
      client.publish("outTopic","Hello World");
      String clientID = "ESP32Client-";
      ClientID += String(random(0xffff),HEX);
      if(client.connect(ClientID.c_str(),MQTT_USER,MC
      {
          Serial.println("Connected");
```

```
Sketch uses 6494 bytes (20%) of program storage space
Global variables use 375 bytes (18%) of dynamic memor
```

That's it, this is the reconnect function for Van Kutty server. Now we can have this call toward the end, however for the time being, this is all that we require. To begin with, we need to ensure that the customer isn't associated. On the off chance that it's not associated, we need to compose that you are endeavoring to interface and we need to set a customer I.D.. Presently, on the off chance that we have

154

sent the customer as of now and cutesie client name and secret key, it will associate if there is any issue. There is no Internet association or some other issue. It will print fizzled and it will print the condition of this customer and will print that. You should attempt again in almost no time and will add a postponement to guarantee that you are sound after a decent measure of time. Presently, in the event that we didn't check our code, we would get an OK and all that land, it isn't characterized on the grounds that we have little.

```
                    }
                }
            }
void setup() {
    // put your setup code here, to run once:

}

Sketch uses 6494 bytes (20%) of program storage space
Global variables use 375 bytes (18%) of dynamic memor
```

So let's make it a capital. OK, Duncan, darling, everything is correct, and the next , we are going to start the set up and look function coding, but that's it for now. If you have any questions.

HALL SENSOR

```
//Simple sketch to access the internal hall effect detector on the esp32.
//values can be quite low.
//Brian Degger / @sctv

7
8   int val = 0;
9   void setup() {
10    Serial.begin(9600);
11    }
12
13  void loop() {
14    // put your main code here, to run repeatedly:
15    val = hallRead();
16    // print the results to the serial monitor:
      //Serial.print("sensor = ");
      Serial.println(val);//to graph
    }
```

ESP CODING PART3 READ DATA ENTER FROM ARDUINO

Presently, how about we should call a stop work. The primary thing that we need to do is starting ICRA correspondence. Kasprzyk depicted a similar representation and Alduin report. At that point we need to set an opportunity for the sequential correspondence.

```
void setup() {
    // put your setup code here, to run once:
    Serial.begin(115200);
    Serial.setTimeout();
}
```

```
Sketch uses 6494 bytes (20%) of program storage space
Global variables use 375 bytes (18%) of dynamic memor
```

It will be 500 milliseconds, so half a second is enough. Then let's call the set up wi fi function, ensure that we have the right name. This is it. Set up Wi-Fi. After that, we need to call the client, the server to past the server parameters and will take them

```
    // put your setup code here, to run once:
    Serial.begin(115200);
    Serial.setTimeout(500);
    setup_wifi();
    client.setServer(mqtt_server, mqtt_port);
    reconn
}
```

```
Sketch uses 6494 bytes (20%) of program storage space
Global variables use 375 bytes (18%) of dynamic memor
```

Kutty worker connection and pollution port as information, at that point we should call the capacity reconnect. Presently how about we check our code. Extraordinary, we don't have any issues now we need to characterize another capacity between the set up and look, how about we call it distribute. So we distribute. Syrian thatta. Presently, this capacity will take. Sequential information as info. Also, subsequent to taking Syria, that has been purchased voluntarily. Ensure that then local area worker is associated utilizing an if proclamation.

```
if(!client.connected())
{
    reconnect();
    }
    |
}
```

```
Sketch uses 11114 bytes (34%) of program storage spac
Global variables use 657 bytes (32%) of dynamic memor
```

No, inside that assertion will right if customer that associated. Presently, it's not associated. Call that iConnect capacity to associate it currently whenever it's associated. What we need to do is distribute the information, so distribute the distribute will take the MQ Titi Serial Publish channel. As both and will likewise take the sequential information from here, and this is now characterized here. See our public channel. Furthermore, you can transform it to your own distributed diagram. In any case, for the present, we should return. Alright, presently plan to distribute darkland will distribute this. Sequential information to this channel subsequent to ensuring that the PC worker is associated. Presently, this is the expulsion from this capacity inside the world. We will call this capacity so inside the oilor we will inquire. To start with, how about we consider a customer that lub work. Presently we will inquire as to whether. That oat that accessible is more than nothing or over nothing, it implies that we have approaching oat information and all things considered, on the off chance that we have approaching cereal, that is the thing that we need to do, is take the grain that are introduced and a variable. So we will characterize our character. How about we call it Mafa. Deathtoll. What's more, you can make it. This will be a variety of characters and its size will be 500, at that point you can change the choose whatever meets your requirements. In the wake of doing this. We will utilize a capacity as a capacity called me, set the Killara work by name, said

Koby's, the character to the first in quite a while of the string pointed by the cluster. Presently I will record it. At that point I will disclose to you. And keeping in mind that you are utilizing it here, the main thing that you need to compose here is me set inside it. It will accept the cradle as information. What's more, zero, at that point the cushion information of this size, which is 510 now, what this capacity will do is the accompanying. The primary thing, that support information. This is the pointer to the square of New Autofill. So we need to fill this square of limmer with information. Presently, the subsequent boundary, which is this number zero, this is the worth to be set. The worth is passed as whole number, however the capacity fills the square of a request utilizing the unsigned roast transformation of the worth. Presently we go to the last factor or the last component, which is 500 and ten, this is the quantity of bytes to be said to the worth, which is essentially the size of the early. Furthermore, this capacity will return a pointer to the region where support information is told. Presently we need to peruse the information until we see another line, which is fundamentally what we did, not our agreement, we say we have sent information and toward the finish of each square of information, we are adding another line. So. Right, sequential the exchange chomps until. What's more, here are going to different conditions. First thing is LaShun, which is another line and the information that we will peruse will be put away here in the

```
client.loop();
if(Serial.available() > 0)
{
    char bufferData[510];
    memset(bufferData,0,510);
    Serial.readBytesUntil('\n',bufferData,500);
}
```

Sketch uses 11114 bytes (34%) of program storage spac
Global variables use 657 bytes (32%) of dynamic memor

Wild ox information and the information size, we should make it 500. We as of now have a cluster with a size more than 500, 510. So 500 is a similar worth to be embedded here. Typically you need to set a worth that is beneath Baddeley size after this and afterward you need to distribute this information. So bubblish sequential information, this is the capacity that we characterized here. Also, we'll take that that that we got as information, which is the over our information. So this capacity will peruse the approaching sequential information and saw it here until another line is, uh, sent from arguin to E.S.P. At that point it will send the information to the distributed sequential information work, which takes that that has info and this capacity and ensure that time Kutty worker is associated. Subsequent to ensuring that it's associated, it will distribute the information to the promptly sequential channel. What's more, from your perspective, this is the sequential that which is the primary capacity of our coding practice here. Presently, once more, what we have done here, let me zoom out.

We have made characterized a few factors and we have utilized them Kutty Library, the out of control fire library to set up fire to ensure that we are interfacing or we are associated with our Wi-Fi organization and we are on the web. That iConnect work is to ensure that we are associated with the PC worker and we have the set up work where we have interface with Wi-Fi and to the PC worker. At that point we have the circle, which will ensure that we are all we have approaching sequential information. Furthermore, it will store the approaching sign that are inside this variable before that, which is essentially a variety of character and will send it to the distributer and information work, which is this one first, we will ensure that we are associated with the PC worker. At that point we will distribute the information to this channel that we as of now find here. So this is our principle coding practice for Legazpi 32. The following , we will figure this out and ensure that it's turned out great. On the off chance that you have any inquiries in regards to any of these lines, kindly ask precisely what empowered. Presently, just to ensure that we don't have any mistakes, we should confirm our code once again.

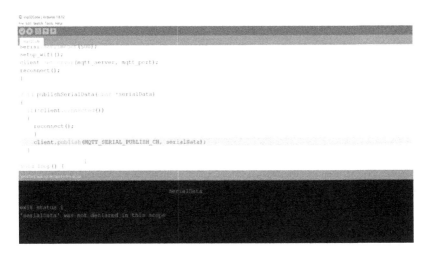

Alright, presently we have an ear, as should be obvious, Cyril, that was not proclaimed, it's here. So we have a spelling mistake. Check once more. At that point joining with no blunders. That is it. Presently, we may need to change the qualities for our Wi-Fi network name and secret phrase and for the username and secret phrase and the channel or the worker joins relying upon our requirements.

```
esp32Code | Arduino 1.8.12
File Edit Sketch Tools Help

esp32Code
Serial.setTimeout(500);
setup_wifi();
client.setServer(mqtt_server, mqtt_port);
reconnect();
}

void publishSerialData(char *serialData)
{
    if(!client.connected())
    {
        reconnect();
    }
    client.publish(MQTT_SERIAL_PUBLISH_CH, serialData);
}

void loop() {
```

```
Sketch uses 12410 bytes (38%) of program storage space. Maximum is 32256 bytes.
Global variables use 683 bytes (33%) of dynamic memory, leaving 1365 bytes for local variables. Maximum is 2048 byte
```

Presently, in the event that you are utilizing your own API, you can essentially send the sequential information to your own API utilizing Jason coding or whatever other technique that accommodates your need, your necessities. Yet, for the present, I'm utilizing the PC to worker. So this is the coding practice for this worker. It's a very notable and broadly utilized one. So I will change that Wi-Fi network esteems and the username and secret key qualities with mine. At that point we will test this code out. A debt of gratitude is in order for imparting to us on this asharaf from instructive designing group.

TOUCH READ

```
void setup()
{
  Serial.begin(115200);
  delay(1000); // give me time to bring up serial monitor
  Serial.println("ESP32 Touch Test");
}

void loop()
{
  Serial.println(touchRead(T0)); // get value using T0
  delay(1000);
}
```

CIRCUIT CONNECTION EXPLAINED

The recreation, and I'm simply going to associate E.S.P first to board with Arduino. We will utilize Fritzing Software. It's a very notable programming for making circuit plan, and it's an awesome programming for showing the wiring design for any electronic circuit. So how about we go to breadboard mode here.

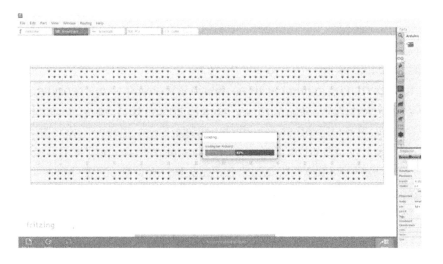

Presently we need to add Arduino board so you can go here and select contending. This is the board. Presently, the following stage will be. Getting a part to board. This is it here we have our indeed, we need to ball. Presently we need a rationale level shifter. You can purchase rationale and you will get huge loads of results. Qualitest. Alright, presently we have, as should be obvious, a little convertor, we have this one. What's more, we have others too. However, this one will be sufficient for us now. To begin associating, we should kind of this by 90 degrees at the present time, we need to interface the three point three volt from the E.S.P load up, which is the game to our rationale level shifter. So this is the three point three ball and we need to interface it to. The low voltage canister, this one, Elvie. Furthermore, we should make it at the present time, the subsequent stage is interfacing the five miles from our old Linebaugh to the HIV or significant level the twist. So how about we attempt this one here. That is it. No. We need to interface the ground from our Arduino with the rationale of a converter with a USB port so the ground from here should be associated with the ground of the level. Contact on the ground from here should be associated with the ground from our level shifter. Presently, we should change the tone to dark here. Around here. Rundown that this arrangement. Alright, presently. Proceeding onward, how about we approach this. Presently, we have associated the force underground and everything is associated accurately. We need to associate the sequential correspondence wires and the initial step is going to our Arduino ready. What's more, since we have instated and as per PIN two and three for the association, we need to interface that up in number three, which is the twist to our sensible level converter. What's more, we need to ensure that we are picking ATX, H.V. or on the other hand high voltage. So you need to go to the X. HIV, and as should be obvious, we have more than one T X. This is T to its V, we need to X S.V., which is dispo. No. How about we move it up here. Alright. Presently, we should show the tone to yellow. Presently we have associated. Number three has now been called, we have said number two and 340, Xander X. Presently the craftsmen from here, which has been number three, is associated with the T x h.

We ensure that you are picking the correct band. At that point you need to interface the R x D zero from your ISP board. So as you can see here, we have Artex zero.

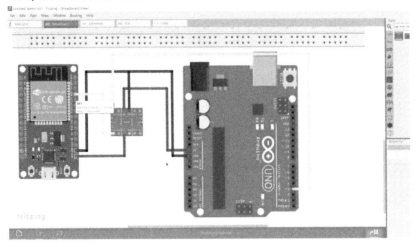

So now we should proceed to get the ah x pen and interface with the T X LV. Here. Alright, presently, as should be obvious, this is the three X. LV, and we have the Arduino pin associated with 3x HIV, and this is fundamentally the transformation it will take for Arduino, convert it and send it to different individuals without consuming the ball. Furthermore, this is the fundamental objective from the converter. Presently, you can see the schematic by clicking here, as should be obvious. These are the two sheets.

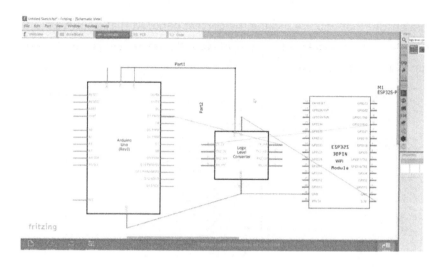

You can move these balls this way and we can turn, as should be obvious, by 90 degree ensured by one hundred eighty degree. Alright, presently the ground is associated between these two balls. What's more, as you can see, we have this twist optics and the as individuals associated with the T SLV PIN six, and we have been not the same as our Arduino associated with that really. What's more, we have in reality high voltage associated with the five volt and the low voltage. All the Elvie associated with the three focuses rotated. That is it. This is our association, ensure that you have everything associated, that we don't blend things up, attempt to twofold check your association prior to pushing ahead and interfacing your part, since, supposing that you have associated any wire and alongside it may harm your bond. Twofold check prior to proceeding onward. A debt of gratitude is in order for sharing this . In the event that you have any inquiries with respect to anything of this association, you can ask on the air terminal. This is Ashenoff from instructive designing group.

CONNECT ARDUINO BOARD AND MAKE SURE IT WORKS

Now, the first thing that we need to do is upload the Arduino code to your Arduino board, make sure that you are selecting Arduino horno.

Also, ensure that you reserve the option to lift it, at that point transfer your code and I will reveal to you how to know whether what you are doing is right or not. Also, I mean it whenever that was transferred to our Alduin done transferring. Presently proceed to tap the chronic screen. In the event that you are getting these readings, as should be obvious, some I.D. what's more, ADC worth and this.

Format, then your Arduino is good to go and it's ready to be connected with or a sport, that's it. And the next we are going to upload, they are code and test their connection before moving forward to connect these two boards together.

ESP32 CODE UPDATE AND UPLOAD

The simulation in which you are going to edit our E.S.P 32 code and uploaded to our E.S.P board now to do this all, what you need to do is go to the M.

Kutty website, which we have created our account. And here, as you can see. We have. The requested data, we have the username and password, for our instance. Go back to the details page, and as you can see, this is our server.

Now, if we want to hear. This is our SilverLink. Now, the next step is the port, make sure that you have the right port here. We have this port, which is copy and paste the port. We have a user and password.

So we need to choose a username and secret word and you can even choose the username and secret phrase for. Your position from this menu, and we as a whole realize that we have this username. What's more, we can right any identification here, the visa that we use to make our record. That is it. Also, we have this as the distributed channel. Presently, to ensure that that tells that you have and thought are turned out great, you can attempt and sweetie, which is an open source utility expected to assist you with checking action on uncute themes, and you can without much of a stretch download it from GitHub. You simply need to ride and dollface.

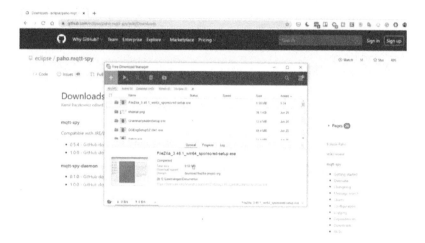

Also, here's the adaptations that are accessible, you can download any of these. We should get how about we get this one. This one. This is a task find. As should be obvious. Presently to test this out. You need to download a product called Uncute Explorer, and the product will assist you with interfacing you to your PC or distributed computing prior to pushing ahead with entering the information inside your ISP code.

Now, choose your platform, download the software for Windows, and once you download the software, you can easily. Connect to Cutie, and as you can see, I have connected here. Let's let's disconnect. OK, now this is.

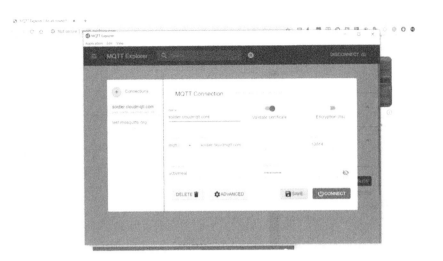

Our cloud and Kutty, you can go to the Download or the Tales page kobie the name of the worker and based it here and the host Kopitar. What's more, here we have the board 10,000 fourteen and based level with the client name from his place level and code with the secret key and spot here. These are the very subtleties that we need here in our code. As should be obvious, this is the part this is the worker you. This is the username we need to change. It was or this username from this page. A go. Of this space. As should be obvious, here is the username lobectomy of code based here with a secret key from here and based it here, at that point save your code. Presently, to ensure that our distributed computing is working, when you interface with Computer Explorer, Click Connect subsequent to entering the subtleties and now, as should be obvious, it's associated, return here and select WebSocket. You I we will attempt to communicate something specific.

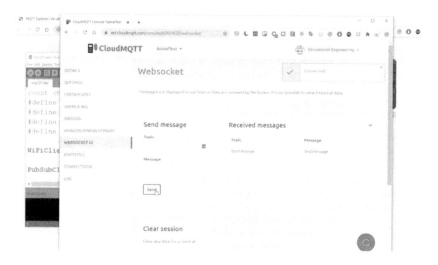

How about we call it instant message. Furthermore, Clexane now, as should be obvious, we have it here. Presently, as should be obvious, we additionally have it here, an amputee traveler, which implies that the data that we entered turn our E.S.P record is right. Try to pick the correct amputee support interface for username and secret key to ensure that you are associated. We should limit this. Presently, this is our code. I would based my own previous 40 years. That is it now, when you have every one of the subtleties your Wi-Fi network tells composed inaccurately and your PC worker subtleties everything effectively, what you need to do now is go to the apparatuses, ensure that you are choosing the correct board, FASB 32, the form one, and ensure that you are choosing the privilege homeport and just snap transfer. That is it.

```
#include <SoftwareSerial.h>
int sens[] 13 = 1;
SoftwareSerial sw(2,3);   // Rx and Tx

void setup() {
  // put your setup code here, to run once:
  Serial.begin(115200);
  Serial.println("Project for Interfacing Arduino with ESP32");
  sw.begin(115200);
}

void loop() {
  // put your main code here, to run repeatedly:
  Serial.println("Send Data to ESP32 Board");
  int adcValue = analogRead(A0);
  Serial.print("{\"sensorid\":");   // if sensor data and sensor id
  Serial.print(sensorid);
  Serial.print(",");
  Serial.print("\"adcValue\":");
  Serial.print(adcValue);
  Serial.print("}");
  Serial.println();
}
```

Presently, whenever that was transferred, simply open up the chronic screen, and in the event that you get this message, it implies that you are currently associated with the amputee worker in the wake of being associated with the Internet utilizing your Wi-Fi organization. Furthermore, you should see your IP address. This is the manner by which you ensure that everything is turned out great. What's more, similarly as made arrangements for the U.S. individuals, the subsequent stage is interfacing these two balls together so they can begin trading data. Also, you will peruse enumeration information on the online ascribed worker. A debt of gratitude is in order for sharing this . This is Ashar from instructive designing group.

LOAD WIFISCAN

```
   /*
5  *  This sketch demonstrates how to scan WiFi networks.
6  *  The API is almost the same as with the WiFi Shield library,
7  *  the most obvious difference being the different file you need to include:
8  */
9  #include "WiFi.h"
10
11 void setup()
12 {
13   Serial.begin(115200);
14
15   // Set WiFi to station mode and disconnect from an AP if it was
16 previously connected
17   WiFi.mode(WIFI_STA);
18   WiFi.disconnect();
19   delay(100);
20
21   Serial.println("Setup done");
22 }
23
24 void loop()
25 {
26   Serial.println("scan start");
27
28   // WiFi.scanNetworks will return the number of networks found
29   int n = WiFi.scanNetworks();
30   Serial.println("scan done");
31   if (n == 0) {
32     Serial.println("no networks found");
33   } else {
34     Serial.print(n);
35     Serial.println(" networks found");
36     for (int i = 0; i < n; ++i) {
37       // Print SSID and RSSI for each network found
38       Serial.print(i + 1);
39       Serial.print(": ");
40       Serial.print(WiFi.SSID(i));
41       Serial.print(" (");
42       Serial.print(WiFi.RSSI(i));
43       Serial.print(")");
44       Serial.println((WiFi.encryptionType(i) == WIFI_AUTH_OPEN)?"
45 ":"*");
```

```
46      delay(10);
47    }
48  }
    Serial.println("");

    // Wait a bit before scanning again
    delay(5000);
  }
```

FINAL ESP32 SERVER TEST

Now, to make sure that our ISP has connected to our Cloud and Kutty
server. I already mentioned that you have to download them to
Explorer.

What's more, as you can see here, we have one subject and around 11
messages. Also, on the off chance that we opened the messages, we
can see that icey presence, Yasui 32 and the message is Hello World,
which is the message that we sent utilizing our code. In the event that
you. Investigate our coding, you can see that here we have Hello World

and we have Icey Presence E.S.P 32. Alright, presently on the off chance that we returned, as should be obvious, we have around 11 messages and this is our E.S.P manure. I will visit E.S.P board and you'll see that the 11 messages will become 12 messages. When I get the board, I will flick it now. As you can see currently, it's 12 messages, and in the event that I navigate it once more, it will be 13 messages. So each time we turn on our E.S.P load up, it will reach out to our PC worker. Also, when we associate it to our Arduino board, it will begin sending sensor information to this point. Furthermore, once more, all what we need to do now is adhere to the circuit plan guidance in the following area to interface Arduino board and indeed, individuals together to begin sending sensor information from Arduino to E.S.P 30 to and from that point to that PC itself. That is it.

HARDWARE AND SOFTWARE REQUIREMENTS

Presently, we should discuss the equipment and programming prerequisites. In the first place, you need the temperature and moistness, Sentsov, and you can get a discretionary water level sensor and dampness sensors. You will likewise require drove and obstruction as markers for your venture. What's more, you will require a breadboard to interface these things together. You need wires with the goal that you associate, you can interface these modules and sensors to the E.S.P 32 board, which is the mind of this task. It's fundamentally the microcontroller that we will code. You need an advanced mobile phone so you can download the UpLink application and you'll likewise require the flicker, which are accessible in the App Store and both Google and Apple Store. You can without much of a stretch download it. We will likewise require Arduino I.D. to compose our code for E.S.P 32 baud. This will be shrouded in the Codding area, so don't stress over that.

WORKING PRINCIPLE

Presently, we should discuss the functioning head. What's more, this arrangement, we are observing the sensor information and interfacing control high transfer modules to control high voltage gadgets like mortars, bombs and different things through the squint. We can distantly screen different boundaries in our nursery and we can convey controlled messages. Presently, let me show you this in a sketch. Presently we have our E.S.P 32 here. E.S.P. 32. Also, Here we have Sonsoles. Suppose that this is the principal sensor, a temperature sensor. Furthermore, suppose that we have a human and true. Alright, presently we have these two sensors currently suppose that we have a knock. What's more, this will be inside our nursery. This will be our nursery. Presently, the opposite side, we have our cell phone. Furthermore, we are busy working. Inside our cell phone, we have. That flicker up. Introduced. What's more, we have a temperature scale and we do the scale. Also, on of all the knock. Also, caution framework. Presently, the temperature will be appeared here. Suppose that we have 30 degree temperature line, which is 80, so we can enter our squint system utilizing Internet association and our ISP will interface. Suppose that our home is here or we have a Wi-Fi network here. Our Espanol all associate with the Internet utilizing our Wi-Fi organization or versatile organization, so information will be shipped off an Internet worker and this Internet worker will send the information to the connection up that you have introduced in your telephone. Presently, when you have the entirety of this data, your application, which is clear, you can screen your nursery progressively. You can see the temperature, the moistness, and you can kill on or the water siphon on the off chance that you feel that your nursery needs more water. Alright. This is fundamentally the primary thought and the principle working standard for this venture, and it's simple and direct. Presently, once more, this can be applied to whatever else inside your home. You can screen a room, change your nursery to see the temperature inside this room. You can't handle. In the event that you have a motor inside your home, you can handle it. You can handle your entryway if there is movement. So if movement is recognized, you can have movement sensor here and you can advise the exploding to send you a caution on. Movement is distinguished and you can even interface a camera. So it's fundamentally a similar working standard. What's more, we will be in a bit by bit model how to code your ISP 32 and how to set up your flicker to begin getting information from this specific ISP board.

CIRCUIT CONNECTION

This you will plan our circuits now, we will utilize our dirt dampness sensors to quantify the volume of water content in the dirt. What's more, we will for the most part utilize that the H.T. 11 sensor, which we will use to quantify temperature and mugginess levels in the plant's environmental factors, and the water level sensor will gauge the water level in a little tank. Also, this is a discretionary sensor. You can decide to add it or not, contingent upon your water, say, state. On the off chance that you have a persistent water supply, you shouldn't stress over the tank level. Presently, to plan our circuit, what we need to do is straightforward. We should open up. Amazing up that we just downloaded Double-Click on it. Presently, this will reenact the genuine association, so you need to think, go to the breadboard see up here and you will see a Bridport. Presently, shift this to the side, we will require SB 32 Balde. Also, as should be obvious, we have a ton of yes individuals we need an ASPEY 32 on board this one. Alright, presently we will likewise require a decision with you.

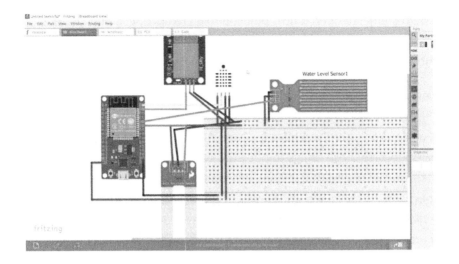

Presently, you can see that here we have a ton of actually module's out segments, we will take this one. We will require the H 11 Sencer DHT. Alright, how about we attempt another. We. Gay, when you deal with this issue, when you attempt to puberty, you don't discover it by another name. This implies that this sensor isn't here. Furthermore, as you can see here, we have one of these sensors. It's called, ah, a sensor. Also, we can see that it nearly have the very terminal's ground and PTC and that signal. So we can utilize it for this association. What's more, you can either search for option or you can download it on the web. A ton of libraries are now accessible by individuals who are making these segments. So you can download it and add it. Be that as it may, this will take a ton of time. So we will utilize this rather now. Presently we need the dirt, more dampness sensor and this is it, we will require the water level sensor and when you search for it, you will not discover it. So for this situation, you need to go to Google here and in here. Right. Water level, Centonze. Fritzing. As should be obvious, you'll get water level. Alright, this is all pointer, how about we search for them. Strip search. Alright. That is mutiple. The Lesli distorter liberal. Fritzing objective, OK? The principal result is this, as you can see, this is the water level sensor and this is the flooding that we will download. It has a water level sensor associated with our drill and we just need this thing. So download the fritzing record from here. Here it is. Presently, to open it up, you need to go to Fritzing. Simplified the record on that, on your open flooding programming, you will see that now you'll have

another window. What's more, this is the water level sensor. Presently, what you need to do is basic. Reorder the sensor. Furthermore, here you have it. Sorry. Alright, presently now how about we interface these things to our E.S.P board. We'll begin with the edge sensor. We realize that we need ground association, which is the dark one. What's more, we will likewise require. Five volts, so to get five volts, we need to ensure this vent will furnish you with five volts. Furthermore, you need to ensure that you will be, you know, what you are doing, since, supposing that you associated your ISP more through your ISP, you will get five volts from this veltman. Else, you need to associate an outer force source that gives five volts. Presently we need to associate the first and fourth, which is that the edge sensor. Presently, as you can see here, we have an excess to interface and relying upon that terminal that you are attempting to associate. Presently. We need to interface the VXI and ground. Presently, the explanation he should be associated here, however we need to interface. That is expected around here and the dark a long distance over here. Just to ensure that we have our up there, that, OK, presently the Viscusi will be associated here. So now we have different other options. This is the letter sign and we will send it to our ISP 32 Balde. How about we send it to this twist. Convey a spoon and how about we go close to Ben, number 32. Change the tone to yellow. Furthermore, here we have the ground pen and we should keep on establishing the vehicle to obstruct and this one turret. Presently, this boycott is the subsequent ground and you can interface it to the ground. You relying upon the module that you have, you can check the information sheet for the association, yet this is the association for the one that we have here at this point. Presently, to associate the transfer module, we can't utilize this one as it has a great deal of information yield boards and it's a committed module. So how about we eliminate this. I previously downloaded a hand-off module and I'll give a connect to you to utilize it. This is it. You can drag it. Also, Robert on your fritzing. What's more, as you can see here, we have it. You simply need to drag this module and Roberte. Presently we have these three twists. The sign should be associated with your board. What's more, how about we pick an alternate tone. Suppose green and the impact should be associated with the five volt. The excavators should be associated with ground. Also, we can't permit him to obstruct. Angela. Or on the other hand OK, presently. We result in these present circumstances module, which is the water level module, we need to associate the glass to five volts, the dark. The ground, which is the less. Also, the sign can be associated with the 21. We should show this to, suppose all us now, we have three signs, one yield and two contributions from sensors. We additionally have other sensor. Which is this one? The dirt dampness sensor, presently how about we interface the ground. To the ground that we see. To the recency and the sign to the 19. How about we show the distinctive shading. Also, That is it. I will show the tones to peruse. On this one. I will transform it to dark. Presently we have associated the dirt dampness sensor, the water level sensor, the stickiness and the sensor as info, and we have finished the hand-off as yield. I will say this are. How about we call it circuit plan. I will give this circuit plan and assets so you can get these modules for your fritzing plan. Presently. Once more, ensure that you observe the entirety of this and furthermore now we have completely associated with a number 22. So let me open up a notebook. A daily existence click new, not awful, we should call it Penns. Presently, inside it, we need to ensure that we have everything now the sensor.

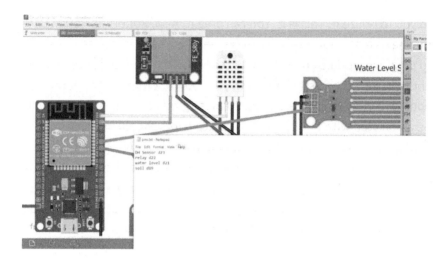

It's connected to the 23 relay is connected to the toilet all and water level. It's connected to the. To anyone and soil is connected to the 19. As you can see here, the 19, the 21, the 22 and 23, this will be used in the coding section. Now you can see the schematic for your design here, as you can see. You can't read these components. And you can also make the wedding. No cattle trade these items.

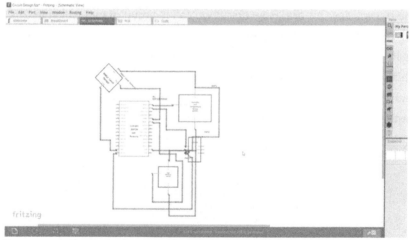

You can go through them so that they are connected with wires. As you can see, Fritzing is trying to wipe out these components together. As you can see here, we have a problem, so we need to all with this and you can't even create a PCB design. By moving these components.

182

Or at the very least, increasing the size of this layout. Now, as you can see, it's a piece of cake.

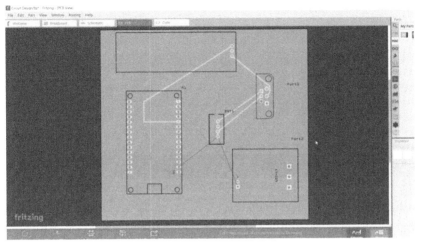

Furthermore, you can likewise utilize. Potoroos. Snap on to Ruth. We'll take some time, at that point you will prepare your PCB plan for assembling. Presently, there are still a few miles that you need to do physically, as you can see this one. We need to interface out from one here to another physically. Also, you can do likewise for most of these wires, and as should be obvious.

CODING ESP32 PART1

The stimulus one in which we are going to start coding using Arduino Edesia. We know only the. Now. Now, we will start by including some libraries. First, we know for sure that we will need let me increase the font size. We will need the wi fi library. So right. WI fi detects and we also need the Wi-Fi client library.

```
#include <WiFi.h>
#include <WiFiClient.h>
#include <DHT.h>
#include <BlynkSimpleESP32.h>

#define DHPIN
#define DHTYPE
void setup() {
    // put your setup code here, to run once:

}
```

The takes and we will need that DHT censored library, so we have to include it. And we need to blink, yes, be 30 to library, so let's include that to. Planked. Symbol E.S.P, 32 not. Now, these are the main levers that we need. Let's define some variables, and if we need more labels, we will add them as we go. And according now define the Ich bin. And define the the edge. The type, so let's define again.

```
#include <BlynkSimpleESP32.h>

#define DHPIN 23
#define DHTYPE DHT11

const int relay = 22;
const int waterLevelSensor = 21;
const int SoilSensor = 19;

int waterLevelData;
int Soil
```

The edge type, a feeling of type. Presently the sensor tab is DHT 11 and the PIN, as we previously referenced in the content report, that that the expen is number 23. So here we are, 23. Presently we need to instate a few factors for the truly. What's more, different segments that we have in the framework now, we know without a doubt that Verilli is associated with a PIN 22. Furthermore, we likewise know. That

that water. The level is associated with Ben. No. He is 21. What's more, we will characterize our variable for the dirt sensor, and it's associated with a PIN 19. Presently, on the money senseor here and directly since we're here to ensure that. Presently, how about we characterize two new factors what a ultra liberal. Also, the other one, all the dirt since or. Live in that. Presently we will utilize that DHT library, yet we should initially save our code. Since we have saved the code, how about we check and ensure that we don't have any mistakes, we will in all likelihood confront a library or as you can see since the library isn't perceived. So you need to go to the apparatuses. Alright, presently incorporate library and without any preparation incorporate library oversaw libraries.

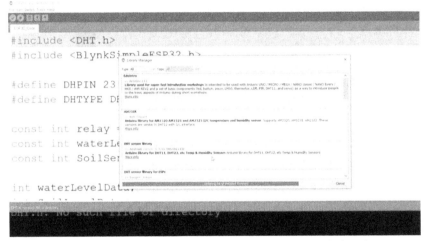

Also, we need to incorporate these libraries now. Search for the principal library. The DHT. Library, as you can see here, we have the downtown area library click introduce. Introduce all. Presently, as should be obvious, the cameras introduced. Snap close, click check, presently you can see that the DHT is perceived. Presently we have this library playing image E.S.P and go sketch incorporate library oversaw libraries and do exactly the same thing to incorporate this library. Presently, based here, hit the intel button. Also, pause. Presently, you may have to change the watchword that you are utilizing to search for the library here we have the clear library and the help for E.S.P 32. Also, click on. Presently, as should be obvious, and it's told. Presently click close and attempt to check to check whether this works or not. As should be obvious, Blinkx Simbel Library is as yet vague. So we need to do this at this point.

The issue that we have here is that E.S.P is written in capital letters. How about we attempt little lotter and we should confirm. Alright, presently, as should be obvious. This code currently perceives the public library, however since we are picking, contending on our own board, we are confronting an extremely fine blunder. So proceed to change this to E.S.P 32. Kay. Indeed, how about we search for the one that we have. Indeed, be troublesome like this one, do it. Indeed, be 32, troublesome veteran one five, could you see? That you don't have any blunders. Furthermore, ensure that you have S&P and little letters here. It's requiring some investment and we have disclosed how to empower indeed, we need to do when you are doing Idy, you need to look at this on the off chance that you can. As you can see now, Duncan Barling, which implies that every one of the renegades are characterized and all is functioning admirably. Presently we need to ensure, OK, here we have an issue now. We need to ensure that we make another article from the Apache sensor, and it's called DHT. What's more, it will take two factors that the first is this one, DSG Ben, and the subsequent one is that type. Presently. We need to during a period of. Let's.

```
#define DHTYPE DHT11

const int relay = 22;
const int waterLevelSensor = 21;
const int SoilSensor = 19;

int waterLevel;
int moistureLevel;

DHT dht(H)
```

```
Sketch uses 312837 bytes (23%) of program storage space. Maxim
Global variables use 18276 bytes (5%) of dynamic memory, leavi
```

Make another playing Time Out for the flicker. We will clarify why we are doing this later. Doublecheck prior to proceeding onward, we need to realize that for flicker up to perceive our E.S.P world, we need to have a verification key which will be given by the squint up once we see the top and the coming s. So for the time being, we need to characterize a character for the confirmation. Also, here you need to enter. Your partnership. Court. Presently. Since our E.S.P board is utilizing Wi-Fi to interface with the Internet, we need to ensure that we have the Wi-Fi setting set up accurately. So characterize another character for the organization name. Also, here we will add Wi-Fi. This to the side, and another character for the secret word. It wi fi secret word. You need to see segment toward the finish of these two lines. Presently we need to make another strategy to send our statistics information to the up. Presently, we know without a doubt that we have like three or four Sonsoles that are called for. This is quite clear. We will utilize that DHT since our library to get the temperature and stickiness

```
char auth[] = "Enter Your Auth Code";

char ssid[] = "WiFi SSID";
char pass[] = "WiFi Password";


coid

void setup() {
  // put your setup code here, to run once:
```

```
Sketch uses 312837 bytes (23%) of program storage space. Maximu
Global variables use 18276 bytes (5%) of dynamic memory, leavi
```

readings and the water and soil dampness levels are simply simple perusing. So we can utilize the simple capacity to peruse the approaching information and mastermind to change over it and send it to our application. Contingent upon your current circumstance and sensor or obliges the simple qualities from the water and soil dampness level sensors can be dealt with and planned into orange. Presently we will make two capacities to send information to. The flicker of the main capacity will help send the temperature and dampness esteems since we are depending on the DH library and the subsequent technique will send the water and soil dampness levels, sensors, readings, which are essentially simple readings. It will send these readings to weblink up. So we should begin with the primary capacity like void. Cynde. Senseor DH. Presently. This is the main strategy, and how about we characterize the subsequent technique, at that point we can begin composing the code, send salt water, soil. Alright, presently we have these two strategies and the following we will call these two techniques and continue with volume and voice at Wohlstetter capacities, yet that is it for this . How about we do a speedy amendment.

```
#include <WiFi.h>
#include <WiFiClient.h>
#include <DHT.h>
#include <BlynkSimpleEsp32.h>

#define DHPIN 23
#define DHTYPE DHT11

const int relay = 22;
const int waterLevelSensor = 21;
const int SoilSensor = 19;
```

Sketch uses 312837 bytes (23%) of program storage space. Maxim
Global variables use 18276 bytes (5%) of dynamic memory, leavi

We incorporated the Wi-Fi and Wi-Fi class libraries for the Wi-Fi association that the city library for that temperature and moistness sensor, the Blink Symbol E.S.P library, so we can undoubtedly interface our E.S.P 30 to board with the Blink workers. We characterized these to ensure that we have the right PIN for that d.h sensorially water and soil sensor. Furthermore, we made two factors to store the approaching information from the water and soil sensor. Since they are simple readings, we additionally characterized an article called DHT from the DHT library and we made a clock utilizing the Blink Time Library and the Blink Symbol E.S.P 32 library and we will utilize it at our capacities. Presently, we previously referenced that bending over has a confirmation key for every client and for one another. So you need to introduce the verification key here and we will disclose how to get it. Furthermore, the reasonable with respect to the UpLink AB, we previously referenced that we are utilizing Wi-Fi association. So we characterize two factors. One, for the Wi-Fi network name and the other one for the secret key. Presently we have two capacities. The first will be coded to send the temperature and mugginess sensor readings and the subsequent one will be coded to send the water and soil dampness level readings. That is it for this .

CODING ESP32 PART2

This new Arason. Presently how about we start by citing the principal technique. To begin with, we need to peruse the approaching information. So light moistness, low mugginess rises to DHT, which is the article that we as of now discover, seed dampness. Furthermore, the following one is for coast for that temperature. By DHT speck read. At that point, Richard, presently we have the mugginess and temperature to send them, we can without much of a stretch utilize the Vishwa light capacity. The first Blinkx Library has a strategy called Vishwa Right, which is utilized to drive the sensor adding something extra to virtual receptacles. We have or we will characterize and arrange and our connection up. So to do this, basically compose clear speck virtual. Right. Presently, first, characterize the virtual pen, how about we call it V.. Five, and we will send dampness. Also, we will do likewise for the temperature. We should consider it the V for.

```
void SendSensorDH()
{
    float humidity = dht.readHumidity();
    float temperature = dht.readTemperature();

    Blynk.virtualWrite(V5,humidity);
    Blynk.virtualWrite(V4,temperature);
}

void SendSensorWaterSoil()
{
```

```
Sketch uses 312837 bytes (23%) of program storage space. Maxim
Global variables use 18276 bytes (5%) of dynamic memory, leavi
```

And let's and the temperature in which. That's it. Now, this is the first function, now the second function, what we will do in the second function is basically the same thing. We will be the water level. And we already define two variables here and here. So the water level will equal unallowed read function. And this will equal analogueue.

```
void SendSensorWaterSoil()
{
  waterLevel = analogRead(waterLevelSensor);
  waterLevel = map(waterLevel,0,2000,0,20);
  moistureLevel = analogRead(SoilSensor);
  moistureLevel = map(moistureLevel,0,4000,0,20);
  }

void setup() {
  // put your setup code here, to run once:
```

At this moment, we need to bring the two factors here, water level, sensor PIN and the salt and salt and no. Presently we have two simple readings, and to plan them, we can without much of a stretch utilize this capacity you cut at water level. Equivalent crowd and inside the horde, you can add water level and the reach zero 2000 zero. 25 now, exactly the same thing should be possible for the. Dampness level will rise to mud and we will do exactly the same thing, we will compose more Circleville and we will add zero 4000 zero 25 or we should make it 20 hundredths. Make this one. Presently, this these qualities are relying upon my sensor readings and the reach that I need to get. Presently, contingent upon your kind of sensor information sheet, you need to ensure that you are picking the correct qualities. Presently to know. The Arduino breakdown.

We should investigate its portrayal now, the guide is essentially an approach to make maps, a number starting with one territory then onto the next that is accessible from law would get guide to law now. It doesn't oblige qualities to inside the reach on the grounds that out of reach esteems are now and again planned and valuable, that compels capacity might be utilized either previously or after this capacity if cutoff points to that energies are wanted, contingent upon your ultimate objective. You can either utilize the limitations work or don't utilize it. Presently, I can see here the guide will take a worth and from law from high to low and excessively high. So it will divert the worth from one law to another. As you can see this to this and from one high to another, as you can see from this to this. Presently the worth is the base up from low, the lower bound of the qualities current reach from high, the upper bound of the qualities current reach to low, the lower bound of the qualities target range, the one that we need to high, the upper bound of the qualities target range. Presently, as should be obvious, this is a model code. We are planning a simple worth to eight pieces, zero to 255. As you can see here, we are perusing the worth and here we are getting the readings from zero to 1,000 23. Furthermore, we need them to be guide to zero to 255. So 1,000 23 will give a yield of 200 55 and it will be put away the worth here. So it's fundamentally an approach to transform from this reach to this reach, as should be obvious. Also, we are utilizing exactly the same strategy here. We are moving the qualities from this reach from zero to 2,000 to this reach from zero to twenty. Furthermore, here we are moving the qualities from zero to 4000. So this reach from zero to twenty. Also, it's a simple, clear and simple to execute approach to change the reach from an extremely enormous reach to a little one. What's more, the two of them will give exactly the same end-product. Presently, this is in regards to the planning, and since we currently have the water level and dampness level, we can without much of a stretch send the qualities utilizing the uplink, the virtual. Right capacity here we have seven. Walter Lippmann. What's more, here we have. Suppose v six. To send the most. Hi. Presently, we should check the code to ensure that we don't have any spelling or. Missing a.m. section for pushing ahead.

```
BlynkTimer timer;

char auth[] = "Enter Your Auth Code";

char ssid[] = "WiFi SSID";
char pass[] = "WiFi Password";


void SendSensorDH()
{
    float humidity = dht.readHumidity();
```

expected ',' or ';' before 'BlynkTimer'

OK, now, as you can see here, we have another. We have seen here.

```
waterLevel = analogRead(WaterLevelSensor);
waterLevel = map(waterLevel,0,2000,0,20);
moistureLevel = analogRead(SoilSensor);
moistureLevel = map(moistureLevel,0,4000,0,20);

Blynk.virtualWrite(V7,waterLevel);
Blynk.virtualWrite(V6, moistureLevel);
 }

void setup() {
  // put your setup code here, to run once:
```

```
Sketch uses 313369 bytes (23%) of program storage space. Maxim
Global variables use 18876 bytes (5%) of dynamic memory, leavi
```

Alright, here we have another critical on the grounds that I'm citing and see Python and Java. Once in a while. Such missteps happens in light of the fact that, as you most likely are aware, Python doesn't have a semicolon toward the finish of each sentence. Alright. Presently, done joining everything is at this moment, we can add an additional progression here and this additional progression will ensure that we are getting readings from the DH sensor. However, on the off chance that you have associated effectively, you will not need this progression.

```
#include <WiFi.h>
#include <WiFiClient.h>
#include <DHT.h>
#include <BlynkSimpleESP32.h>

#define DHPIN
#define DHTYPE
void setup() {
  // put your setup code here, to run once:

}
```

You can add an if explanation. Assuming you are getting readings from the stickiness and temperature, proceed onward. Assuming not, plant a cereal line, neglect to peruse information from the sensor and you can do likewise here. Yet, I don't believe that we need them now. We need to ensure that we retain these numbers. We will reward them in the squint clarification . Presently, we are finished with this. Capacity and we are finished with this capacity. The following stage is it's arranging the set up and the circle capacities and this will be something simple to do. At that point we'll look again. This called Bartletts Memrise, or we should cause a fast outline of what we to have done here. We have utilized the ESTIE object to make the dampness and temperature sensor esteems, and we have sent them to the flicker up utilizing V5 and V4, which are the virtual pens. So now we have utilized simple to have to peruse the water liberal and most liberal sensors esteem. Furthermore, we have utilized the guide capacity to plan the reach from zero to 2000 to a lower range, which is zero to 20. Also, in the most liberal sensor, we have utilized the guide capacity to plan these qualities from zero to 4000 to zero to 20. And afterward we have a few qualities utilizing the virtual right capacity in the public library and we utilize V six and seven as virtual pens for the flicker up. What's more, the following we will set up, we will compose the code inside the arrangement and the capacities to complete this coding cycle.

CODING SETUP AND LOOP PART3

The recreation where we will continue with the coding of this E.S.P, first utility belt, presently in the arrangement work, we need to begin the sequential correspondence for troubleshooting purposes at 9,000 600. Baudrillard And we need to start the squint up association utilizing the flicker to start. It will take the verification key, that to the side, for the Wi-Fi organization and the secret word as info and we need to begin DHT since our library, at that point we need to set as far as possible span. Call the first and second clock, so a clock that set. Tavel. Addressed questioner Now that said, stretch capacity for the clock will take two boundaries, the first is the time we need to send the DH esteems Western qualities each a few seconds. Also, you need to characterize the capacity, yet you need to send so since thus the engraving. Furthermore, the subsequent one, we will send it we will send the liberal answer and most liberal sensor information at regular intervals or seconds. Presently go this and base Bastia. That is it now inside the circle work, we need to compose flicker.

```
void setup() {
    // put your setup code here, to run once:
    Serial.begin(9600);
    Blynk.begin(auth,ssid,pass);
    dht.begin();
    timer.setInterval(3000L, SendSensorDH);
    timer.setInterval(6000L, SendSensorWaterSoil);
}
```

```
Sketch uses 313369 bytes (23%) of program storage space. Maxim
Global variables use 18876 bytes (5%) of dynamic memory, leavi
```

Duran, The Bling Connection, and we need to run the opportunity to. Presently, just to ensure that we have item clock are extraordinary. Presently click check to ensure that we don't have any mistakes. We will return to the court once we set up the flicker up and we have our validation code and we will enter our Wi-Fi as a general public name and secret key. What's more, the reasonable toward the end, and that is it for this , what we have done here is essentially we have begun the correspondence that flicker, stop or start greatest capacity and that the Tucson library, we have set the clock span for the principal technique and the subsequent strategy. So we will get the feeling of qualities like clockwork and we will get the water and soil dampness levels thus esteem at regular intervals. Also, inside the circle we run, we utilize the round work for the flicker and the hour of libraries. All things considered, this is all that we require to do. On the off chance that you have any inquiry with respect to any of these means, I'm here to help you

MOBILE BLYNK APP DOWNLOAD AND SETUP

The improvement cash. Presently it's an ideal opportunity to set up the bling application to screen on qualities, and the initial step will introduce getting serious about your cell phone. Presently go to your cell phone and go to the App Store. Contingent upon the sort of cell phone that you have, that may be Google Play store or Apple Play store or App Store Android playing. As should be obvious, you will get it and it's the main outcome.

This is our uplink and Internet of thing for Arduino E.S.P 32. Presently, as should be obvious, I as of now have the application, so I will flick open. Yet, in the event that you don't have it, you need to click, introduce or download. It will stand by some time and you will surrender. Furthermore, as you can see from the depiction, this application is utilized to control Arduino. Raspberry Pi E.S.P is 266 and E.S.P 32 and a great deal of different sheets is the solitary simplified portable manufacturer for microcontrollers and Internet of Things. Snap open and as should be obvious, you have more than one alternative to sign in. You can sign in on the off chance that you as of now have a record, you can make new record or you can sign in with your Facebook.

Presently you can make a record by clicking here and adding your email and secret phrase. Presently, subsequent to putting your identification click, make new record, it shouldn't take a ton of time. Making another record will give you an interesting verification code and will be shipped off your email. What's more, this is vital since we are doing this to control our fare now. Presently, subsequent to making a record, you need to make another undertaking and select your equipment. Presently click the new undertaking. Also, as should be obvious, you need to name your task. I would call it Smart Ghanim, and you need to choose your board. What's more, as you can see, you have a great deal of surveys that you can browse. Also, the one that we need is the E.S.P. You have are improving by different sheets we need to address to this board and you can pick that association type. As you can see here, we have Wi-Fi association and you can either pick dull or light. I would pick light as since it's simpler and I at that point click make a venture. Presently, as should be obvious, validation. Tolkien was shipped off my email and you can likewise discover it by tapping on this thing on the upper right corner. Snap OK, and we will get it from our email. Presently, the validation code is a vital code that you will use to control your task. Presently we need to make our brilliant Goldwing checking framework inside this connection up. Presently you have a vacant material, as should be obvious, and we need to add four check gadgets to screen temperature, dampness, water level and soil dampness level sensor readings and to do that tap on the material to open up the gadget box. Presently you can pick a check. As should be obvious, we have a ton of measures and you need to pick one of these. You can pick any of them. As you can see here, we have controls. We don't need these here.

We have showcases and we can pick this measure, the one that is called check. Also, when you pick it, as should be obvious, you can handle the size of the check by moving, utilizing these four focuses in the corners. Also, when you type in the gadget, you can change its settings. So on the off chance that you click once, you can see that you can change the name size, take size and shade of the measure. Presently you can change the name and you can change the reach and you can change the text dimension and text. As should be obvious, we need a bigger text dimension. We can pick this tone, that blue one, and you can pick the revive span. Presently, the two most significant things are the torment and the baffle. You need to set a virtual pen for each check with two seconds or three seconds or six seconds of reflash time. Furthermore, since we pick three seconds for the temperature and stickiness, as should be obvious, we don't have it as an alternative here. So we will transform it in the code to two seconds and snap, OK? Furthermore, we will enter the code to coordinate with that. Presently, two seconds and the subsequent stage is choosing the PIN. Presently, when you click the PIN, as should be obvious, OK, click the pin. At the point when you click on the pin, you can see that we have V, which is essentially a virtual pen and we know without a doubt that for our temperature.

Furthermore, maybe, since we are getting these readings vulnerable, in the event that you returned to our cool, you can see that the temperature is V4. So change the story for. Also, as should be obvious, you can change the name, however we would prefer not to do that, and here we have the reach now subsequent to changing the fridge and the PIN, you can return to your material and make it look. The manner in which you need, so click OK, and as you can see here, we have temperature previously and it's in blue. You can. Move it anyplace and you can change its size now, I would add the temperature here. You can't change the size now. We need another check. For the lowliness and sense we have for how about we limit this and have them close to one another. Presently, we should move this one. Up here and this one, we should call it. Stickiness. What's more, the under are baffled two seconds make a fonsi as extensive as they've been, number two V5 since we have the five. Also, as you can see when you click here, you can see that change is occupied. So we pick the five. Refaat is occupied on the grounds that we have utilized it. Presently, as should be obvious, this is that newgrange from zero to 1,000 focuses three. We can change that later. In any case, until further notice, stickiness at V5, very much like an hour cold and the cooler is two seconds. Presently we need two home loans. We should add our water level measure and how about we add another check for the dirt dampness. This one is for water. Live in. Furthermore, we know without a doubt that the water level is seven. Alright, so now. We attempted the revive rate five seconds, at that point click, it can change the shade of the cigarette case and make it blue. Presently the last one is for the spirit and it's the six. Presently, that is changed by plans and that if to five. That is it.

OK. And make sure that you have everything correctly before V5 for the temperature and humidity, V seven and V six for the water level and soil moisture. Now, the next step, we need to add a button widget to control thoroughly. Now click here, go up and choose button. And this is our button. Click once and change the button bin now,

as
you can see here, you can choose a digital or virtual button. Now. Change the name of the button first and call it necessarily. Control. After changing the name, you can change the button tied on the bill that is the general purpose and outward pain of the E.S.P 32 that is connected. And we already mentioned that Ali is connected to PIN twenty two.

22. Presently we need to send this. So we need to go to the stick and pick g.P 20 to. As you can see here now, you can pick either switch or press Button, I will pick the switch and that is it. Presently. Alright, presently the squint we can change, OK, can change this shading now the flicker. Totally. We have four markers and one catch to control the

hand-off and everything is picked accurately. That is it for the flicker set up. Furthermore, the following one, we will take the verification code and we will embed inside our E.S.P 32 code and we will add the Wi-Fi and you name and secret word to our ISP to standardized tag and we will commend Dakotah E.S.P board with the goal that we can begin controlling and checking this. As should be obvious, that is near. In any case, on the option to side, when you click on it, it will begin attempting to associate with E.S.P. What's more, on the off chance that it is associated on the web, you will get three things.

DOWNLOAD AND BLYNK
APPLICATION SETTINGS

Presently it's an ideal opportunity to set up the bling up to screens and social qualities, and the initial step will introduce getting serious about your cell phone. Presently go to your cell phone and go to the App Store. Contingent upon the kind of cell phone that you have, that may be Google Play store or Apple Play store or App Store and. Right. Who flicker. As should be obvious,

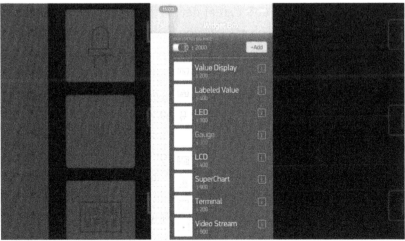

you will get it and it's the main outcomes. This is our eyeblink and

Internet of thing for Arduino E.S.P 32. Presently, as should be obvious, I as of now have the application, so I will flick open. Be that as it may, on the off chance that you don't have it, you need to click, introduce or download. You will stand by some time and you will surrender. Also, as you can see from the depiction, this application is utilized to control Arduino. A Raspberry Pi E.S.P is 266 and E.S.P 32 and a ton of different sheets. It's the sole simplified portable application manufacturer for microcontrollers and Internet of Things. Snap open and as should be obvious, you have more than one alternative to login. You can log in the event that you as of now have a record, you can make another record or you can login with your Facebook. Presently you can make a record by clicking here and adding your email and secret key. Presently, in the wake of composing your secret word, click, make new record, it shouldn't take a great deal of time. Making another record will give you a remarkable validation code and will be shipped off your email. Furthermore, this is vital since we are doing this to control our esport now. Presently, subsequent to making a record, you need to make another undertaking and select your equipment. Presently click new venture. Furthermore, as should be obvious, you need to name your venture. I will call it Smart Ghanim. What's more, you need to choose your board and as. You can see you have a ton of balls that you can look over. What's more, the one that we need is the E.S.P, you have Arduino Raspier Pi and a great deal of different sheets. We need E.S.P 32 Dev Board and you can pick the association type. As you can see here, we have Wi-Fi association and you can either pick dull or light, I will pick light as since it's simpler on the eye. At that point click make a venture. Presently, as should be obvious, verification. Tolkien was shipped off my email and you can likewise discover it by tapping on this symbol on the upper right corner. Snap OK, and we will get it from our email. Presently, the validation codes are vital code that you will use to control your undertaking. Presently we need to make our savvy guarding observing framework inside this connection up. Presently you have a vacant material, as should be obvious, and we need to add four measure gadgets to screen temperature, mugginess, water level and soil dampness level sensor readings and to do that tap on the material to open up the gadget box. Presently you can pick a check. As should be obvious, we have a ton of measures and you need to pick one of these. You can pick any of them, as you can see here, we have controls, we don't need these here. We have showcases and we can pick. This is the one that is called Cage. Furthermore, when you pick it, as should be obvious, you can handle the size of the pen by relocating, utilizing these four focuses on the corners. Also, when you tap on the gadget, you can change its settings. So in the event that you click once, you can see that you can change the name. Size takes size and shade of the enclosure. Presently you can change the name and you can change the reach and you can change the text dimension and text. As should be obvious, we need an enormous text dimension. We can pick this tone, the blue one, and you can pick the revive stretch. Presently, the two most significant things are the pen and the refrigerate. You need to set a virtual pen for each GigE with two seconds or three seconds or six seconds of invigorate time. Furthermore, since we pick three seconds for the temperature and stickiness, as should be obvious, we don't have it as a choice here. So we will transform it in the code to two seconds and snap, OK, and we will do the code to coordinate with that. Presently, two seconds and the subsequent stage is choosing the PIN. Presently, when you click the PIN, as should be obvious, OK, click the pen. At the point when you click on the pen, you can see that we have V, which is fundamentally a virtual pen and we know without a doubt that for our temperature. What's more, dampness sensor, we are getting these readings vulnerable, on the off chance that you returned to our code, you can see that the temperature is V4. So change this to previously. Furthermore, as should be obvious, you can change the mark, yet we would prefer not to do that, and here we have that range now in the wake of changing the cooler and the PIN, you can return to your material and make it look. The manner in which you need, so click OK, and as you can see here, we have temperature previously and it's in blue. You can. Move it anyplace and you can change its size presently would add the temperature here, you can change the size. Presently we need another check for the mugginess. What's more, since we have four, how about we limit this and have them close to one another. Presently, we should move this one. Up here. Furthermore, this one, we should call it. Stickiness. Also, the compelled to two seconds make the text dimension huge change the PIN to V5 since we have five and as you can see when you click here, you can see that before is occupied. So it shows the five. Refaat is occupied in light of the fact that we previously utilized it now, as should be obvious, this is the simple reach from zero to 1023. We can change that later. However, until further notice, stickiness at V5, very much like an hour cold and the cooler is two seconds. Presently we need to contracts. How about we add our water level measure and we should add another check for the dirt dampness. Presently, this one is for water. Live in. Furthermore, we know without a doubt that the water level is. V. seven. Avieson now. We attempted the invigorate rate five seconds, at that point click, OK, you can change the tone. The steroids case since kind of makes it blue. Presently, the last one is for ASOL. Furthermore, it's V six. Presently, president, as per Orange, and that if to five. That is it currently we should look OK and ensure that we have everything effectively before we five-overlay the temperature and stickiness V seven and we six for the water level and soil dampness. Presently, the following stage, we need to add a catch gadget to control completely. Presently click here, go up and pick button. What's more, this is our catch.

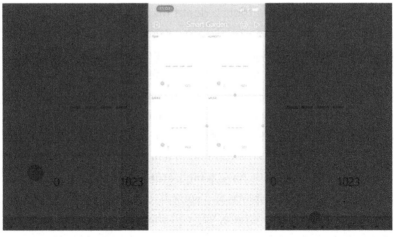

Snap once on the catch canister. Presently, as you can see here, you can pick an advanced or virtual catch now. Change the name of the catch first and call it fundamentally. Enthrone. Subsequent to changing the name, you can change the catch, Taieb, and the container, that canister is the universally useful information yield pin of the E.S.P 32 Weatherley is associated and we previously referenced that it is associated with a PIN 22, the 22. Presently we need to send this. So we need to go to the stick and pick g.P 22. As you can see here now, you can pick either switch or push, I will pick switch and that is it. Presently click, OK, presently that squint, we can change, OK, we can change this shading now the flicker abs prepared, we have four pointers and one catch to control the hand-off and everything is picked effectively. That is it for the uplink set up in the following , we will take the validation code and we will embed inside our E.S.P.

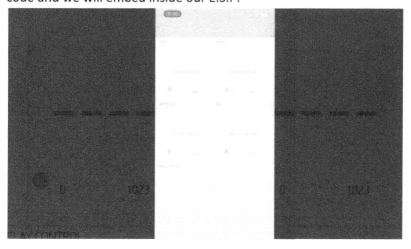

Thirty two code and we will add the wi fi and you name and password to our ISP hoped to board bar code and we will applaud Dakotah E.S.P board so that we can start controlling and monitoring this. As you can see, that is around. But on the right to bright side, once you click on it, it will start trying to connect to your ISP and if it is connected online, you will get the readings

AUTH CODE AND WIFI SETTINGS

The stimulus on and also are going to copy the authentication talking code that we just received from the link up to our ISP 32 code. Now, as you can see, this is the authentication token and I'm copying it now. You need to go, let's call this final code.

```
DHT dht(DHPIN,DHTYPE);
BlynkTimer timer;

char auth[] = "                              ";

char ssid[] = "
char pass[] = "


void SendSensorDH()
```

```
Sketch uses 641030 bytes (48%) of program storage space. Maxim
Global variables use 39552 bytes (12%) of dynamic memory, leav
```

Now, you need to go here and you need to have this authentication talking with your own board, and you need to have the wi fi as a side with your Wi-Fi network name. Priority's.

Could be the name. And based here. OK, let's go back. Let's call it the Wi-Fi network name.

And the password. Now we have our cold up and ready, we need to go down and change the refrigerator two and five seconds, as you can see here, and the interval function changed this to two and this to five. Now, verifier code.

```
    // put your setup code here, to run once:
Serial.begin(9600);
Blynk.begin(auth,ssid,pass);
dht.begin();
timer.setInterval(2000L, SendSensorDH);
timer.setInterval(5000L, SendSensorWaterSoil);
}

void loop() {
    // put your main code here, to run repeatedly:
Blynk.run();
```

```
Sketch uses 641042 bytes (48%) of program storage space. Maxin
Global variables use 39568 bytes (12%) of dynamic memory, leav
```

Now done compiling and the next hour we are going to hook up our E.S.P to board and we are going to upload the code and start receiving the values from SENSEOR and you will see how that Blinkx will control the relay and how everything will work.

HP PART - HOSTING YOUR WEBSITE

As of now, the target of this is to have your own space name and encouraging record that grants you to store sensor or catch or LEDs data from the HP 32 board and view them on your site. You can picture the readings from wherever in the world by getting to your own specialist zone. Additionally, to do accordingly. I propose using an encouraging, there is a huge load of paid options that I will show you on this and I will in like manner show you a free decision. Free is adequate for this thing. Regardless, if you are building a business or building a certified errand that has tricky data, I recommend purchasing an encouraging like Blue House Digital Oshin Eyepatch, GoDaddy. I will show you some in a second. By and by what about we check the things that I did the first. As of now there is more than one encouraging. One of them is called GoDaddy and. As you can see from this whole thing, you can look at a man with a hose thing, I think for twelve dollars for the essential year. It's an incredibly modest house thing that is furthermore blue. Moreover, there is eyepatch, as you can see, south from three dollars every month and there is furthermore eyepatch. These are the three. Most by and large used encouraging this one is the most economical one. It's one point 99 consistently. For the fundamental year. So. Right, zero Web cost. Additionally, this is sans it web encouraging, post our website for nothing out of pocket with board and BHP, and we need that BHP board, so click once. We should close this one down. As ought to be self-evident, this is our free encouraging.

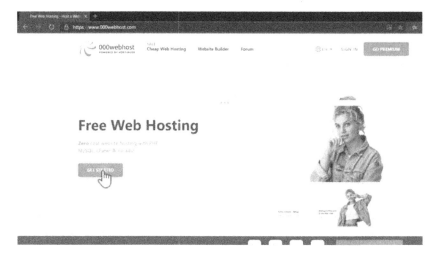

As of now, what you need to do is basically snap and start. Moreover, by and by showing you the plans, as ought to be self-evident, zero dollar, one 300 megabyte circle space, confined information move limit, up to three gigabyte.

There is no email account and no assistance. Furthermore, it's OK now in case you need there are various decisions you can give them. Nonetheless, I envision that the icing is everything necessary. Explore. Join. By and by you need to enter your record nuances, I by and large login with my Google account. As of now, undoubtedly, you need to pick the Google account that you need to get with. That is it. This is it as of now what about we make some wizardry click here. Also, as of now it's asking you for your staff to kick you off.

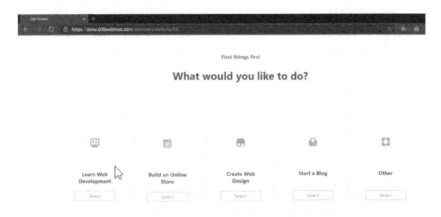

You need to make your own to learn web advancement or fabricate online store, make website composition, start a blog or other select other. Our site name will test E.S.P 32 and. This is our secret word, and we should conceal the secret phrase and pick another. Presently click submit. It appears to be that we were stuck on this page just to invigorate the page and select, it's not my first re-try. Take me to the ocean board. We have issues with their sign up page. Presently click submit again utilizing the secret word that was given by the site you can choose and you'll see them or some other thing. Presently utilize our web designer, introduce WordPress or transfer your website. We need to transfer our site.

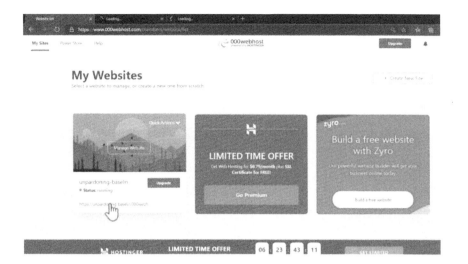

As you can see, this is. Our hosting, and this is the domain, they give you a free domain, so if you click here, you can see your freedom and it will be something. Zero zero zero host of dot com. Just click Manege website. And now you are on this page, go to the file manager. OK, now you need to enter the login details for Europe site. Now, let's say that you did forget that username and password, you can all always go here to this location and click manage website.

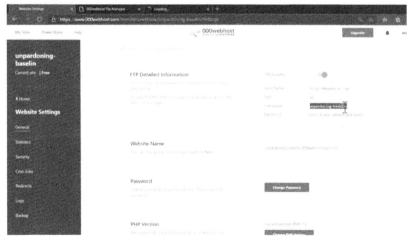

And from here, you can easily go to your website settings, select general, and from here you can get your username. And your password, you can change it from here, just click change password and enter your password. Anyway, I'll go with my username from here and I'll post it here and enter my password. Now just click login. And you should be good to go. Now, everything went OK with you, you should see this page and this is where you upload your files and folders inside the public e-mail folder.

Now, on a page that you upload here, we will upload our PSP files will be or can be accessed using your website domain. Now, the next step that you need to do is prepare your actual database. And this we are going to explain in the next . If you have any questions or you faced any problem creating an account, you can send us a message and I will help you create our website for free on this one posting. I recommend it just for testing purposes. And if you are or if you have more serious business, you should consider buying a hosting.

CREATING SQL TABLE

The simulation and this , you will learn how to prepare yourself a secure database after signing up for a hosting account and setting up your domain name.

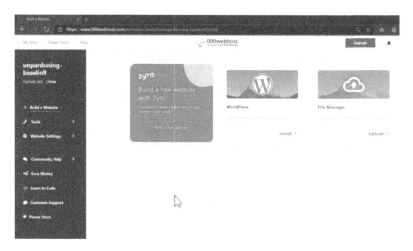

You can sign in very much like we disclosed in the past to your board or the comparative dashboard. From that point onward, you need to follow my means to make your data set username, secret phrase and your Ezekial table. Presently we should initially make an information base and a client. The initial step is go to the instruments area and select a data set chief. As should be obvious, this is the information base director, simply click another data set, and here you need to enter your data set name and data set client name and data set secret key. The initial step that we need to do is pick your data set name and our model, it will be E.S.P information since we are dealing with E.S.P 32 information. At that point we need to pick our secret key and our username. So we should call them now, I typically incline toward picking the information base username name astutely and make it significant. Presently, our information base username will be E.S.P board. What's more, you ought to enter your secret word here. I will enter my secret phrase and you ought to record it. Alright, yet you need to ensure that you are utilizing a capitalized letter and that your secret word is at any rate 12 character long and incorporate no exceptional characters. So you can make that secret phrase or pick an irregular one. As should be obvious, it will make one for you and you should take this data and save them. In workmanship, not legislative issues awful. So here's not terrible, what you need to do is duplicate the username best it very well may be the. So that is the best name, username and secret phrase. That is it presently click make subsequent to replicating this data. Hello, I would prefer not to save. Alright, presently here's our information base and now it's making the data set. So you should stand by a little while. The data set cutoff is one gigabyte and you can make up to 100 table. We just need one table. Furthermore, this is all that could possibly be needed again for testing.

You can make two information bases utilizing the free facilitating. So I believe it's an excellent method to begin testing. It shouldn't take long. Presently you can utilize localhost as a condition hostname. Furthermore, you can duplicate this data and set them in the notebook that you made before. Alright, since we made this is the thing that you need to do is make an expertise table, click here and go to HP, my administrator, you can erase the space or change your secret phrase or see the insights from these two lines. Simply navigate my administrator. Furthermore, you'll be diverted to this window, and this is the PSAP, my approaches, a well known interface to control your information base and make tables, erase tables, make inquiries and other stuff. Presently, making the real information base is the subsequent advance. Subsequent to making your data set and utilizing what you need to do is go to one side of this information base,

as should be obvious, and this will be your data set name. Presently, ordinarily we named E.S.P information, yet they don't give you, suppose, admittance to this name. So they add a thought previously. So this is our data set name. Presently you need to click it. Furthermore, when you click it, you approach your data set, you need to proceed to tap on the genuine tab. This is Hilltop will assist us with making our table and ensure we have open the data set that you have made, at that point click the black-top up. In the event that you haven't chosen this information base and snap the genuine tab, it will take you to another or an overall data set that you don't have command over. On the off chance that you don't follow these definite advances and run the real question, you may make a table in some unacceptable information base. Presently, to make the question, inquiry is fundamentally a straightforward lines of code that you execute utilizing this window. You will glue them here and once you click go, it will execute this inquiry and this question will make the sections of our table and will make another table for us with the name that we do pick. Presently to make that question, you need to do the accompanying. See, Muscleman. The initial step is attempt to make and as should be obvious, it's perceiving and trustable then sensor information or some other thing, you can basically compose S or E.S.P information, at that point you need to open and near enclosures. Presently you need to compose your question in the middle. Presently, this will compose the E.S.P information, which is essentially making another table and naming it E.S.P information. The subsequent stage will be is I make the segments inside this table. The initial step is making the thought segment. It's a typical one that will be end. Also, we should make it six presently to be unsigned, so left unsigned thus I auto augmentation. We expected to increase. We don't have to enter it physically and pick essential key. So it will be the essential key for our table. This is a protected UL information base inquiry, so on the off chance that you are curious about it, it's OK. You can simply reorder the code that I will accommodate you in the assets talk of this part. So no concerns. On the off chance that you don't comprehend what I'm doing now, I will glue the lines and afterward I will disclose them to you so we will not sit around idly making a circle. Then, we need to make, suppose, esteem one. What's more, we make it far character. How about we give it our first. Furthermore, ensure that it's perceived as not typical. Alright. Presently, this should be 30, not 10 and unsigned here has a red line under it since, OK, how about we make this stem since we incorrectly spelled it, OK, and sign. Marked, OK? Presently all is Great, presently how about we proceed onward, we need to make different factors too. The subsequent one is called worth to a third one. We can call it esteem three, contingent upon the number of qualities we need to make. We can make different qualities just as we go with this code. Presently, the following stage will be. Adding a timestamp, so we should add understanding time and make a period stamp default and pick current time. Remain on update on timestamped. This will ensure that we have a section that will print the time at which these qualities were gotten. Presently, the subsequent stage is making different factors, in the event that we in the event that we need, we can make a variable and call sensor so it will be sensor information. Also, it will be truly factor character and we should give it an estimation of 10 or how about we make it 30 and ensure that it's not. We can be something similar.

Also, based it here to make another variable and how about we call it area information. Alright, area information accessible shot 30 Natnael. That is it. Presently how about we audit what we have done here. We made a table and named it E.S.P information. You can change this name. We made an I.D. which will auto addition. It's fundamentally the possibility of the table. It will be one, two, three, four, five and will continue to increment. It's the essential key that we will use to get to any of these qualities. Presently we have made a character named Census Data and another character named Location Data. We made worth one to three to pass different qualities. In the event that we need, we can leave them to be zeroes or we can pass information. So these are essentially factor creation. Presently here we are making a timestamp. At whatever point we make or send our new enumeration information, it will print out the time at which this evaluation information was sent. That is it for this .

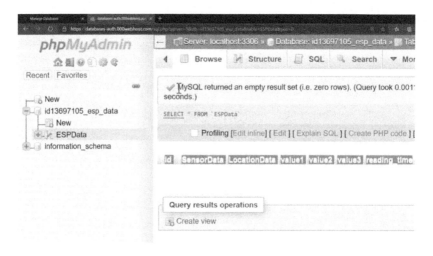

Now, before moving on, we need to click the goal button to create this table, and it will take a minute, as you can see, my security and an empty ResultSet, which is Xeros. And as you can see now, this is our database and this is our table. If you click once on your table, you can see that you have already since data location data value one value to value three and the reading time. So that's it. This is our table and these are all columns. If you got this smashers and you got this this result, it means that you have done everything correctly.

HP SCRIPT TO INSERT DATA IN DATABASE

The simulation, and you are going to handle that BHP HTP request or post. They are going to create a new script. So let's go back here.

And click tools go to your file manager, and this is the place where you can upload files. You can click here and start uploading files to your website.

As you can see, go here, the five measure, and once you are in this window, in this section, we are going to create a BHB script that is responsible for receiving incoming requests from the E.S.P 32 ball. And it will be also responsible for inserting the data into my actual database, the one that we just created here. And if you are using a facilitating supplier with a board like this one, you can just explore to the document administrator the manner in which I did then choose public HDMI choice. Presently, this fall, that Double-Click it once you are in this organizer, click the in addition to sign and make another record. Presently it will request that you name the new record. So what you need to do is call it past information. Not it will be manhandled BHP document and will present information on the ISP data set, so click make. This is our first BHB record presently to enter this document and to enter your code, you can essentially tap on it and snap, I marked. Presently you can compose your HP code here and this window. Above all, how about we compose it on another proofreader, at that point we can reorder the code to this window. We should download the superb content manager. It's an extremely modern content manager. That you can use to compose codes.

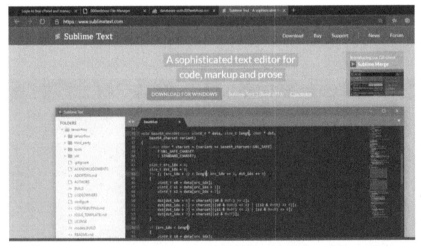

It will require one moment to download, as should be obvious, it has a graphical and shading. Uh, you can undoubtedly compose codes and it will finish autocomplete, the harmonies while you compose and you can look through the code. So I suggest that when you compose any kind of code, it upholds practically the entirety of the programming dialects. Alright, that is it. Presently open the arrangement record, click, yes. Alright. One night from now. That is it currently go to the beginning menu, click heavenly or glorious content. Presently, this is it, you can utilize the control button and the mouse look to expand the text dimension and to pick the programming language that you are managing. You can essentially do that by going to get the view. Furthermore, from the sentence structure, you can check any programming language that you will compose your code in. Furthermore, for our situation, it will be PSP. Presently, the main thing that you need to do when you are making another HP document is correct, HP, and you need this is known as the tag and you need to close it. When you made. Presently we need to pass the primary inconstancies last name. Also, the common name will be localhost actually like 60 minutes. Text document with me, check. Alright, let me open up the content document and as should be obvious, use localhost as an association hostname so the worker name will be localhost. Presently, the subsequent stage will allot the information base name and username and secret word. So the dollar sign and the B name until you need to pass the name. What's more, we likewise need to pass the username data set username. What's more, the information base pass. Furthermore, these qualities will get from the content record that we utilized, this is the secret key and this is the username. Furthermore, this is the data set name. Presently, we generally have a prefix before this, however we will return to that toward the finish of recording meeting. Presently, what we are doing is making an API.

```php
1  <?php
2
3  $servername = "localhost";
4  $dbname = "esp_data";
5  $username = "esp_board";
6  $password = "4TOc7~@ba9Ie]Xs*";
7
8  $api_key_value = "4TOc7~@b";
9  $api_key = $sensor
```

So we will make an uncommon key that nobody knows and use it for our API to permit association among E.S.P and our PSP or our site. So. Right, that sign and compose API underscore key, underscore worth and you can compose any key worth. How about we duplicate this and glue it here and we will utilize a similar code in our E.S.P coding measure. Very much as we did in our secret word, we did reorder the secret key precisely equivalent to in our site. So this will be an uncommon key that will be utilized and ESB code. Presently, the API key will pass a couple of factors. Furthermore, these factors will be the focal variable. Alright, let me realize the dollar sign sensor. Also, to give these factors, we need to return to our. Called Let me. Open up the article at the. As should be obvious, this is the code that we did. Execute. What's more, we need to get the names from that, the table here, so we need the registration information, we can duplicate it from here and based it here, and we will likewise require the excess factors. So we should duplicate every one of them and how about we based them here. Alright, at a little sign, equivalent dollar sign for every single one of these. Alright, presently, child, I will pass these factors and toward the end add equivalent and how about we pass them as unfilled content. Presently we need to inquire as to whether there is a post solicitation, and since the vast majority of you will not be acquainted with HP, I will play stuccoed and I'll clarify it. Presently, as you can see here, here we have an assertion, assuming the worker got a post solicitation, check the IP, on the off chance that it coordinates with the IP that we have here. Which is this one at that point begin taking qualities, as you can see here, we have the statistics information, which is the main worth on our table. The subsequent worth is the table or the area information and the worth one worth to add esteem three or more the understanding time. Presently, the perusing time will naturally be made by the worker since we did. Make it auto made and our real inquiry so we don't need to pass the I.D. or on the other hand the understanding time. That is the reason we are just passing these qualities. So these qualities, the ID and the perusing time will not be passed on the grounds that they will be consequently made by our site once it gets another information. So it will name one and will make the time, at that point it will record these qualities that it got from the ISP. However, this is the call to check the post solicitation presently to make an association for the information base. We need to utilize this code, as should be obvious, this is a variable called KCON from Connection, and it's making another article from the my genuine information data set item, and it's taking worker name, username, secret word and data set name. These qualities are introduced here, as should be obvious. So if any of these qualities isn't right, there will be no association with the information base. So in the event that you passed the correct qualities, the association would be set up. Else it will print out association fizzled. As you can find in this message currently, proceeding onward, in the wake of making an association with the data set, we need to begin passing the qualities presently to begin passing the estimations of the data set. We need to utilize the addition, we should embed order. What's more, as you can see, the response to embed these qualities that since the area, the worth on worth to add esteem three, which are essentially these qualities that the take from this.

```
18        $value3 = test_input($_POST["value3"]);
19
20  // Create connection
21        $conn = new mysqli($servername, $username, $password, $dbname
22        if ($conn->connect_error) {
23            die("Connection failed: " . $conn->connect_error);
24        }
25
26
27  $sql = "INSERT INTO SensorData (sensor, location, value1, value2,
        value3)
28        VALUES ('" . $sensor . "', '" . $location . "', '" . $value1
              . "', '" . $value2 . "', '" . $value3 . "')";
```

An association, so the qualities will be composed and this genuine question will be executed, which will essentially embed these qualities into the table, and we will make another BHP document to show these qualities. Yet, until further notice, this is fundamentally a real question that passes the estimations of the sense or area, worth and worth to and esteem free. Presently, the following stage will be to check if another record was effectively made in our information base or not after we passed these qualities. So to do that, what we need to do is check with an if articulation. This assertion will inquire as to whether there is an association with the Ezekial and on the off chance that it is valid, it implies that new record was made effectively. In the event that there is any difficult that will not be made and will print out a blunder. You don't need to retain any of these things. You simply need to reorder, however you need to understand what you are reordering. Presently, whenever you are finished. With the question, you need to close the association, so. We will close the association utilizing association, close strategy, else we need to approach that, we have gotten a solid API key. So if the supplement didn't work and we didn't get the information, this implies that the API key that we got. Isn't right, and all things considered, it will not permit us to take the or and area and worth information so it will print out wrong Iraqi gave and this is to investigating reason. You need to see it on the screen and I will tell you the best way to see it in the event that there is any issue.

Presently. There is another situation where no information is posted with a YouTube post, if the eSport is disconnected or on the off chance that it isn't sending any information. We need to print that. No information was gotten to ensure that the client realizes that we didn't get any information from the ECB board and it is anything but an API key issue. Presently, that is a capacity that we can utilize, which is to test and board and to ensure that this info is correct.

```php
36        $conn->close();
37        }
38    else {
39            echo "Wrong API Key provided.";
40        }
41
42        }
43    else {
44        echo "No data posted with HTTP POST.";
45    }
46
47    function test_input($data) {
48        $data = trim($data);
49        $data = stripslashes($data);
50        $data = htmlspecialchars($data);
51        return $data;
52    }
```

Presently, this capacity will test the info and ensure that the information was composed accurately and was passed effectively. Presently, as you can see that this info will accept the information as info and will it will manage whatever isn't viewed as information, at that point it will make some change and return the information that we need, which is fundamentally that since or the perusing of the character. So if there is some other space in the approaching information, it will eliminate it and it will eliminate and unique characters and pass just the qualities that we need. What's more, this capacity was brought in our code here, as should be obvious. So when we get that API key, we are ensuring that we get the key with no spaces or any unique key that may not be right or that may be passed in an incorrect manner. So this is vital to pass this off, to utilize this capacity. I will furnish you with the full code so you can reorder the code and you need to ensure that you change these qualities relying upon your code. So change that ISP data set, name ISP board and the secret phrase and the API key worth, contingent upon your readings so this code can be usable for you. That is it for this . Presently, one final advance is fundamentally select the code, select all.

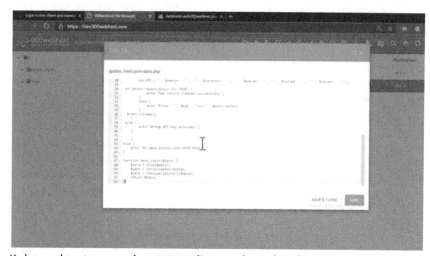

Kobe and go to your document director based code and snap Save. As should be obvious, this is our code snap, save and close. Presently you have this document with your code, however prior to saving the record, you need to ensure that you altered the data set, name the username and secret key factors with your remarkable subtleties in the wake of adding data set, name, username and secret phrase, save the record very much as I did and proceed with the court's guidance. On the off chance that you attempt to get to your area name utilizing this record, you can see the accompanying outcome. The initial step is objective and could be your site. You are, as you can see, this is your site. You are currently at Slash and you need to compose a similar name post information, DOT, PSP or post information spot BHP. Presently, as you can see now that are posted with HTP Post since we haven't yet posted any information. On the off chance that you got this message, it implies that you have done everything accurately and that you have compose your code effectively. Presently in the following class we will compose a content to the Sibley information base substance, yet that is it for this

PHP SCRIPT TO DISPLAY READINGS

Presently we will compose our HP content to the Sibley data set substance, which is essentially sensors perusing and various qualities that we passed utilizing E.S.P. So how about we make another image before the public email envelope. So click here and we should name it E.S.P. Information not be. Subsequent to making the document click make, presently we have it here, ESB information. What you need to do is just snap it and snap alter to begin altering your code. Presently we should save our past code and make another record. Ensure that the grammar is BHP. Presently, how about we begin composing, the primary thing that you need to do is compose the email fundamental code so you can get it on code. Also, as should be obvious, this is the principle line that you can compose your ascherman. So you can basically duplicate this.

I will give you that source code and I will provide links to download it and just copy from three schools. And base, this is basically Asham Alcalde, and here we have the body inside the body.

```
 1  <!DOCTYPE html>
 2  <html>
 3  <body>
 4
 5  <?php
 6
 7  $servername = "localhost";
 8  $dbname = "esp_data";
 9  $username = "esp_board";
10  $password = "4TOc7~@ba9Ie]Xs*";
11
12  </body>
13  </html>
```

We will make a HP code, so like PSP, and now we need to begin
composing our code and it will be fundamentally the same as our past
code. So how about we move these two lines. We need first to
duplicate this data. The worker name, which is localhost the
information base, name, data set, username, data set, secret phrase,
and suppose the code, how about we call it ISP information show.
Alright, since we since we have this code, we can change once more,
the grammar to PSP. I imagine that it transformed it naturally to expect
all since we composed a Shyamal code. Presently we can move to PSP
once more. Presently, whenever you are finished with directing your
worker name, data set, name, username and secret phrase, you need
to make an association and check it once more. We did that and this
code so you can essentially duplicate this extraordinary association.
What's more, the tears. Presently, the association neglected to
association, fizzled in the event that you and any of this data en route.
From that point forward, we need to make a genuine variable and pass
along the qualities. Furthermore, to do that, we can essentially. By the
accompanying. We compose it that path here, however we write in an
alternate route here, correct? Try not to ask you all then the
equivalent sign here you need to compose, select. Heidi. Sensor
information. Area information esteem one worth to esteem three and
the understanding time. These are fundamentally the qualities that we
need to get from our information base and compose the data set table

230

that you need to peruse the information from. So from. What's more, presently you need to ride the table name. So how about we return here. Our table name is E.S.P. Thatta, so Cobbett E.S.P. Girl, return and here, E.S.P information now, right. Request to arrange the information by I.D. in satisfactory request. Alright. Presently this line is fundamentally calling the I.D. from the data set. That is called E.S.P information. It's calling IDs. Furthermore, since all that area information esteem on worth to esteem three and perusing time from this data set table, and it's requesting the qualities by previously beginning from the norm, essentially from number one and proceeding onward to number two, three, four, five and proceed onward. Presently, subsequent to doing that, we can rise to the qualities we need to make a table to show information. What's more, without going into subtleties of that real coding, since this isn't impossible or BHB coding you can essentially duplicate my code. Also, this code is essentially making a table. As you can see it will has ID since all information area information esteem enhance Vilo three and timestamp. This will be the name of the sections and we will have these segments.

```
16              die("Connection failed:    $conn->connect_error);
17          }
18  $sql = "SELECT id, SensorData, LocationData, value1, value2, value3
            reading_time FROM ESPData ORDER BY id DESC"
19
20  echo '<table cellspacing="5" cellpadding="5">
21          <tr>
22              <td>ID</td>
23              <td>Sensor</td>
24              <td>Location</td>
25              <td>Value 1</td>
26              <td>Value 2</td>
27              <td>Value 3</td>
28              <td>Timestamp</td>
29          </tr>';
30
31
```

As should be obvious, the dispersing would be five and the cushioning will be five. Essentially the space among Searls and in vertical and even. Presently, in the wake of making the table, we need to begin passing qualities to this table. Also, to do as such, we need first to ensure that we have an association with the information base and call things by ID. Presently, to do that, what you need to do is fundamentally utilize this code. Presently, in the event that the consequence of the association is through, proceed to call the I.D. furthermore, dole out it to the ideal called the evaluation information and allocated to the sensor considered area that and appointed to the area and call the qualities and dole out them each to an alternate variable and BHB. Presently the subsequent stage will be to approach these qualities and we can just do that by utilizing this code. We will approach every one of the qualities that we got from the table into this table that we have made here. So it will print out the entire thought that all sensor information and area information that all worth one, two, three and the understanding time. Presently, subsequent to doing the entirety of this, we need to ensure that we are shutting the association that we property association. So association close. Also, this is the end tag for our PSP code, which is fundamentally here. We open it here and we shut here. Presently, subsequent to doing that, we need to ensure likewise to right the table that we made a table so we can essentially add this tag. Here and this will flor's the table label that we opened here and this region, as should be obvious, this is the launch of the table tag and this is the end. Presently, this is our code and I will give the code to you and this talk assets so you can utilize it. Simply ensure that you alter the worker name, the information base name and the username and secret phrase to what you have on your site. Presently select all. Could be the Cold War here. To your document director, the code snap, save and close. Presently you are finished. Presently, in the event that you attempt to get to this code utilizing very much like language, actually as we did our past model and we call E.S.P information, it's called E.S.P information. PSP, not all now, as should be obvious, we are accepting a mistake line 20, how about we check for the blunder. Alright, as you can see here, and our code line 20, there's an issue, which is essentially we didn't in this line utilizing a semicolon.

So I had a simple on here, copy the code, go back edit tier. But what I provide you with the correct code. Now, check if there is any other error. OK, we have a problem with constructing connection line 14. As you can see, the connection failed and this was expected. I already told you that when you edit your database name, this is not the database name that's here. As you can see, this is our database now.

So you need to duplicate this information base name and put together it with respect to your code. It has the speed at which is the name that we picked, however they ordinarily add I.D. prior to that. Alright, with me. Show us. Alright, presently this is the name for the data set, yet they added their own ID for assurance, presently for the client name. It's normally a similar case. Presently, we should check the client name for this data set. As should be obvious, this is the data set ID. Also, it has this table, it's called E.S.P information, so the table name is right, we don't need to transform it now. Presently, typically you need to add a similar prefix for the username.

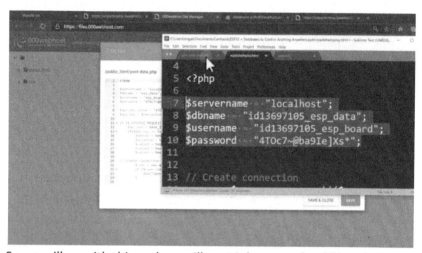

So we will go with this and we will post it here, as should be obvious. Presently we have the thought, at that point the client name and how about we go with the code. We should put it this. Presently, we can't base that here protected and close. On the off chance that you revive the page. Simply return. Put together save with respect to garments. As should be obvious, the I.D. also, Soledad, that area information worth and worth to esteem three and the timestamp. So our page is turned out great. Also, this page. The first additionally should be altered. We need to alter these three lines. We should go with them from here. Furthermore, put together them with respect to our unique code, which is this one, and how about we based them here, the data set USA and the data set name should be changed presently, save and close and you are all set now in the event that you don't care to proceed to compose the code yourself. You can basically duplicate our code and simply alter the data set and those of name and secret phrase and you are all set. You can add more qualities and more factors. It's simple.

```
13  // Create connection
14         $conn = new mysqli($servername, $username, $password, $dbnam
15         if ($conn->connect_error) {
16             die("Connection failed: " . $conn->connect_error);
17         }
18  $sql = "SELECT id, SensorData, LocationData, value1, value2, value3
        reading_time FROM ESPData ORDER BY id DESC";
19
20  echo '<table cellspacing="5" cellpadding="5">
21       <tr>
22          <td>ID</td>
23          <td>SensorData</td>
24          <td>LocationData</td>
25          <td>Value 1</td>
26          <td>Value 2</td>
27          <td>Value 3</td>
28          <td>Timestamp</td>
```

You can essentially add more qualities here utilizing these lines and calling them utilizing this line. So relying upon your venture or what you are attempting to accomplish, you can basically alter the entirety of this code to meet your requirements on the off chance that you have any inquiry concerning any line of code. I'm here to help you. Once more, this isn't seem, by all accounts, to be Arashiyama cause that is the reason I didn't go into subtleties of the BHB coding or shamal coding. You can basically reorder our code are accommodated you and there's likewise a talk. That is it until further notice. This is Ashara from Educational Engineering Team.

CODING ESP PART1

This and your last one, and we will program E.S.P 32 utilizing Arduino IDE. You should have the Arduino thought introduced and E.S.P, a 32 AdOne introduced, as we clarified in the download and introduce segment. Presently, subsequent to introducing the important Bolt Adams Cobie. The I don't prefer to contend, no thought, similarly as clarified then you can't just open Arduino. To begin coding. Presently, the initial step that we will do is. Make another document on your

235

sketch. Presently we need to incorporate a few libraries, so we should incorporate the wi fi library. What's more, we additionally need to incorporate. Their city customer library.

```
#include <WiFi.h>
#include <HTTPClient.h>

const char* ssid = "Ashraf TV";
const char* password = "asm@05666600099";

const char* serverName = "https://unpardoning-baselin9.000webhostapp.c

void setup() {
```

```
Sketch uses 266573 bytes (20%) of program storage space. Maximum is 13
Global variables use 15124 bytes (4%) of dynamic memory, leaving 31255
```

Also, we need to incorporate. Whatever other work that we may require for our undertaking, for the present, I will simply stay with these two. Presently, in the event that you confirmed your code, it would request that you save the code at a specific area. So here we will save it. We should call it E.S.P. Gold and silver here. Done consolidating now what you need to do is make a couple of factors, we need to make factors for our remote organization certification, so make a steady character and call it as of now. Also, here you need to enter your organization name. Furthermore, my organization name is called I figure I ought to have TiVo. Presently add a semicolon, add a different line. Steady character for the secret word. What's more, I think my secret word is this. Something to that effect. In any case, I'll change it later. Presently we should proceed onward to the worker name, make a predictable character. For the worker name and in the worker name will put are for the most part the space name and they are all way, the entirety of the IP address with the way relying upon your facilitating. What's more, for our situation, we need to duplicate this. We need the post information documenting, which is fundamentally this one. Alright, let me check this one. Our area name and postdated BHP. So return here, recorded here relying upon your space name. This may be unique, however this is the thing that you

236

need to do. Presently. The following stage is making the API key worth, and we previously referenced that key on the Fabulous on. Also, it should be indistinguishable from the one you use when you're upbeat, and to do as such, we should open up or be called. Also, search for the. Programming interface key worth. Alright, here it is, a bickie esteem. It is this one Lobach duplicate and based Diabolik esteem. Presently you can make some other variable that you need. You can make a variable for the Zinser name. How about we call it contact sensor. Furthermore, since of area,

```
const char* password = "asm@05666600099";

const char* serverName = "https://unpardoning-baselin9.000webh

String apiKeyValue = "4TOc7~@b";

String sensorName = "Touch";
String sensorLocation = "HomeOffice"
```

```
Sketch uses 266573 bytes (20%) of program storage space. Maxim
Global variables use 15124 bytes (4%) of dynamic memory, leavi
```

how about we call it home office since we are at home at this point. What you need to do is go to the void arrangement technique and start the sequential module at a particular rate and how about we make it a hundred fifty fifteen thousand 200. Presently we need to begin the Wi-Fi association wi fi that started utilizing the ID and the secret phrase that we utilized from that point onward, we need to print the chronic screen line expressing that we are interfacing so. Right. Interfacing with the Wi-Fi organization. Alright, presently, to ensure that we don't have any mistake, we need to check and to print the neighborhood IP address that we get from our Wi-Fi organization. So we should add this one assertion, incidentally. You can duplicate the Wi-Fi code from the models in the event that you need here models and on the off chance that you need the ISP.

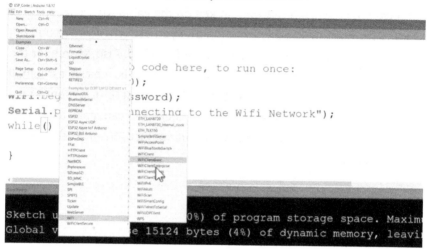

You can't just. Search for the Wi-Fi. What's more, as you can see here, wi fi, on the off chance that you check the Wi-Fi filter, you can see. Code for wi fi. Also, as you can perceive any reason why in the event that I separate wi fi mode and you can alter the code or use it. Furthermore, presently it's checking and printing, that is a Saudi you can utilize this code or you can duplicate our code. The two of them work a similar currently with respect to Wi-Fi, yet you need to alter them or alter the code to permit a Stoebe post and BHP association. At any rate, we should continue. Presently, the Wi-Fi, we need to watch that. The Wi-Fi, the status. WI fi associated. To ensure that we are associated and afterward we can't to execute the brackets. Presently, between these two carbon burdens, how about we add some deferral to ensure that we are giving all yes individuals sufficient opportunity to interface and we should print embrace to demonstrate that we arrived at this point. Alright, presently.

```
// put your setup code here, to run once:
Serial.begin(115200);
WiFi.begin(ssid,password);
Serial.println("Connecting to the Wifi Network");
while(WiFi.status()!= WL_CONNECTED)
{
    delay(500);
    Serial.print(".");
}
    Serial.println("");
```

Sketch uses 266573 bytes (20%) of program storage space. Maxim
Global variables use 15124 bytes (4%) of dynamic memory, leavi

After the wild proclamation, we can lease an unfilled string. At that
point we can print different lines expressing that we are associated
with the Wi-Fi with a specific IP address to ensure that we have an IP
address. Alright, presently Wi-Fi is associated and utilization of this IP
address. What's more, presently to print the IP address on Wi-Fi
organization, we can utilize Siri on that forefront and inside it we need
to call Wi-Fi DOT nearby IP. So it will print the IP that our ISP got from
the Wi-Fi after. Presently, in the wake of doing the entirety of this, we
can. Start the TB cycle currently to begin HCB measure. You need to go
to the Void Laub and compose a basic if explanation inside that on the
off chance that we need to ensure that our Wi-Fi is associated
effectively, so we will utilize Wi-Fi status, equivalent remote
associated. Presently, whenever detached, what we need here. Is first
make a Stoebe.

```
void loop() {
  // put your main code here, to run repeatedly:
IF(WiFi.status() == WL_CONNECTED)
{
  HTTPClient http;
  http.begin(serverName);    I

  http.addHeader("Content-Type", "application/x-www-form-u");
```

Sketch uses 266573 bytes (20%) of program storage space. Maxim
Global variables use 15124 bytes (4%) of dynamic memory, leavi

Customer item and name it is GTP now, your area name, who they are on way or IP address should be passed to the HTP object, be utilizing this line Huckerby start and inside it you got a worker name, which is fundamentally the worker name that we composed here. Make a point to compose it effectively. We have in capital. Alright, from that point onward, we need to indicate content sort here to ensure that we are passing the correct qualities to our Web page, the feeling of qualities and other perusing. Presently, right htp dab advertisement header. This technique is the one that we will use to send information. Presently, inside it, you need to compose content sort, at that point add a section. Also, right, this line battle application cut x, w structure and you are all. Encored. Presently, this line can be discovered on the web, it's simple and you need to send it before you begin composing that. Presently, the subsequent stage is to set up our FTB demand information and the information that we will send in that solicitation is essentially the way to Ikki, the sensor area on the sensor name and the worth number one worth. Number three, two and three. Furthermore, these that are will be sent in a string. So we need to set up that strength, make another string group of four, a city B, demand information and begin passing the qualities. The principal worth will be a B, I underscore key and exceptional to the in addition to sign and compose API key worth. Which is fundamentally the key worth that we alloted toward the start of our. Codes here. Presently, you need to attempt similar factors now, in addition to sign what we are doing now is we are linking a string with the qualities that we need to send. So from that point onward, we need to send the registration information. So we were correct and focus. Dr.. Equivalent and you are the in addition to sign and send many. The variable we've called since her name. From that point forward, we will send us your area, you can add on and sign and compose that area equivalent. Furthermore, we will add since that area. Here they add another impact sign and begin adding various qualities and worth, one equivalent. Furthermore, we will add a string, how about we call it esteem one, we can add some other variable here, yet since

```
if (WiFi.status() == WL_CONNECTED)
{
  HTTPClient http;
   http.begin(serverName);

   http.addHeader("Content-Type", "application/x-www-form-urlen

   String httpRequestData = "api_key" + apiKeyValue + "&SensorD
 + sensorLocation + "&value1=" + "value1" + "&value2=" + "value
}
```

```
Sketch uses 266573 bytes (20%) of program storage space. Maxim
Global variables use 15124 bytes (4%) of dynamic memory, leavi
```

we haven't assigned any variable, we can simply write value one and you can keep doing this for the other two. OK. Now, the value three for this one value two for this one, so it will send value one value to one value. Three, we can assign variables for this one, but let's leave them to this at this point.

```
http.addHeader("Content-Type", "application/x-www-form-urlen

    String httpRequestData = "api_key" + apiKeyValue + "&SensorD
+ sensorLocation + "&value1=" + "value1" + "&value2=" + "value

Serial.print("httpRequestData: ");
Serial.print(httpRequestData);

}
}
```

```
Sketch uses 266573 bytes (20%) of program storage space. Maxim
Global variables use 15124 bytes (4%) of dynamic memory, leavi
```

Presently, after we set up this solicitation. As should be obvious, we need to add a semicolon here and we need to add sequential dab print and. We will print is this ECB demand information. So we should attempt it once more. So it will be mentioned that at this point. That is it for this in the following , we will continue with the. With composing our code and ensuring that it works for individuals and that it will send information to our site.

CODING ESP PART2

Presently, to ensure that you comprehend that a reasonable solicitation information that we just made, what we did is essentially the accompanying. We made factors and we have sent qualities or the estimations of these factors to the ACTU demand. Presently, you can't remark this line, the news, this ACTU demand that a variable and as should be obvious, without the factors, you can really pass the information straightforwardly. So the key here is this. This is our API key. Furthermore, the worry is that Atchinson that you previously referenced, its area is at home office and it depreciates one, two and three out of these arbitrary qualities. This can be utilized for testing purposes. You can come this and utilize this line. The two of them work something similar. Yet, on the off chance that you have issues or on the off chance that you are suspecting something, you can utilize this one for testing. In any case, I will leave it to you in the event that you wish. Presently, to send the HTP post solicitation, we need to make a whole number and consider it a P reaction called equivalent htp speck post. Presently the post will take. This variable, the one that we made the information and it will send it through the HDTV, in the event that you need a gauge demand with a substance type text or plain, you can change the header. In any case, this is something I need to suggest on the grounds that what we are doing here is further developed.

```
String httpRequestData = "api_key" + apiKeyValue + "&SensorD
+ sensorLocation + "&value1=" + "value1" + "&value2=" + "value

Serial.print("httpRequestData: ");
Serial.print(httpRequestData);
//String httpRequestData = "api_key=4TOc7~@b&sensor=Touch&loca

int httpResponseCode = http.POST(httpRequestData);
}
```

```
Sketch uses 266573 bytes (20%) of program storage space. Maxim
Global variables use 15124 bytes (4%) of dynamic memory, leavi
```

We are sending factors now. I will add alternate approaches to add, suppose, text or plain content or adjoining record to the city demand. Yet, what we are doing here is just sending sensor readings and factors so you can adhere to the substance header that we made, which is fundamentally application and this is its sort w we are totally encoded and this is the encoding part. Presently. To ensure that our solicitation did go and we don't have any blunder, we introduce a number so the aftereffect of this solicitation can be put away and this variable. Presently, to check this variable, we need to inquire as to whether proclamation and Is now. How about we do this presently, they've said and will be if the Stoebe reaction code is over nothing, this implies that we have seen information and we got a worth over zero as a reaction to the post solicitation. What's more, that case we need to print on the Syrian screen. Brent HTP reaction code. Furthermore, we need to print the code to know whether there is an issue so I don't print.

```
if(httpResponseCode>0)
{
    Serial.print("HTTP Response Code: ");
    Serial.println(httpResponseCode);
    }
else
{}
}
}
```

```
Sketch uses 266573 bytes (20%) of program storage space. Maxim
Global variables use 15124 bytes (4%) of dynamic memory, leavi
```

Furthermore, the reaction, quote, presently, else, we need to cover this, as well, if the worth isn't over nothing, it implies that there is a blunder. So all things considered, we will utilize the Ayles and we will see mistake code. Code and words print a similar code toward the end. We need to end our solicitation. So we need to add Test-tube and. This will end the city demand interaction and we need to close this. Presently. Else, as should be obvious, this is our F proclamation that we did close. Presently, if the Wi-Fi is associated, it will do the entirety of this, else it will forestall that wi fi isn't associated. So we can compose sequential, spot, print, new line and we can essentially compose wi fi disengaged. From that point forward, we need to ensure that we are not getting that constantly, so. How about we move this one. Alright, we need to one or the other postponement. 30,000 milliseconds, which is fundamentally 30 seconds.

```
else
{
   Serial.print("ERROR Code: ");
   Serial.println(httpResponseCode);
   }
   http.end();
}else {Serial.println("WiFi Disconnected");}

delay(30000);
}
```

```
Sketch uses 266573 bytes (20%) of program storage space. Maxim
Global variables use 15124 bytes (4%) of dynamic memory, leavi
```

So this will advise our ISP to send a functioning post solicitation at regular intervals to send since all that. Presently, as I previously referenced, I will post the code, yet you need to alter the accompanying lines. The principal thing that you need to alter is their general public and secret key. Furthermore, the second thing that you need to peruse is the Savani, which is this one, and you additionally need to understand it, the AP Ikki. We introduced the common correspondence for troubleshooting purposes. It's not something you need to do, but rather it's a decent practice with the goal that you can know whether your code has blunders. Presently, subsequent to doing the entirety of this. You can confirm your code. We will check it if that is mistakes. I will address them currently to ensure that we can transfer this code.

```
   Serial.println(WiFi.localIP());

}

void loop() {
   // put your main code here, to run repeatedly:
IF(WiFi.status() == WL_CONNECTED)
{
   HTTPClient http;
   http.begin(serverName);
```

```
'IF' was not declared in this scope
```

OK, now that statements and capital letters. I did this. OK, now I think that we might have some spelling errors because I was writing as I was speaking and explaining so this might happen.

```
© ESP_Code | Arduino 1.8.12
File Edit Sketch Tools Help

ESP_Code §

#include <WiFi.h>
#include <HTTPClient.h>

const char* ssid = "Ashraf TV";
const char* password = "asm@05666600099";

const char* serverName = "https://unpardoning-baselin9.000webhostapp.c

void setup() {
    // put your setup code here, to run once:
```

```
Sketch uses 266573 bytes (20%) of program storage space. Maximum is 13
Global variables use 15124 bytes (4%) of dynamic memory, leaving 31255
```

OK, Duncan Barling, great. We do not have any rules now what you need to do is simply copy this code and based it on your ISP and we are going to do this. And the next to test out our coding and to make sure that the server receives the data and everything is working fine. That's it for this . If you have any questions.

PRACTICAL LIVE DEMONSTRATION OF THE PROJECT

```
    Serial.print("ERROR Code: ");
    Serial.println(httpResponseCode);
    }
    http.end();
}else {Serial.println("WiFi Disconnected");}

delay(30000);
}
```

```
esptool.py v2.6
Serial port COM4
Connecting........
```

Presently we should attempt to turn our code or move our call to our E.S.P board and test this venture, go to the gadget chief subsequent to connecting your E.S.P board, ensure that it's noticeable, as you can see, confort. Presently go to the instruments. Ensure that Conforth is. Associated and pick your board, we are utilizing E.S.P 32. Troublesome Virgin one, presently transfer your code. It will require like a moment, and in the wake of transferring, we will check what's going on utilizing the chronic screen. As should be obvious, it's associating with come for. Presently it's composing the code three percent and it's proceeding onward. Alright, 1790 100, OK, done transferring now our board has the code, presently click here. As should be obvious, we did. Request that the board bring Dot.

```
// put your setup code he
Serial.begin(115200);
WiFi.begin(ssid,password);
Serial.println("Connecting
while(WiFi.status()!= WL_CO
{
    delay(500);
    Serial.print(".");
    }
    Serial.println("");
```

Leaving...
Hard resetting via RTS pin.

Let me minimize this. Now, this means that wi fi is not connected, so it will keep printing dots until Wi-Fi is connected. So let's make sure that we have the Wi-Fi details that it incorrectly Saidee. Now, this is. Corbould of D.V.. OK. And this is the password. OK, let me check, OK, after checking.

I found that my network name has two spaces after my name asharaf two spaces, TV. So we need to add the code and two spaces. Let's upload it again.

Alright, it seems like I have another issue, which is that my Wi-Fi network has two spaces here and one space after many. So how about we go with a similar name here from my little girl and we should glue it here. As should be obvious, it has one space here, two spaces here. So how about we transfer the code once again. I might have recently cut this part, yet I imagine that you should realize that you may have issues associating with I discover it to your Wi-Fi organization and you need to tackle these issues. What's more, the most ideal path is to duplicate your Wi-Fi network name and secret word from your switch administrator page. Alright.

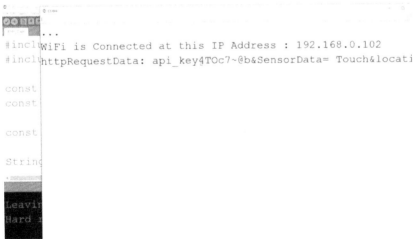

Duncan Barling, now we click here, as you can see, it did connect wi fi is connected this IP address and it's showing my IP address and it did print the HDTV request data. You can see. Now, let's check our database. Now, as you can see, we haven't received any data on our database, so let's see what is the problem. Now, an unusual request was is out. Now, let's first check our database to make sure.

Presently, in the event that you have composed everything accurately, you should see on this page, when you revive it, you should see the qualities here as you can see the area, one, two. What's more, here we get esteem one worth to esteem three. Also, the timestamp. The sensor information and area information are not obvious here, generally in light of the fact that we have the name wrong or PSP record. So we should initially check our information base and as you can find in our data set, we are not getting these names. This implies that we object to the post information document.

So go to the information document, alter it and ensure that you have the correct naming for every one of these progressions to equivalent to in this one. Presently, eSport, as should be obvious, we have since we have area, so how about we share this with Senseor. Also, area so true and here when you attempt to edit and the area, we need to do likewise for the area and here we need to add the area. Presently, same for here. Alright, they are looking accurately here. You need to ensure that they are named something very similar. Invigorate the page and we should sit tight for another solicitation. We should clear the yield.

Alright, we got another solicitation, we can return on the off chance that we will invigorate your data set, you should see the qualities here in your table. Alright, presently, as should be obvious, Touch and Home Office, consequently embed name and area are composed accurately. What's more, on the off chance that you revive the page here, you will see that we have Touch and Home Office. Also, the qualities from our sensors now, since what can be a feeling of sense or appended sensor or some other kind of sensors, and in the following , I will utilize three touch sensors and send their qualities to our Web page.

HARDWARE AND SOFTWARE REQUIREMENTS

Equipment and programming prerequisites. You will require a specialist to board and we are utilizing the word one, you will require a few LEDs and resistors so you can attach them with your E.S.P board to control them. You will require some jumper wires for the associations and we will wind up programming, which is Arduino idée, and we will disclose how to download and introduce the product. This is the ball that we are utilizing, as you can find in this picture. It's called E.S.P 32 and we will clarify this ball momentarily in a different talk. Much obliged for sharing this . Make a point to have these things close by.

WHAT IS A WEB SERVER

What is our observer and how it works? Observer is a place which stores processes and delivers Web pages to a client's.

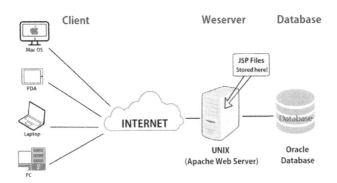

What customers is only our program on our workstations and cell phones? As you can find in this picture. The correspondence among customer and worker happens utilizing an uncommon convention called Hypertext Transfer Protocol, which essentially HDTV. I feel that you know about this one since you see it in practically all length and all pages in this convention, the customer here. Starts correspondence by asking for a particular Web page utilizing ECB convention, and the worker at that point reacts with the substance of that Web page or a mistake message on the off chance that it couldn't do that, similar to the celebrated 404 blunder page, pages conveyed by a worker are for the most part collected records or PSP archives. Presently, how about we take a snappy model. This program is our customer now free, isn't that so? Google website.

It will give HDTV, which we previously referenced, and it will request that the worker convey this Web page, which is Google website. Presently, this solicitation will go from the old customer, which is this program to Google workers and Google workers will react with this page content, which is essentially a picture and two catches. So this is us speaking with Google worker utilizing our old customer, which is this program. I think since this thought is all the more clear and we will move our PSP board to our Web worker and we will compose an email code so that at whatever point somebody sent a solicitation to our fare worker, it will react with the pages that we made inside it.

ESP32 OPERATING MODES

32 working modes. E.S.P, 32 needs to work and needs the station moved or as they moved and the delicate passage moved, every last bit of it's called Eppy. Presently, we should discuss every one of them. Perhaps the best element we have, E.S.P 30 to give is that it can't just associate with a current Wi-Fi organization and go about as a spectator, yet it can likewise set up its very own organization, permitting different gadgets to interface straightforwardly to it and

access website pages. This is conceivable in light of the fact that SB 32 can work in various working modes, typically there's three the station more the delicate passage mode and the third one that consolidates the two of them simultaneously, which give the chance of building organizations. In any case, we will not emerge from that one in light of the fact that the two generally utilized working models are station mode and delicate passageway mode. On the off chance that you are keen on networks, who can. Presently, we should begin by covering the station.

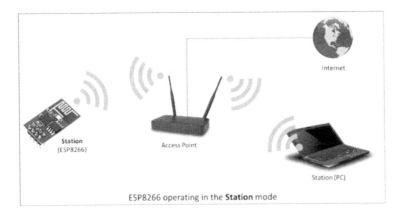

ESP8266 operating in the **Station** mode

What they E.S.P 32 that associates with a current Wi-Fi organization, one made by your remote switch is called station or Station Mode E.S.P. Presently, in Stamford, E.S.P, 32 gets IP from remote switch to which it is associated with this IP address, it can set up our worker and convey all pagers to all associated gadgets under existing Wi-Fi organization. So as you can see here, we have a passageway and the ISP will interface with that passageway so it can approaches the Internet. Presently, the

ESP8266 operating in the **Soft Access Point** mode

second mode is called delicate passage mode in the delicate passageway mode, they SB 32 makes its own Wi-Fi organization and goes about as a center actually out of control after for at least one stations. That is called Access Point or AP. In contrast to Wi-Fi, rather, it doesn't have interface to our organization. So such method of activity is called delicate passage or delicate AP. Likewise the most extreme number of stations that can be associated with its. Organization is extremely restricted. It resembles up to five, a scene, ESP 32 makes another Wi-Fi organization and put in a safe spot, which is fundamentally the name of the organization and IP address to it. With this IP address, it can convey what pages to all associated gadgets under its own organization. Also, from this picture, you can see that this is individuals, us as a delicate passageway and the PC and the cell phone as a station so they can interface with that network that was made by the ISP board. This is the delicate passage mode. While in station Sorin. In the station mode, the ISP needs to associate with the passageway to get to the Internet. Else it will not have the option to get to the Internet and it can't make its own organization. So the PC can associate with the ISP network straightforwardly in light of the fact that it doesn't have any while a passageway methods of passage mode. They ASPEY makes a remote organization that any gadget can interface with. So this is the principle contrast between towards these two moves in this mode, esp go about as a passageway here, esp as a station that associates with a passageway that is as of now there. I will likewise give clarification on the best way to code every one of these two moons and what are the alterations needed to switch between delicate passageway mode and station. This will be in the coding area, however that is it for the present.

Circuit Design

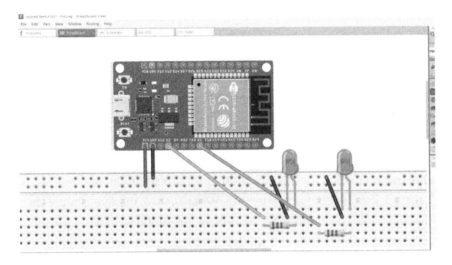

Since we know how the fundamentals of OutServe are or how the Web worker functions and in which mode SB 32 can make a Web worker, it's an ideal opportunity to interface a few prompts E.S.P 32 that we need to command over Wi-Fi. We need to begin by discovering a circuit plan programming. Furthermore, I will utilize Fritzing previously disclosed how to download and introduce the product. So here it is currently, double tap, the uprising that we find so you can begin running the product. Presently go to the breadboard see. Feel free to haul to LED's. You likewise need to resistors. Furthermore, we need, indeed, be strong, so right, E.S.P. Karate viewpoint 32, however you will not discover it, so you need to download it from an online site. Presently to discover the SB 32 board library for Fritzing, right, fritzing. As should be obvious. What's more, we can go to the recreation center subnet, this is the world that we are utilizing the word E.S.P, 32 words and one. Presently, this is the length that you need to download, click on it and you'll have it here. Presently how about we open it up with Fritzing, record open and go to downloads. Open it up. What's more, here you are. Here we have the Fritzing Board. For the E.S.P 32. The library for the SB 32 board. Presently we should zoom out. Furthermore, how about we pivot it, OK? Thate. Presently, first, we need to associate the ground to the ground. What's more, the three direct three fall toward the force. Give it red shading. Furthermore, give this a square, OK? Presently, here we have two covers. This is the first. What's more, As should be obvious, it has two terminals and we need to associate, that is Mr.. Presently, every one of these terma, when you point your mouse on this lesson, you can see that this is a Gethard and this is the A.. Presently we should associate. That is Mr.. To this lake, which is the island, and how about we associate the cathode. To talk around. Exactly. Gethard to ground, and that is an off to the A.. Presently the other terminal that is believed to be associated with our board and for this situation or for our situation, we need to interface it to. These two pens. Dita. What's more, the five. Simply the shading make the green. Also, incredible, presently we have our eSport associated with LED's, and it will tell these two on or off utilizing our page and this will be clarified in the coding area. However, that is it for the present. This is our extremely straightforward schematic, and I will show you how to control your burbles, input yield pens utilizing the entire page and the coding area. Much obliged for sharing this , in the event that you have any inquiries, kindly get some information about and the library for individuals will be added as assets to this talk so you can undoubtedly download it or you can find it on the web.

UNDERSTAND HOW ESP32 FUNCTIONS AS A SERVER

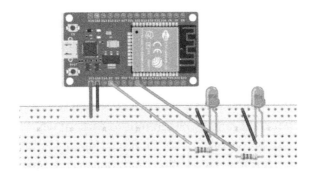

Controlling things from E.S.P 30 to eyewitness. Presently, if things aren't clear yet, you may be asking yourself, how could I be going to control things from Observer that only cycles and conveys what pages? All things considered, at that point you need to comprehend what's happening in the background. Presently. At the point when you type are you are an old program and hit enter the program sends and additionally A.B. demand, which is fundamentally get solicitation to our worker. What's more, in the model we recently clarified, we referenced Google workers. It's a task of Web worker to deal with this solicitation by accomplishing something. You may have sorted it out at this point that we will control things by getting to a particular URL. For instance, assume we enter resemble one hundred 92 point one hundred 68 point one point one drove on. I might want to do that for you so the thought will be all the more clear. Presently, Furat. HTP. Also, we composed a great deal of. One hundred 92 point one six eight point one point one, and afterward we had a cut driven. Presently, in the event that we entered this in the program, the program sends HTP solicitation to E.S.P 52 to deal with this solicitation. At the point when

E.S.P 32 peruses the solicitation, it realizes that the client needs to divert that on from D-line. It turns the top on and sends a unique page to commendation are showing little status on. The entirety of now, this piece of the preliminary can be whatever else that may change the tone. This part can be changed with whatever else, contingent upon the IP that you set for your USB port, and this line out of this world can be changed with some other thing worked out on laid off or turn it on, turn it off. What's more, this is the YouTube demand that we previously referenced. So this is essentially the thing we will compose and our customer, which is the Web program, and this will be shipped off the worker, which is the ISP bar. What's more, all things considered, these individuals will have a code that will be prepared to get this, uh, your URL, and it will attempt to sort out what's composed here. Whenever it's perceived that's it has a cover on directly in here, it will turn on the top. At that point it will convey page showing the situation with that prompted your Web program. So it's essentially customer or program and worker, at that point back to the customer and from the customer, the worker once more. What's more, this law will proceed. This is fundamentally the thing we will do. We will compose a code inside the worker and that code will has a Web page code and it will needs to fasten. Or then again of. When you call it by name, when you compose 100 thousand 800 61 one, it will take you. When you have this in your program, it will take you to this Web page that exists inside the ISP worker. Also, from that point, you can handle these two letters on or off. It's pretty much as basic as that. The ISP is the worker and your Web program is the customer. You will utilize the your customer to associate with the worker and provide it orders to turn it on or off. What's more, it will execute contingent upon the code inside it and will send you the entire page showing your little status. I believe that now the thought is all the more clear and to be significantly more clear with the coding and the coding segment, so stay tuned. See your next. Furthermore, we will begin calling this board to go about as a spectator.

WIFI AND WEBSERVER CODING SETTINGS

Presently, we should address the coding cycle. It will be a long cycle since this code isn't only four or five lines, it's a beautiful long code. However, I will clarify each line and we will compose it together and you will see how everything functions. In this first model, we will utilize SB 32 as FTB worker utilizing Wi-Fi passage mode. We will exhibit how to transform the E.S.P 32 into a passageway and present Web pages to any indicted customer to begin with this. In the first place, you need to plug your ISP first to board, and you need to run the Arduino programming. We previously disclosed how to download and introduce the product and how to get it to perceive your ISP, yet. Presently. Start by making another task. An Arduino and how about we save this undertaking. Presently, how about we call it E.S.P 32 Observer and snap Save. Presently, we need to begin by including the wi fi library, since we will utilize Wi-Fi association, so incorporate Wi-Fi. The Turks now this library gives SPF 30 to explicit Wi-Fi techniques, we are calling to associate the organization. Following that, we additionally incorporate the Web worker. Library impede. Sarah, the at this point. This library has a few strategies accessible that will help us setting up a worker and taking care of approaching ACTU demands without expecting to stress over low level execution subtleties. So these two libraries are fundamental in our coding cycle. Furthermore, to ensure that all is great, you need to arrange. Presently, as should be obvious, the expound isn't coordinated. Presently, this should be capital, so once more, check. Presently, Duncan Barling, as we are sitting VSP 32, a passageway board, it will make a Wi-Fi organization, subsequently we need to put it to the side secret word, IP address, IP subnet cover and IP escape. These are all data that we need to ensure that our ISP will act a passageway. So how about we begin by putting our ID right. Character. What's more, ID, we will leave this. I will compose it when we get done with recording measure now steady character again for the secret phrase.

```
esp32webserver | Arduino 1.8.12
File Edit Sketch Tools Help

esp32webserver §

#include <WiFi.h>
#include <WebServer.h>

const char* ssid = "";
const char* password = "";

IPAddress local_ip(192,168,1,1);
IPAddress gateway(192,168,1,1);
IPAddress subnet(255,255,255,0);

void setup() {
```

```
Sketch uses 267245 bytes (20%) of program storage space. Maximum is 1
Global variables use 15108 bytes (4%) of dynamic memory, leaving 3125
```

Also, we will leave this now from that point onward, we need the IP address boundaries, so IP address. Nearby, I.B.. What's more, you need to enter your nearby I.B. subtleties. Typically there are one hundred 98 168. What's more, you need to add a comma between them. Then, you need to make the escape sitting's. What's more, they are typically very much like that of sitting's. Then, you need to compose your IP address, subnet cover. Presently, I will show you how you can get this data for your organization. Alright, presently, on the off chance that you need to get this data so you can fill them accurately, you need to go to the beginning menu and open up the external shell.

Honda's partial or you can simply to TMD these both Wallwork. Now, if you see Amde, stop when you see Amde. All what you need to do is right, I be config while you are connecting to the wireless network and from there you can see that we have this information.

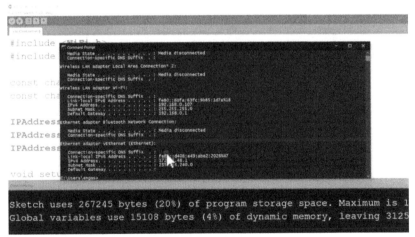

Also, from this data, we can get all that we need. Presently, here I realize that the subnet veil for my organization is 255, 255, 255 zero, very much like this one. Also, the default door is 190 to 168 01. So I would need to change this to zero one and connection neighborhood IP address or the IP address for my PC is one hundred 92 to 200 68 two zero spot one zero seven. So this must be zero and we can change this to 10. Or then again some other IP address, this will be our ISP worker

IP address. So ensure that you pick an IP address that isn't utilized by some other gadget in your organization. So. This is the way you set these things up and you can join your code to ensure that all is well and right. Duncan Barling and the following , we will pronounce an object of the onlooker so we can begin calling our spectator and begin starting controlled activity. That is it for this . What we did is we incorporated the Wi-Fi and notice our library. We made the A Society and secret word for our nearby Wi-Fi organization.

```
#include <WiFi.h>
#include <WebServer.h>

const char* ssid = "";
const char* password = "";

IPAddress local_ip(192,168,0,10);
IPAddress gateway(192,168,0,1);
IPAddress subnet(255,255,255,0);

void setup() {
```

```
Sketch uses 267301 bytes (20%) of program storage space. Maximum is 1
Global variables use 15132 bytes (4%) of dynamic memory, leaving 3125
```

And we assigned the local IP gateway and subnet mask for our Wi-Fi network. Now, if you have a question about anything in this lecture, you can ask and that you aren't able. That's it for this . This is aside from educational engineering team.

HTTP encoding requests and servers

Presently we need to announce an object of notice our library so we can get to its capacities, the constructor of the item to send out what the worker will tune in as a boundary, since A-T is the default port for all that we demand, we will utilize this worth. What's more, you can without much of a stretch do that by composing this basic line. Prior to the arrangement strategy, right eyewitness, and it ought to be called spectator worker and at 80 years. So we have pronounced an item from the Observer with this port 84 HCB demand. Then, we proclaim that E.S.P 32 broadly useful info yield pins to which cover's are associated and we will set their underlying state. Presently, to do that for the set up strategy, characterize a number. Also, call it drove. What's more, one and we definitely realize that we have drawn an obvious conclusion to PIN two and five. So we might want to hear a similar line will be composed for and number five. For the second. Lyd. Presently, how about we give them introductory worth added one status.

```
IPAddress local_ip(192,168,0,10);
IPAddress gateway(192,168,0,1);
IPAddress subnet(255,255,255,0);

WebServer server(80);

uint8_t LEDPin1 = 2;
bool LED
uint8_t LEDPin2 = 5;

void setup() {
```

```
Sketch uses 267301 bytes (20%) of program storage space. Maximum is 1
Global variables use 15132 bytes (4%) of dynamic memory, leaving 3125
```

Turn it off low and something for little. Make it law. Alright, since we have outfitted everything before the arrangement, we figured we will return to our remote organization name and secret phrase. How about we proceed onward to the set up work. We will arrange our HTP solicitation or worker before really running it. Above all else, we open a sequential association for investigating purposes and we will set universally useful information yield ports to yield since they are fundamentally LEDs and we will control them as yield. So inside the arrangement material to start and utilize and direct.

```
bool LED2status = LOW;

void setup() {
  // put your setup code here, to run once:
  Serial.begin(115200);
  pinMode();            I
}

void loop() {
  // put your main code here, to run repeatedly:
```

```
Sketch uses 267301 bytes (20%) of program storage space. Maximum is 1
Global variables use 15132 bytes (4%) of dynamic memory, leaving 3125
```

Next, Pinewood just slightly on Arduino, and they are going to either take the print name Litvin one and make it out or something for the second pen and two, it will be treated as output. Then we are going to set up a soft access point to establish a Wi-Fi network by providing that as the password,

```
bool LED1status = LOW;

uint8_t LEDPin2 = 5;
bool LED2status = LOW;

void setup() {
  // put your setup code here, to run once:
  Serial.begin(115200);
  pinMode(LEDPin1, OUTPUT);
  pinMode(LEDPin2, OUTPUT);
}
```

```
Sketch uses 267301 bytes (20%) of program storage space. Maximum is 1
Global variables use 15132 bytes (4%) of dynamic memory, leaving 3125
```

IP address,

```
D esp32webserver : Arduino 1.8.12
File Edit Sketch Tools Help

#include <WiFi.h>
#include <WebServer.h>

const char* ssid = "";
const char* password = "";

IPAddress local_ip(192,168,0,10);
IPAddress gateway(192,168,0,1);
IPAddress subnet(255,255,255,0);

WebServer server(80);
```

```
Sketch uses 267301 bytes (20%) of program storage space. Maximum is 1
Global variables use 15132 bytes (4%) of dynamic memory, leaving 3125
```

IP subnet cover and IP escape, which are essentially this data that we gave or we added here. What we need to do inside the arrangement strategy is compose wi fi. That delicate. AP And this will take two boundaries, this as ID and the secret word at that point, right, Wi-Fi, the delicate AP config, and it will take three boundaries, the nearby IP passage and the subnet. From that point forward, you can add a deferral to ensure that everything is steady. Presently, that is it, how about we confirm to ensure that we don't have young ladies. I like checking everybody and afterward to ensure that if there is a blunder, I can fix it when it occur. Alright, Duncan Barling, we don't have any principles. Presently we go to the main piece of this court to deal with approaching ACTU demands, we need to determine which court to execute when a specific young lady is hit. To do as such, we utilize one strategy. This strategy takes two boundaries. Initial one is a genuine way, and second one is dunam of capacity, which we need to execute. At the point when that you are is hit, for instance. We should attempt to think of one line and I'll clarify it as we compose it right worker. Not on. Presently, open to enclosures, the principal boundary that will take. Is the slice and consume unit right, KUMAH, why the strategy name that will take control when something occur? Alright, presently this line. At the point when a worker gets a gauge on the development way, it will trigger the handle interface. Capacity, not that they are determined, is a relative way. Moreover, we can do likewise for other are we can here let one on and we can name the capacity drove one on the equivalent for other. We should serve our own and we will compose various qualities here. Slice drove one off and handle drove one of same for prompted. We will change this to the two and same for here. Prompted let to simply to save time and to ensure that we couldn't care less about composition. Presently what will occur here. At whatever point you compose the IP address this one, suppose that you write in your program, I will give you a model, 182 168 one zero by ten. Also, you compose this slice. At the point when they request that individuals get this solicitation, it will run this technique.

```
WiFi.softAP(ssid, password);
WiFi.softAPConfig(local_ip,gateway, subnet);
delay(100);

server.on("/", handle_OnConnect);
server.on("/led1on", handle_led1on);
server.on("/led1off", handle_led1off);
server.on("/led2on", handle_led2on);
server.on("/led2off", handle_led2off);
}
```

```
Sketch uses 713190 bytes (54%) of program storage space. Maximum is 1
Global variables use 39360 bytes (12%) of dynamic memory, leaving 288
```

Presently, on the off chance that you compose, let one on, it will execute this strategy. What's more, we will compose this strategy techniques insider savvy area. Be that as it may, for the present, this is the thing that I need you to see now, we haven't determined what the worker ought to do if the customer solicitations and you are other than the predefined Web worker on other Valdese, it ought to react with an issue, be status 404 mistake, which has fundamentally not discovered a page and a directive for the client. We put this in a capacity too, and we can undoubtedly do that by composing worker that on not discovered, which is one of the capacities that we can without much of a stretch use here. You need to compose the name of the capacity Quantic. It will take just a single boundary. So not found. Alright. To begin our worker, we need to compose worker to start. What's more, don't take any boundaries, and we can battle a line in the Syrian screen to ensure that it will show us SERVERLESS has begun, OK, FTB worker has begun. This is the means by which to begin yourself out once you finish the design. Presently how about we cause a speedy audit of what we to have done here and we initialised that delicate passageway mode and offer it to boundaries, the Wi-Fi network name and the secret phrase, and we give it the nearby IP escape and subnet cover. At that point we can ensure that everything is steady.

```
#include <WiFi.h>
#include <WebServer.h>

const char* ssid = "";
const char* password = "";

IPAddress local_ip(192,168,1,1);
IPAddress gateway(192,168,1,1);
IPAddress subnet(255,255,255,0);

void setup() {
```

```
Sketch uses 267245 bytes (20%) of program storage space. Maximum is 1
Global variables use 15108 bytes (4%) of dynamic memory, leaving 3125
```

From that point forward, we composed these lines. The third on will take two boundaries, first boundary is they are permitted and the subsequent boundary is the technique. So when somebody demands the you are this one. It will call the idea about Connect technique, and when somebody composes lit one, when somebody calls this genuine, it will call this strategy and we will make these strategies on the up and up segment. However, what you cannot deny is that you can add more Yarl's and more demands, and on the off chance that somebody until they are generally that you haven't set here, you can guide him to deal with not discovered a technique on not found. Presently, to settle the social equality time that started, at that point sequential doctorand line and to live this long and the service or showing that the common conflict has begun, we should check. Alright, presently we have a difficult which is taken care of, Internet was not announced, which

269

implies that this technique was not at this point pronounced and we haven't yet proclaimed anything on the up and up segment. So this is a blunder that we can't disregard. Also, in the following , we will begin composing the code inside the circle segment. What's more, that is it until further notice.

CODING CLIENT METHODS

To deal with the genuine approaching HCB demands, we need to call the handle, associate all the handle customer technique on the worker object. We additionally need to change the lead or the condition of ready according to the solicitation. So inside the void circle, you need to compose worker the handle customer. From that point onward, you need to compose two articulations, a substantial one. Alright, we should duplicate the variable from here. Flood, one state's. At that point. We need to ride computerized rights drove when one and make a tie. Else we need to make it law. So it very well may be this line here and make it look. Presently, something for the subsequent cutting edge if. Ilse. No.

```
digitalWrite(LEDPin1, HIGH);}
else {
  digitalWrite(LEDPin1, LOW);
  }

  if(LED2status)
  {digitalWrite(LEDPin2, HIGH);}
  else
  {digitalWrite(LEDPin2, LOW);}


}
```

```
exit status 1
'handle_OnConnect' was not declared in this scope
```

And that if a lived two status is changed, we need to make a tie, otherwise make it look. Now, this will change depending on the request, so that handle client will handle the incoming data and depending on the request, it will turn the light on or off. Now, this will be more clear when we create a function to attach it to the root directory. You are AI. As you can see here, we initiated the handle and cannot handle it one on and one off hand the lid to on and handle it to off and handle around.

```
delay(100);

/// 192.168.0.10/ledlon
server.on("/", handle_OnConnect);
server.on("/led1on", handle_led1on);
server.on("/led1off", handle_led1off);
server.on("/led2on", handle_led2on);
server.on("/led2off", handle_led2off);
server.onNotFound(handle_NotFound);

server.begin();
```

```
exit status 1
'handle_OnConnect' was not declared in this scope
```

These are for the most part works that we need to announce. Presently to proclaim these capacities. Presently, the handle Connecticut will be as per the following toward the beginning of this capacity, we need to set the state or the situation with these two prompts law, which implies that they will be off and print that state on the chronic screen to ensure that everything is turned out great. Furthermore, to react to that demand, we utilize a similar technique. Albeit that strategy can be called with an alternate arrangement of contentions, it's most straightforward structure comprises of the city reaction called the substance type and the substance. For our situation, we need to send that 200 solicitation. How about we initially make the technique now outside the void law. You need to make your new strategy. Furthermore, to do that, what you need to do is basically compose void and the them name handle on Connect. Presently inside this strategy, we will like not many things. The main thing is the let one state status. We will make it law prompted status will likewise be law, sequential, speck, print. We will print a line to ensure that everything is composed effectively. This first line, uh, Lyd or g.P I or two of.

```
{digitalWrite(LEDPin2, LOW);}

}

void handle_onConnect()
{
LED1status = LOW;
LED2status = LOW;
Serial.println("GPIO 1 : OFF and GPIO5: OFF");
server.send(200, "text/html", SendHTML(LED1status, LED2status));
}

exit status 1
'handle_OnConnect' was not declared in this scope
```

Furthermore, GPI, each of the five is likewise off, this one will ensure that at whatever point this technique is called, we will see this line and that screen. You can't disregard it on the off chance that you would prefer not to know. In any case, I favor adding these for troubleshooting. Alright, presently you need this is the main line you need to worker. That sent and between the two brackets, you need to compose the accompanying, the main contention will be the code. We are sending the code 200 for this situation, the unconvicted case. Furthermore, this code will help us from various perspectives. The principal way that this crew will assist us with is there's more than one status code for demands, as you can see on this page. You can compose a rundown of HIV status code, and you can as you can see here, 200 methods, OK, so at whatever point we compose 200, this implies that it's OK to get this. You are separated from everyone else and we can deal with it. So we will utilize it. We resembled 200 here. Furthermore, after 200, you need to compose or to indicate the substance type. For our situation, it will be out page text, cut HTML. Presently the third palmtop that you need to compose is simply the substance. We will send email and this convey a message strategy. We will compose two boundaries. The first is driven one status. Also, the subsequent one will be directed to theaters which are essentially low and low, so it will send low and low ground here. The real technique will be talked about later. Presently. To ensure that you comprehend what occurred here for our situation, we are sending the code 200, which is one of the HCB status demands or codes that compares to the OK reaction, at that point we are indicating the substance type to be is text or email. Lastly, we are calling to convey a message custom capacity, which makes a powerful email page containing status of these two letters. So this will be made later in convenience , however that is it until further notice.

```
void handle_onConnect()
{
LED1status = LOW;
LED2status = LOW;
Serial.println("GPIO 2 : OFF and GPIO5: OFF");
server.send(200, "text/html", SendHTML(LED1status, LED2status));
}

void handle_led1on()
{
LED1status = HIGH;
```

```
exit status 1
'handle_OnConnect' was not declared in this scope
```

This is how to create the first method that will be called whatever we call this.

You are the men you are and it will call hands on Connect. Presently, we need to do likewise for these techniques, as should be obvious. So we should begin. Similarly, we need to make four capacities to deal with the entirety of our solicitations and the 404 mistake page. To do this effectively, we can't just duplicate this strategy and based it down underneath here and here, we can battle late one on. What's more, L'Etoile status will be high. We needn't bother with that little status, and for our situation, this will imply that this line will resemble this on. Presently, the worker sent will send 200, OK, and the time will be text and ascherman, the sender Shamal strategy will send through and the two states will be something similar. Presently, to do this for the subsequent reorder, right, let one off now here hearing it right law. Of I feel that now you got the thought and you can do this all alone, you can finish the excess four techniques. Presently. We need to duplicate these two techniques now, we have four strategies, this will be two and the two. Broadly useful information yield to number five here and five here. The first would be number two here. Furthermore, to hear what we have simply to fix this, since we associated their lives to a number two and five. So two on five. Alright. To five now we need to change these two. This will be cherished one status and this will be valid. This will be. Cherished status, and this would be bogus. Alright, presently we need to change these lines, everything is right, there is one more technique that we need to make, which is the 404 not discovered strategy. Not found. Not discovered, no. The not discovered will have just one. Line not found and we needn't bother with any red states, and here we attempt the code 404 for not found and basically right not found. Alright, that is it. This is the manner by which you can make these strategies. Presently, there is as yet one strategy and email that we need to make, yet we should consolidate the code to ensure that there is no else other than the standard Shamala. Kay.

```
void handle_led2off()
{
LED1status = LOW;
Serial.println("GPIO 5 : OFF");
server.send(200, "text/html", SendHTML(LED1status, false));
}

void handle_NotFound()
{
Serial.println("Not Found");

exit status 1
'SendHTML' was not declared in this scope
```

This is the idea about Connect. Presently, to fix this mistake, we need just to change the tone, we should assemble this line with capital on this. Presently confirm once more. Alright, presently. Alright, presently we have the Sinochem al strategy, which has blunders, and we will fix this while going to make this technique in the following . Be that as it may, how about we cause a speedy synopsis of what we to have done here in this code. Presently, the primary thing that we did here is make inside the void circle. We call the handle customer technique and we bust the top status utilizing this if proclamation late one and prompted high or low, contingent upon the ready one status. Presently, when the deal with and associate techniques are called, every one of them will accomplish something. Presently the interconnect the primary technique for the manual will set that identifies with the heap mode, will turn them off and will print this on the third screen and it will send this 200 methods, OK, this is the substance type and it will send the situation with these two letters and submit them on our Shamal page. What's more, we will disclose how to do that in the following . Same thing for different strategies. These strategies are pronounced dependent on this worker that on line, as should be obvious, if the line was lit, one on implies that it will tell that it one on the subsequent line and one oft implies it will consider the hand an oddball strategy. So we made strategies for these lines. Also, we added our code inside every one of these strategies to kill the top and potentially a sentence that this top is currently off and to send an email page showing that this cover or top one is off, OK? Presently, the following we will make, that is a trick. What's more, you will compose or make our email code or page. Much obliged for inquiring. This is Asharaf from instructive designing group.

WRITING HTML CODE FOR WEBPAGE

Presently we go to the last and most significant piece of the coding cycle, the kin that Axium appealed page the sentence structure glitch is liable for creating page at whatever point that E.S.P 30 to Web worker gets a solicitation from our customer. It only link Etchingham Alcalde into a major string and gets back to the worker doesn't work we examined before. The capacity accepts status of LEDs as a boundary powerfully create stream killjoy. The principal test you ought to consistently send is that DOCTYPE presentation, this DOCTYPE announcement demonstrates that we are sending ASTM uncowed. So how about we start by instating this technique down here. It will hold strength so it will not be void string. Send an email now. This strategy will take. Two boundaries. The first will be that whole number. Let one status. Also, it will take prompted St.. As you can see here on here now, we need to distinguish appointer. So inside it, the main line will string BTR, which is that point or the beginning stage out that we will utilize and the principal thing that we will pass is the DOCTYPE. Ascherman, Doug. Furthermore, in the event that you know about ASML, you'll realize that this is something you need to do, you can't disregard it and you can't leave it, you need to tell the educator that this is an email code utilizing this line. Presently, the determination here implies new line, so the primary thing that will be written in our admirable page is this, and it will not be composed, it will be covered up and the choice will move to the following line so we can compose more things.

```
void handle_NotFound()
{
Serial.println("Not Found");
server.send(404, "text/html", "Not Found");
}


String SendHTML(uint8_t led1stat, uint8_t led2stat)
{
    String ptr = "<!DOCTYPE html> <html>\n";
```

```
exit status 1
'SendHTML' was not declared in this scope
```

Then, we will compose the meter viewport component that makes the
entire page responsive in any Web program while Title Tags sits the
title of the page. So we should do them individually. Furthermore,
you'll notice that at whatever point I compose this, I compose in
addition to rises to in addition to approach implies. Take this and add
whatever composed here to it. Try not to supplant it connected. So I
have the primary position, in addition to the subsequent string, in
addition to the third string, etc. So we will compose a long queue here.
This line will make that email page, header or head and we will
compose the meta labels and you can't just record them or duplicate
them from our code. I will give the source code to this venture.
Presently, right, viewport, how about we slice. I'm about. More than
content, yet equivalent and rights once more. At that point. Also,
another sign right with. Equivalents gadget with this will make our
base responsive and it will change contingent upon our gadget with.
Then, what you need to do is beginning scale. The extreme lethargies,
right, Atia? Scale and 1.0, we don't need it to scale up or down.
Presently the utilization of adaptable equivalent No. Try not to permit
the client to scale our public code, it will auto conform to the program
settings whenever you are finished. You can essentially close the tag,
that meat assault and the correct cut and another characteristic of
this, OK? I realize that this is a long queue. This is fundamentally the
header for page, and we are composing meta labels to ensure that our

old page will be responsive. I don't suggest recording it. Simply reorder this code from our code. Presently, the subsequent stage will compose or setting the title of our page like BTR in addition to rise to. Furthermore, you can't just purchase title. This is the title tag and I title again now between these two, you can compose the label Bullet Control E.S.P 32. This will be the title of our Web page. Presently, our conversation here is to ensure that you have another line now for styling the entire page, we can add us, which is essentially an approach to shading everything on your page and to control the foundation, the width of the strokes and different things. Also, we will add some see as a styling to our gauge bill to make it look more excellent. Furthermore, to do that, you need to pick the textual style type. The edges and other stuff, on the off chance that you are curious about this, simply reorder what we have done and do some alters and you will see the distinction now, right, Peter? Furthermore, equivalent. What's more, two signs, their way of life, right, as Jamal inside that you would now be able to pick the textual style family. You can't zone or some other kind and you can't show. To be in line block. At that point you can't change the edge I would at zero bexell to the edge. Presently. It's half of the zero, so you can add auto now, we can likewise send the content a line. To be representative. After you do the entirety of this, simply add new line to ensure that you have moved to the following line to continue to compose your Astrium alcalde. Presently, this is the vehicles are styling and this is the title of our page. This is the header. Presently, we should proceed onward. Presently. Presently, you can just follow our ride, the accompanying code, these two lines, these two lines will help set that shading textual style and edge around the body labels that every one S3 and P labels. As should be obvious, this will set the text dimension. This will set the tone for the P tag and this will set the edge. Exactly. This is for every one and this is for every three.

```
tring SendHTML(uint8_t led1stat, uint8_t led2stat)

    String ptr = "<!DOCTYPE html> <html>\n";
    ptr += "<head><meta name=\ "viewport\" content=\" width=device-width
    ptr += "<title> LED Control ESP32</title>\n"
    ptr += "<style> html {font-family: Arial; display: inline-block; mar
    ptr +="body{margin-top: 50px;} h1 {color: #444444;margin: 50px auto
    ptr +="p {font-size: 14px;color: #888;margin-bottom: 10px;}\n";
```

```
L' was not declared in this scope
```

You can essentially reorder these lines from our code. Some styling is
applied to the catches also with properties like tone, size, edge, and so
on The on and off button has diverse foundation tone. We can set
diverse foundation tone by utilizing the dynamic selector for catches to
guarantee button click impact. Presently I can record the entire code
gradually, however I will glue it here and disclose it to you. Presently,
as you can see here now are required the catch here, we said the
words and the foundation tone for that catch and we are expressing
that will not have any lines. That shading will be white. The structure
will be 13 pixel and 30 pixel from left, straight here and there the
content enrichment. There will be no content enhancement. The text
dimension will be 25. Furthermore, these are different properties.
Sam, for the foundation tone, you can see that here and you can see
the foundation tone, one dynamic when the twirly doo was put for us
to see another tone. Same here for the on the foundation shading will
be this. Also, when it's dynamic, when somebody clicks it, it will change
to this. This will affect the implement and will be more in the dynamic
stick. We can likewise begin the heading. You can basically lie, Peter.
For that one, issue three. These two lines. Will change the heading of
the old page, you can just change the content inside this H1 and H3
labels to whatever suits your application.

```
ptr +=".button {display: block;width: 80px;background-color: #3498db;b
ptr +=".button-on {background-color: #3498db;}\n";
ptr +=".button-on:active {background-color: #2980b9;}\n";
ptr +=".button-off {background-color: #34495e;}\n";
ptr +=".button-off:active {background-color: #2c3e50;}\n";

ptr +="<h1>ESP32 Web Server</h1>\n";
ptr +="<h3>Using Access Point(AP) Mode</h3>\n";

    }
```

In any case, for our situation, I have composed SB 30 to eyewitness and utilizing passageway code. Presently, to begin showing the catches and comparing state to powerfully created the catches and little state we use if proclamation, so relying on the situation with that universally useful, input yield nails to or off button are shown. Presently, we should attempt this if proclamation here, you need to compose F. What's more, unutilized else. Presently, inside that, in the event that we are going attempt to lead one state and incur one state. Is. On we will attempt this line. Allow me to disclose to you what's going on here now we will add to our Astrium alcalde this that this line drove one state is on. Also, we will pick this class for the fight to come. We will pick button off. Also, lead one off and we're directly off inside the catch, so this line will make another catch. Also, In the following case, if the island state is off. We will attempt exactly the same line, yet kind of on we will directly off here, Sam,

```
{
  ptr +="<p>LED1 Status: ON</p><a class=\"button button-off\" href=\",
  }else {
    ptr +="<p>LED1 Status: OFF</p><a class=\"button button-on\" href='
  }

  if(led2stat)
  {ptr +="<p>LED2 Status: ON</p><a class=\"button button-off\" href=\",
else
  {ptr +="<p>LED2 Status: OFF</p><a class=\"button button-on\" href=\",
```

tus 1
L' was not declared in this scope

for the second if proclamation, which has prompted state, we will
have exactly the same lines. Down here, as should be obvious, a to sit
on drove two states off and relying upon the state, it will add this line
to our public code or this line for the red one and for the complete at
this line or this line. Presently, when we compose the entirety of this.
The following stage will be returning the string, so toward the finish of
this strategy, we are going to close the labels. Ensure that everything is
set by. Alright, presently, before we end this, we need to compose
BTR. Also, equivalent, and here you are going to close the Bundestag.
Also, slice and. And afterward we are going to close the email by and
large. And afterward slice and.

```
    }

  if(led2stat)
  {ptr +="<p>LED2 Status: ON</p><a class=\"button button-off\" href=\",
else
  {ptr +="<p>LED2 Status: OFF</p><a class=\"button button-on\" href=\",

  ptr += "</body>\n";
  ptr += "</html>\n";

  }
```

tus 1
L' was not declared in this scope

From that point forward, we should attempt to return BTR, which will return this spring when this strategy is called, and once this thing is returned, it will be sent and shown on our Web program. Presently, that is it. This is the entire cycle. That is shamal coding should be possible consequently. You can just go at this point. You can just in the event that you need to compose your trustworthiness and code, you can essentially go here and. Go the Schimel five Ed, good, on Google online task editorial manager, and utilizing any of these editors, you can essentially compose an email could without much of a stretch. Presently, you can begin by composing, Lyd. On and you can begin adding various things. Sort of clean the code, as should be obvious.

Furthermore, you can add a connection or simply click on add your hyperlink to this, and whenever you are finished with the coding interaction or composing your Web page or how you need your Web page to be, you can basically duplicate these lines. However, you need to add. When you duplicate these lines, I will tell you the best way to do it. Text. Whenever you are done unsatisfied with your code, you can just glue these lines and here you can do the accompanying, as BTR in addition to approach before every one of these lines. Also, toward the end, add this. What's more, and. Furthermore, I see my you can essentially duplicate this rundown here, here and here toward the start, we need this content sign. That is it, at that point you can essentially duplicate this code and put together it with respect to your

Arduino, on a product. This will be a lot simpler path for you to make your own page. Also, the catches that you need to show, however there are a great deal of strategies that you can do this where there are more visual editors or programming that can compose email calls, yet I incline toward cutting them. Furthermore, the Arduino thought and this is my code. Presently, what you need to do, in the event that you felt overpowered with disgrace, I'll call. You can essentially duplicate my code and base it on yours and you can change it relying upon your necessities.

```
ptr +="<h3>Using Access Point(AP) Mode</h3>\n";

if(led1stat)
{
    ptr +="<p>LED1 Status: ON</p><a class=\"button button-off\" href=\",
    }else {
        ptr +="<p>LED1 Status: OFF</p><a class=\"button button-on\" href='
    }

        if(led2stat)
```

```
tus ]
ML' was not declared in this scope
```

Alter your home, your page name utilizing this line. Allow regulator to talk 332, alter the headers, added enhancing catches, add more fastens, contingent upon your necessities, you can do anything you need with this code. Furthermore, the following , we will distil this code and associate our Wi-Fi organization and run the ISP worker. That is it for this .

PRACTICAL

Now, the start code, let's first verify the code and make sure that we don't have any errors. OK, Duncan Barling, now we have to go back and write our network name, that society has to be the same as this network. It's called Asharaf. OK, I would fill out this information.

```
#include <WiFi.h>
#include <WebServer.h>

const char* ssid = "Ashraf TV";
const char* password = "sam@0566660009";

IPAddress local_ip(192,168,0,10);
IPAddress gateway(192,168,0,1);
IPAddress subnet(255,255,255,0);
```

```
Sketch uses 720618 bytes (54%) of program storage space. Maximum is 1
Global variables use 39384 bytes (12%) of dynamic memory, leaving 288
```

Alright, presently, when you round out these data. Return and aggregate your code. Presently, how about we feel free to associate our board. Presently, when you interface the world. The subsequent stage will be going to the apparatuses and choosing the board, ensure that you have chosen the board, which is the IT board. Do it. Indeed, we need to get form one, at that point you can essentially transfer your code. Alright, presently you need to make another passageway name I called my passageway Ashrafi E.S.P. Furthermore, this is the secret phrase for this, uh, ISP passageway. Furthermore, these are IP designs. Presently, what you need to do once you transfer the code is go to the Wi-Fi organizations and ensure that you are associated with this organization asharaf ISP or whatever you called it. When you compose the secret phrase, you will be associated with this organization and here and there it doesn't take the IP arrangements

that you gave here. So when you have a go at wanting to op
program and keep in touch with one hundred 98 or one six ei
one six five, it will not interface. Also, to attempt to sort out wh
happening here, you can essentially proceed to tap on properties
see the Wi-Fi network abilities head down until you see this.

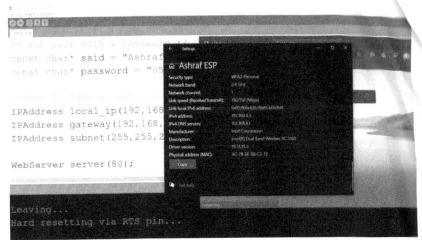

Server address, 192 to 268 for that one. Let's try this line. That one,
once you click into. As you can see here we are on our Web page, SB
32, a browser, and these are the two buttons that we created. These
are the heading one and two. And we can simply turn that on or off
using these buttons.

We have two LEDs and I will concentrate, which is going to be number

d we already have this button to control it. And now let's go to
mmon board so that we can see what's here. Now, once we
up this page, as you can see, the lids are off and we got this line
en you click on,

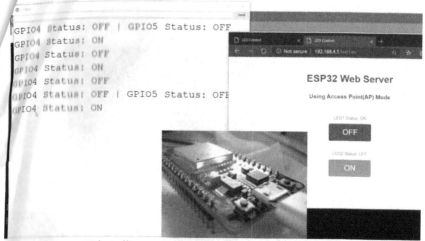

as you can see, it's telling you that this lid is on. It's not not my fault.
It's number two. the blue lid is on. Now, if you clicked again, the blue
lid will be off. And if we have another connected to PIN five, it will be
on. And again, it will turn off if we clicked the button again. So this is
how easily you can turn your ISP to our Web server and control it and
connect to it.

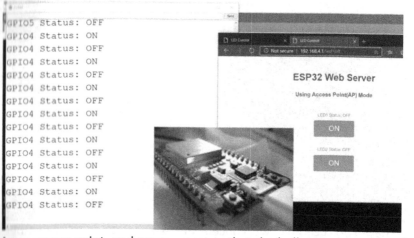

As an access point, and as you can see, that the bullets turning on and off. And as you can see, this is the line that was called when we clicked here. It's that easy. Again, if you want to the main page, it will print Turn-off bobsleds and print this line. That's it. This is how the code works in action. You can change this. You can add more, you can add more buttons. You can change the graphical user interface of that Shyamal code depending on your needs. If you have any questions, please ask. And if you aren't able.

WHAT IS SMTP SERVER

What is A.B. Silver? Presently, a SMTP implies straightforward mail move convention, and it's an Internet standard for email transmission. It assisted with sending messages utilizing an E.S.P 30 to. What's more, you need to associate your SPF 30 to one as MTBE worker, and most email suppliers like Gmail, Hotmail, prohibit Yahoo! Have their own assumptive workers and they give the data that you need to utilize these workers free of charge or what you need to do is make a record, ie, Hotmail, Gmail or some other record and get this A.P. worker data. And the entirety of this is clarified. In the coming s, you will figure out how to make a Gmail account. Also, what are the Gmail or assumptive worker subtleties for Gmail accounts now? What's more, the following will disclose how to utilize the SB 32 Manicaland library and how to introduce it on your Arduino IDE, on the off chance that you have any inquiry, you can ask it in the district board.

INSTALL ESP32 MAIL LIBRARY FOR ARDUINO

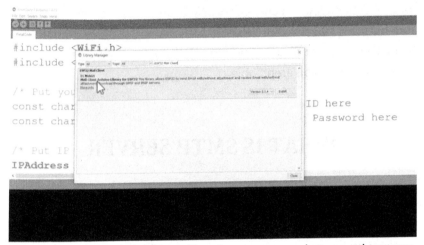

Since we have Arduino and ISP libraries empowered, we need to open up Arduino once again and prior to continuing, we need to introduce the ISP 32 primary customer library. Since we are sending messages, this library can be introduced through the first thought library administrator. So on your Arduino, you need to go to Sketchers. Furthermore, incorporate library, at that point oversee libraries. Presently, in this window, what you need to do is fundamentally look for E.S.P 32 male customer. Furthermore, as should be obvious, this is our library, and it's by Mobilicity, the tea click once and click introduce. It will not take long and. It will be finished. Effectively, as you can see currently, it's introduced and that is it. This is the way you can without much of a stretch introduce the E.S.P to Mail Client Library.

SMTP SERVER SETTINGS

SMTP worker settings now, as I previously referenced, every one of this MGB worker suppliers give settings to you to utilize and on the off chance that you are utilizing Gmail account, these are the SMTP worker subtleties that worker area is assumptive to Gmail website. The username is finished Gmail address. You need to compose your email address in full like Ashraf Agema website and the secret phrase. You need to compose your Gmail secret phrase also. Presently, on the off chance that you are utilizing reveal to US ports, you need to utilize 587 and in the event that you are utilizing SSL port cert, you need to utilize 465 and we will utilize SSL. So we are utilizing 500 or 400 65. Presently is it needed to utilize the US or SSL? Indeed, it's required and it's empowered as a matter of course via the post office customer library. That we previously referenced. Presently, on the off chance that you are utilizing live or Hotmail assumptive worker settings. These are the worker settings for live or Hotmail accounts, assumptive life that come. Furthermore, you need to utilize your full location at live website or at Hotmail website. Also, here you need to compose your secret key. This is the report number 587, and it's needed to have tearless and SSL declarations for your lady customer. Presently for Outlook clients or Outlook accounts, you need to compose assumptive Office 365 website. Compose your full email at Outlook website and your secret key. At that point you will 587 as a post and you are likewise needed to advise us and SSL empowered mail customer. Presently, on the off chance that your mail worker wasn't one of these, you need to look for its assumptive worker settings. Presently you have all you require to begin sending messages utilizing speedballs. So in the following Larsons, the fuel coming Larsons, we will figure out how to code your E.S.P board to begin sending messages. Much obliged for sharing this . On the off chance that you have any inquiries, kindly ask and take you on the board.

DOCKING PROJECT ESP32 EMAIL ALERT PART1

The improvement, one in which will begin composing our statement, the statement that we will compose and this will help send an email through us A.P. worker with email or text or whatever other thing that you need to send now for testing. We are possibly sending an email once when they request that you board boats and we can change this later relying upon our venture or our particular properties or what we need. Presently, you ought to have the option to make the code without any problem. I will go with you on a bit by bit way and we will begin by making another Arduino project. At that point we should save this undertaking. To ensure that we save our work. We should call it code now. The main thing that we need to do is incorporate a few libraries, so it will begin with hashtag incorporate, at that point we can add the library name, which is E.S.P 30 to underscore male customer TotEx, which is fundamentally the library that we did, and utilizing the oversaw libraries. We did that in a past class on. The principle library now we need to embed our organization qualifications, so how about we add two factors. The first is a consistent character for the organization certification as a side, and my organization name is Ashraf TV. Furthermore, we additionally need to enter a secret key, so we'll need to compose consistent characters. Secret phrase. Furthermore, we'll need to enter our secret phrase. I don't recall my secret key, however I will. Alright, I will utilize this one at this point. We need to enter our email settings, so you need to enter that email account and the secret phrase for the messages and their record. So you need to characterize your factors. So how about we attempt characterize email sender tally. What's more, we definitely realize that our email is you and Angie group and Agema website. Presently we likewise need to characterize the secret phrase. So email Cynda. Passwords, we need to have the secret key here. I need to work it out like that when we are trying. Presently you need to enter or you should enter that SEIP email account or the person who got the email account from your ISP board. This is the email that we got, that email sent by our ISP to do that by plan and afterward by email subbrand, at that point compose the email. I will send the messages to my. You and your group at Gmail website, which is our. Email, OK, presently you need to enter your location and TB settings, and we clarified in the past Lassonde that some TB worker settings for Gmail standpoint and Hotmail account, they are steady qualities given by every one of these organizations. So you simply need to reorder the qualities. Furthermore, since we are utilizing Gmail, it will be simple. Presently, how about we start by adding some TEEB worker. So I characterize then FTB worker and I expect to be the Gmail website. Then, we need to allot the help for this assumptive worker.

```
const char* ssid = "Ashraf  TV ";
const char* password = "asm@05666600099";

#define emailSenserAccount "eduengteamen@gmail.com"
#define emailSenderPassword "Password"
#define emailRecipient "eduengteam@gmail.com"
#define smtpServer "smtp.gmail.com"
#define smptServerPort 465
```

So I characterize a TV worker port and afterward compose the number 400 65. Presently we need to compose the email subject so we can likewise utilize characterize, characterize email subject and we can. Be that as it may, E.S.P 32 simply think email. Since we have done the entirety of this, we need to make a wonderful TB information article and we can consider it a TB information that contains the information to send by means of email and any remaining arrangements. So just right as TB information and name it as TB information that said. Presently inside your set up. This is it for the arrangement before the arrangement work. Presently, inside the arrangement, we need to begin the wi fi association utilizing lifeguarded start, and we need to pass this to the side for the organization and the secret phrase to ensure that it will interface with our nearby Wi-Fi organization. Presently. We will utilize and if why not if proclamation, I need to ensure that we give individuals sufficient opportunity to associate so and address this, we will utilize the condition of rocket status in the event that it isn't equivalent. Remote associated, at that point it implies that Wi-Fi isn't associated at this point.

```
// put your setup code here, to run once:
WiFi.begin(ssid, password);
while(WiFi.status() != WL_CONNECTED)
{
    Serial.print("*");
    delay(200);
}
smtp|
```

Furthermore, all things considered, for investigating, we can print something, we can print a dab or a star. At that point you need to add some deferral to give it sufficient opportunity to interface. Presently, if it's not associated, it will continue to print stars until it interfaces. Possibly your Wi-Fi is disconnected or your username as ID or secret key aren't right. Presently. After that. After we get done with checking and ensuring that we are associating with our Wi-Fi network inside the arrangement, we need to set some TB information object subtleties. So you should have some TB information. All things considered, Logan, we need to set the login data that we previously characterized here. So we will begin with the first, which is a SMTP worker, all things considered it's Google worker and we need that worker board, Stoebe Server Port, and we need the messages and that account. Furthermore, we need the email Cynda secret word. So we need to pass these four qualities to this MTV information object, from that point forward, we need to set that Zindani and send the email. So. We can utilize this MTV information. That sits in the capacity and will take E.S.P further to anything you desire to name it, Cynda, at that point we can give that email Cynda account. Presently we need to send the email need and we have a high, low or medium, it's something you can't disregard, however I incline toward adding high need to ensure that we send it as high need email. Presently you can enter high, low, medium, or you can utilize numbers. Alright, in the wake of doing that, we can send the email subject so as MTBE information that said, subject the subject for our email and we will utilize the one that we previously found. Email subject will characterize this here, email subject. So we are utilizing these factors. Presently. We need to send the actual message, so we need to utilize assumptive information. It message. Furthermore, inside to can plain content like Hello World, this is indeed, we email this thing.

```
    }
ntpData.setLogin(smtpServer, smtpServerPort, emailSenderAcco
ntpData.setSender("ESP32 Sender", emailSenderAccount);
ntpData.setPriority("High");
ntpData.setSubject(emailSubject);      I
ntpData.setMessage("Hellow World This is ESP Email Testing",

oid loop() {
```

To send crude information and need to add bogus here, or you can send email information and we will clarify this in the following , yet that is it for this . How about we sum up. We incorporated that, indeed, be my customer, BlackBerry, the Wi-Fi network name and secret word that is in the record. Email the sender secret word that got account, the person who got the message, the TB worker data and port and the email subject. From that point forward, we began the wi fi association cycle and we held up until Wi-Fi is associated. We can add the line here. We can say sequential, the print Wi-Fi is associated.

```
// put your setup code here, to run once:
WiFi.begin(ssid, password);
while(WiFi.status() != WL_CONNECTED)
{
   Serial.print("*");
   delay(200);
   }
   Serial.println("WiFi is Connected");
```

Can then we passed the assumptive server details. So this that object that we already defined here as some TV data we did said that get information, the sender e-mail the priority of this email, the email subject and the message in plain text that said for this, listen to your next and what's your next and what you are going to continue writing.

CODING THE ESP32 PROJECT WARNING EMAIL PART2

Since we have made a plaintext email, we should figure out how to make. My message, an email, you will utilize exactly the same coding information, the message, and inside here, you add your initial yearly add through to implies you will you are passing Astrium Alcalde. Bogus methods you are passing plain content now since we did well through here. How about we eliminate the remark. We can add email here and two extra code. We need to get a basic code in any case. So here is an online code manager and you can utilize this one or this one W three school or the online code supervisor. This one. So in the event that you need to utilize this one.

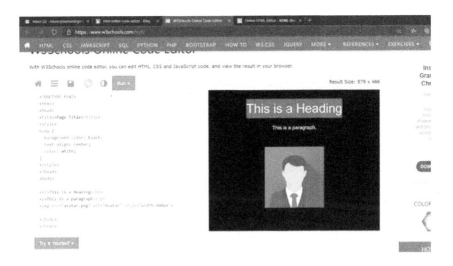

As should be obvious, this is the online editorial manager for this site, you can compose your content and. Here and see it here, see what's going on here. So to this content, you can alter the heading, this is the headings, you can compose your name and snap run and will be noticeable here. Same for different things. Or then again you can basically attempt this one. You can begin composing Hello, World. E.S.P, 32 a.m. this thing, and you can basically duplicate this code. This is a straightforward code for this line, you can add other data, you can. What amount of time it requires to be in the center, you can expand the text dimension or change the textual style tone. You can pick various configurations in the event that you need to create it as should be obvious. That is more the foundation tone and add a red tone for the actual content.

Now you can copy all of this and simply based it inside your code, right. Click and copy. Then go inside your code. Base it right here. As you can see, this is our Astrium alcalde. Now. You can use this or you can use the raw text, it's up to you in my case, I will start with the raw text, then we can text with e-mail. Now, let's move on with code editing. Now, the final step is setting the recipient email address.

```
© Code | Arduino 1.8.12
File Edit Sketch Tools Help

    Serial.println("WiFi is Connected");

smtpData.setLogin(smtpServer, smtpServerPort, emailSenderAccou
smtpData.setSender("ESP32 Sender", emailSenderAccount);
smtpData.setPriority("High");
smtpData.setSubject(emailSubject);
smtpData.setMessage("Hellow World This is ESP Email Testing",
//smtpData.setMessage("<h2 style="text-align: center;"><span s
//<h2 style="text-align: center;"><span style="background-colo
```

So like a Stoebe information dab and the beneficiary. Also, inside it, okay, email re sibilant. That is it since we have every one of the subtleties of this and T.B. information, we are prepared to send the email. So to send the email, you need to compose if. Proclamation and inside, in the event that you need to compose this Manicaland, don't send email. We are utilizing the send email capacity and we are passing this MTBE information that we previously filled here and these lines. Presently. From that point forward, we can print Syria, not print, Alan. On the off chance that there is a mistake, we can see blunder. Also, sending the email and we can give the blunder code from the mail fly and you can light mail customer dab as MTBE or Rezo.

```
tpData.setMessage("Hellow World This is ESP Email Testing", fa
smtpData.setMessage("<h2 style="text-align: center;"><span sty
<h2 style="text-align: center;"><span style="background-color:
tpData.addRecipient(emailRecipient);

(!MailClient.sendMail(smtpData))
Serial.println("Error in Sending the Email" + MailClient.smtpE

smtpData.empty();
```

This is the way you can give that email all, it will doubtlessly print out a code that you can look into utilizing Google to know precisely what's an issue. In the wake of sending the email, you can clear all the information from this MTBE that object. Furthermore, we can do this utilizing one single line, which is MTBE, that void the unfilled capacity is the one that we can use to send void messages. Presently we are sending the email and the progression work, this implies that the email will be sent once and you need to delay to unplug, at that point plug it once more. They request that individuals send another email. In the event that you need to send the email more than once, you can just utilize this strategy to send email methode inside the circle work. Presently, for instance, the circle work is vacant. Presently we can begin this thing, this cold out, however we can add considerably more stuff on top of it work now you can make a callback capacity to get the email sending states to do that. There is a very. Simple technique, you can essentially characterize a callback work like void. Allow me to show it to you. We should make another capacity and name it send get back to. No. The callback capacity will have a straightforward harmony. We will compose the sequential masterbrand plan and here we will compose the message that four. Also, we need to pass the message here. Send a status message now when the ServiceMaster is sent. We consider it an assertion and this assertion will incorporate the message is achievement in sending. At that point we need to compose, I think, for the irritating inside.

```
© Code | Arduino 1.8.12
File Edit Sketch Tools Help
Code 1
}
```

```
void sendCallback(SendStatus message)
{
    Serial.println(message.info());

    if(message.success()){Serial.print("++++++++");}
}
```

Alright, we can't light the signs. This implies that the message was sent effectively, in any case the message will we will get a code or a. MTV illegal intimidation approached our chronic killer. Presently, this is the way you can make a callback capacity to get the email sinding status. Sorry. Presently, that is it, what you need to do next is basic, you need to confirm the code to ensure that it doesn't have any mistakes, at that point we will transfer the code to our ISP board. It will require a couple of moments to order the code. Alright, as you can see here, have a bolt as MTV support was not characterized in this school. How about we ensure that we have.

```
// put your setup code here, to run once:
WiFi.begin(ssid, password);
while(WiFi.status() != WL_CONNECTED)
{
  Serial.print("*");
  delay(200);
  }
  Serial.println("WiFi is Connected");
```

```
exit status 1
'smtpServerPort' was not declared in this scope
```

That SMTP server port. Oh, we have some T.P. Let's go back and fix it. As A.B. Spellman reports. OK. That's right. Now, let me also add my e-mail passwords here. Now, let's combine it. OK, now done combining the next step is uploading the code to our E.S.P board and see if the email is sent or not. Now, we will do this in the next , but that's it for this

PRACTICAL TESTING

Now that I have hooked up my ass people, let's go to the device manager to make sure that it can recognize the ball supports as some comfort. Let's go to the tools menu and make sure that we have everything right. Come for that E.S.P 32 defectively one all everything's OK. And we have the code compound. Now, let's upload a code.

```
#define emailSenderAccount "eduengteamen@gmail.com"
#define emailSenderPassword  ████    ████
#define emailRecipient "eduengteam@gmail.com"
#define smtpServer "smtp.gmail.com"
#define smtpServerPort 465
#define emailSubject "ESP32 Testing Email"

SMTPData smtpData;
```

```
Leaving...
Hard resetting via RTS pin...
```

It will require a couple of moments. For Arduino to transfer the code to our E.S.P board. Alright, I planned to see transferring three were sent up to, I think, 100%. Alright, presently, 100% done transferring now in the event that we go here to our email account and invigorate. How about we open up Arduino and see the serum screen. Alright, we should show the moderate. What was the spending year 92? Alright. We have it here. Alright, we don't have this here. Presently, this is the sender email account, and as should be obvious, this message was sent from the sender email account, which is our record. At that point you account that we made and we ought to get the email on our other record, which is you and your group. That is it, we have another email. This is the new email that we got from the sender who is which is named SB 332 sender, and this is that a beneficiary email and we have this plain instant message. Presently we can change the code so we can get a comparable message. We can uncommented these two and we can remark the plain instant message.

```
smtpData.setSender("ESP32 Sender", emailSenderAccount);
smtpData.setPriority("High");
smtpData.setSubject(emailSubject);
//smtpData.setMessage("Hellow World This is ESP Email Testing"
smtpData.setMessage("<h2 style="text-align: center;"><span sty
<h2 style="text-align: center;"><span style="background-color:
smtpData.addRecipient(emailRecipient);

if(!MailClient.sendMail(smtpData))
```

Then upload the code again. To receive an e-mail encoded message. OK, let's. Make them a cell phone in one line. That's right. No blood again. OK, now, as you can see here, we have an e-mail encoded message. This is the plain text message or the plane or roll text message. And this is an e-mail encoded message that we did send using our E.S.P board.

So if you want to send a plain text message, you have to pass the false value as a second parameter for the message body. And if you want to send a signal code, you need to paste your code then through the second parameter for the ECB message this and that's it. This is how you can easily send e-mail messages from your people to your email address. And we can configure this to send census data and any other type of information from E.S.P to our email. Thanks for answering this .

SENSOR ALERT VIA EMAIL

Since we have sent an email, we can arrange this email to incorporate sensor information. So what we need to do now is return to our code. How about we save it. We should call it called funny bone. Presently we have this code that we can alter. What we need to do is to peruse the touch sensor that is inherent our SSP board, you can utilize that temperature sensor or some other sort of sensor. Simply associate with the correct pen. Presently. The primary thing that we need to do is make new factor, simply make it number and we should name it contact esteem. Presently, inside this strategy, we can. Into the circle and take this variable, which is such worth inside the circle. What's more, make it equivalent that really it's capacity and how about we accept that we are utilizing the substance or that PIN for the present to get the perusing letters imprinted on serum matter grain that print on. Also, we should print out. The touch sensor esteem. No stable, not a citation. Alright, next, we should add grain, not plant alone.

```
void loop() {
    // put your main code here, to run repeatedly:
    touchValue = touchRead(4);
    Serial.print("The touch sensor value: ");
    Serial.println(touchValue);
    if(touchValue >= )
    {

    }
```

```
Sketch uses 940242 bytes (71%) of program storage space. Maxim
Global variables use 40328 bytes (12%) of dynamic memory, leav
```

And let's pass the touch value. OK, now that we have the touch value, we can add a condition. If statement, you can choose the very same thing for temperature sensors or any other type of sensor. Now let's say if the touch value is above or equal 100, we need to send us an email and we need to send the message and this email to be. Let's go this. The school this year. So we need the message to be. And plaintext. Now, Sid, the message we need to write to the Dutch since sensor value. Is above 100 now, we will receive an email stating this after receiving the email Atalay.

```
Serial.print("The touch sensor value: ");
Serial.println(touchValue);
if(touchValue >= 100)
{
  smtpData.setMessage("The Touch Sensor value is above 100", tr
delay(1000)
  }
}
```

```
Sketch uses 940242 bytes (71%) of program storage space. Maxim
Global variables use 40328 bytes (12%) of dynamic memory, leav
```

Presently, let me postpone 1000 seconds, at that point we need to make this, which is fundamentally ensure that we don't have any mistakes and. Add that a second. Back here. Presently, what will occur here when we get an email with this message, one fundamental worth is over 100. You can add a temperature sensor and if the sensor esteem is over 50, you can get an email with an alarm to ensure that, you know, there is high temperature in the area and you can look at it after that. We are adding the beneficiary and we are sending the email with the A.P. information and afterward we are printing this and the sheer measure of we have a mistake, at that point we are discharging that MTBE information. That is it. This is the way you can send an email to this segment of code. Presently, how about we test this out to ensure that it works and you can move these to the void circle area. So how about we move them, we should duplicate the entirety of this.

```
delay(200);
}
Serial.println("WiFi is Connected");

smtpData.setLogin(smtpServer, smtpServerPort, emailSenderAccou
smtpData.setSender("ESP32 Sender", emailSenderAccount);
smtpData.setPriority("High");
smtpData.setSubject(emailSubject);
//smtpData.setMessage("Hellow World This is ESP Email Testing"
```

```
Sketch uses 940242 bytes (71%) of program storage space. Maxim
Global variables use 40328 bytes (12%) of dynamic memory, leav
```

Also, stuck over this line. Here. Presently we have the login subtleties, we have the email, the sender, the need and the email subject, we are perusing the feeling of significant worth and we are printing a similar kind of significant worth on the. So then we are checking in the event that the sensor esteems are over 100 or equivalent to 100, we are communicating something specific, an email message. Also, how about we remark these parts from here. Add this to remarks. Alright, presently how about we confirm the code, at that point transfer it to our kin. I will connect my board to my ISP. Alright, presently the ISP is snared now we should proceed onward to now how about we transfer our code to the E.S.P board that we just associated with, ensure that we are getting the sensor information. Presently. As should be obvious, the court is commending and the is interfacing through com until further notice, it's transferring the code to the ISP memory. Presently, done transferring. That is it. Presently. We need to ensure that we have. The control perusing. How about we browse that email to ensure. Alright. We are accepting an email. What's more, as you can see, that much feeling of significant worth is over 100, and I got a similar email on my cell phone, so that amount feeling of significant worth for this situation is over 100. You can likewise send that feeling of significant worth on the actual email. It will be something simple to do. In any case, this is the central matter, and we have an issue here. We got more than 10 messages. This is on the grounds that in our code insider savvy, inside the circle work, we just added 1,000 milliseconds, which is essentially one second. So

```
if(!MailClient.sendMail(smtpData))
    Serial.println("Error in Sending the Email" + MailClient.smt

    smtpData.empty();
delay(100000);
    }
}
```

```
Leaving...
Hard resetting via RTS pin...
```

we will keep receiving emails every second. We can increase this number to be. Like 10 or 100 seconds, then we can't upload the code. OK, now what I did hear is basically I have seen that sentence, the touchstone of value is above 100 plus that adds value. It will send the touchstone sort of value with the email. And I added 100 second between every email and the next one. So let's check to see. What we did receive.

Now, as you can see here, we are receiving their sense of values, a 99 and we didn't get that line, which is the first sense of value above 100 because it's not above 100. That's it. This is basically how easily you can send census data to our to your email or how to get an email alert when the value goes above a certain value.

THE END

Made in the USA
Middletown, DE
12 June 2023

32462936R00176